WHICH ONE'S PINK?

AN ANALYSIS OF
THE CONCEPT ALBUMS OF ROGER WATERS
AND PINK FLOYD

By
PHIL ROSE

We acknowledge the financial support of the Government of Canada
through the Book Publishing Industry Development Program
for our publishing activities.
Published by Collector's Guide Publishing Inc., Box 62034,
Burlington, Ontario, Canada, L7R 4K2
Printed and bound in Canada by Webcom Ltd of Toronto
Which One's Pink? / Philip Anthony Rose
ISBN 1-896522-47-5

The World Memorial Fund was founded in 1988 by the late Leonard Cheshire VC who had been a famous British Bomber pilot in World War II and who had, following the war, established a network of residential homes, throughout the world, caring for the needs of the chronically sick. Leonard Cheshire set up the new charity as a tribute to those who had lost their lives during the 20th century as the consequence of the effects of world disaster, both natural and man made.

The Charity has now devoted its full financial resources to the work of the Leonard Cheshire Department at University College London, which comes under the auspices of Leonard Cheshire Care Homes and the centre devotes its working activity to providing medical support in those areas of the world where post-conflict support is required.

The author of this book, in memory of Leonard Cheshire, has most generously gifted the sale proceeds to be used by the centre in the continuance of the work being carried out by its personnel. Independent proceeds can be forwarded in the form of cheques made out to the Leonard Cheshire Foundation and sent to the attention of Caroline Kennedy at the address below:

The Leonard Cheshire Department of Conflict Recovery
University College London
St. Martin's House
140 Tottenham Court Road
London W1P 9LN
http://www.ucl.ac.uk/~rmhkjar/

"...There are two ways of settling disputed questions; one by discussion, the other by force. The first being characteristic of man, the second of brutes...".
(Cicero)

"...It is easier for a camel to go through the eye of a needle, than for a rich man to enter into the kingdom of God...".
(Jesus Christ)

"...The most fundamental value of art is that it can strip us of our selfishness and lend us tears for sorrows that are not our own...".
(Oscar Wilde)

"...The pessimists are right. But only the optimists change the world...".
(Bertrand Blanchet—Bishop of Gaspésie, Québec)

"...I'm in no sense going to Berlin to celebrate what I consider to be a victory of capitalism over socialism, or the West over the East, or anything like that. I'm going there to celebrate the victory of the individual over the bureaucracy—and specifically, a victory of the East German individual to rise up against some of the more uncomfortable layers of dogma under which he [sic] was living...".
(Roger Waters)

ACKNOWLEDGEMENTS

I should like to express my gratitude to a number of people who have assisted me in the completion of this project: Anthony Casciano—for his insights, and the loan of his computer in addition to vast portions of his time; Fabrizio DelMonaco—for his astute sound engineering capabilities; Susan Fast—for being my incentive to complete this project in its current form, and for the countless hours she gave to this undertaking; Mark Fenwick—for his constant assistance in bringing my work to life; John Ferns—for the incredible generosity with which he donated his time, and for his invaluable friendship; George Kandalepas—for sharing with me his film insights; Jeff McFarlane—for his critical feedback; Gerry Salvatore—a secondary school English teacher who encouraged my interest in these works years ago; Steve Skrobot—for our numerous eight-hour-long conversations about these works, during which he shared with me his enthusiasm for them; Brian Stapley—another secondary school English teacher who originally inspired this pursuit; John Paul Szarak—for initially being the eyes in the back of my head, and then showing me how to see with them for myself; Roger Waters—for his incomparable artistry, and for allowing me to "beat the dogs"; Noel Uzelac—for shifting the universe.

This project is dedicated to my parents, Gordon and Barbara Rose—whose continued presence in the world the works here considered have helped me truly to appreciate, and whose continued encouragement, support and assistance is beyond thanks.

TABLE OF CONTENTS

ALBUM INFORMATION

1) The Dark Side of the Moon

Produced by Pink Floyd, recorded at EMI, Abbey Road, June, October 1972, January, February 1973, engineered by Alan Parsons, assisted by Peter James, mixed by Chris Thomas and (quad. version) Alan Parsons, released March 24 1973.

David Gilmour—Vocals, Guitars, VCS3; Nick Mason—Percussion, Tape effects; Richard Wright—Keyboards, Vocals, VCS3; Roger Waters—Bass Guitar, Vocals, VCS3, Tape Effects

> Speak to Me *(Mason)*
> Breathe *(Waters, Gilmour, Wright)*
> On the Run *(Gilmour, Waters)*
> Time *(Waters, Wright, Gilmour, Mason)*
> The Great Gig in the Sky *(Wright)*
> Money *(Waters)*
> Us and Them *(Waters, Wright)*
> Any Colour You Like *(Gilmour, Mason, Wright)*
> Brain Damage *(Waters)*
> Eclipse *(Waters)*

All lyrics Roger Waters

Backing vocals—Doris Troy, Leslie Duncan, Barry St. John; Vocal on 'The Great Gig in the Sky'—Clare Torry; Saxophone on 'Us and Them' and 'Money'—Dick Parry.

2) Wish You Were Here

Produced by Pink Floyd, recorded at EMI, Abbey Road, January 6-July 1975, engineered by Brian Humphries, assisted by Peter James, released September 15 1975

> Shine On You Crazy Diamond
> Part I *(Wright, Waters, Gilmour)*
> Part II *(Gilmour, Waters, Wright)*
> Part III *(Waters, Gilmour, Wright)*
> Part IV *(Gilmour, Wright, Waters)*
> Part V *(Waters)*
>
> Welcome to the Machine *(Waters)*
> Have a Cigar *(Waters)*
> Wish You Were Here *(Waters, Gilmour)*
> Shine On You Crazy Diamond
> Part VI *(Wright, Waters, Gilmour)*
> Part VII *(Waters, Gilmour, Wright)*
> Part VIII *(Gilmour, Wright, Waters)*
> Part IX *(Wright)*

All lyrics Roger Waters

Vocal on 'Have a Cigar'—Roy Harper; Backing Vocals—Venetta Fields and Carlena Williams; Saxophone on 'Shine On You Crazy Diamond'—Dick Parry.

3) Animals

Produced by Pink Floyd, recorded at Britannia Row, London, April-November 1976, released February 4 1977

> Pigs on the Wing *(Waters)*
> Dogs *(Waters, Gilmour)*
> Pigs—Three Different Ones *(Waters)*
> Sheep *(Waters)*
> Pigs on the Wing—Part II *(Waters)*

All lyrics Roger Waters

4) The Wall

Produced by David Gilmour, Bob Ezrin, Roger Waters, recorded at Superbear, Miravel France, Producers Workshop, Los Angeles, CBS, New York, April - November 1979, co-produced and engineered by James Guthrie

> In the Flesh? *(Waters)*
> The Thin Ice *(Waters)*
> Another Brick in the Wall—Part I *(Waters)*
> The Happiest Days Of Our Lives *(Waters)*
> Another Brick in the Wall—Part II *(Waters)*
> Mother *(Waters)*
> Goodbye Blue Sky *(Waters)*
> Empty Spaces *(Waters)*
> Young Lust *(Waters/Gilmour)*
> One of My Turns *(Waters)*
> Don't Leave Me Now *(Waters)*
> Another Brick in the Wall—Part III *(Waters)*
> Goodbye Cruel World *(Waters)*
>
> Hey You *(Waters)*
> Is There Anybody Out There? *(Waters)*
> Nobody Home *(Waters)*
> Vera *(Waters)*
> Bring the Boys Back Home *(Waters)*
> Comfortably Numb *(Gilmour/Waters)*
> The Show Must Go On *(Waters)*
> In the Flesh *(Waters)*
> Run Like Hell *(Gilmour/Waters)*
> Waiting for the Worms *(Waters)*
> Stop *(Waters)*
> The Trial *(Waters/Ezrin)*
> Outside the Wall *(Waters)*

All lyrics Roger Waters

Other engineers—Nick Griffiths, Patrice Quef, Brian Christian, John McClure, Rick Hart; Sound equipment—Phil Taylor; Orchestra arranged by Michael Kamen and Bob Ezrin; Backing vocals—Bruce Johnston, Toni Tennille, Joe Chemay, John Joyce, Stan Farber, Jim Haas, Islington Green School.

5) The Final Cut

Produced by Roger Waters, James Guthrie and Michael Kamen, recorded in England at Mayfair, Olympic, Abbey Road, Eel Pie, Audio International, Rak, Hookend and The Billiard Room, July-December 1982, engineered by James Guthrie and Andy Jackson, assistant engineers—Andy Canelle, Mike Nocito, Jules Bowen

> The Post War Dream
> Your Possible Pasts
> One Of the Few
> The Hero's Return
> The Gunners Dream
> Paranoid Eyes
> Get Your Filthy Hands Off My Desert
> The Fletcher Memorial Home
> Southampton Dock
> The Final Cut
> Not Now John
> Two Suns in the Sunset

by Roger Waters

Performed by Pink Floyd, David Gilmour, Nick Mason, Roger Waters with Michael Kamen—piano, harmonium; Andy Bown—hammond organ; Ray Cooper—percussion; Andy Newmark—drums on "Two Suns in the Sunset"; Raphael Ravenscroft—tenor sax; the National Philharmonic Orchestra, conducted and arranged by Michael Kamen.

Preface

As a younger person I discovered the music and lyrics of Pink Floyd and Roger Waters. Never before had I heard music which had been recorded with such distinct attention to sonic detail; nor, previously, had I heard rock songs that consistently contained such cleverly crafted and socially relevant lyrics. That the ideas presented in these songs were sustained throughout an entire album, however, was the trait which made them most intriguingly exceptional. For this illustrated something which, aside from the rare exception, I had found notably absent from popular culture—namely, *prolonged thought.*

In my ebullience I began to purchase books that had been written then about the band and its work, but I was continuously disappointed by these volumes. None of them ever seemed to contain anything more than short and rather insufficient comments about the conceptual content of the recordings, and I had just begun to regard such knowledge as essential in order for one to possess a deeper understanding and appreciation of them. It was for this reason, as well as for the sympathy I felt for Waters' fears and frustration about apparently being unable to communicate his ideas to his audience, that I was motivated to complete the present volume.

Before I began to write, it was suggested to me by a friend that I not overlook in my study of these albums the significance of their musical aspects, and how these also contribute to interpretations of the works' overall meanings. At first this seemed a strange idea. Had I not been taught at university that music had no meaning—at least none that was "worth talking about"? It didn't take me long to decide that this clearly was an inaccurate belief, and one which became more obviously so as a result of the particular music with which I was dealing. Throughout the writing of this book, in fact, I was often truly startled to find out exactly how meaningful this music really is when one takes the time to think about it.

I have had reservations about including some of my observations in this volume however: this is solely the result of my inability to discuss some of the occurring processes without requiring recourse to technical musical vocabulary, some of which undoubtedly will alienate many potential readers. Although it is my belief that the essence of the ideas I have tried to elucidate will still be understood by non-musical readers, I wish to stress that it is not at all necessary for one to comprehend these discussions in order to be able to appreciate the majority of the analysis. In addition, I have attempted to keep these sections very short so as not to disrupt the flow too much for a general readership.

In the first section of the book's introduction, I attempt to provide readers with the background necessary for them to understand the direction from which I approach my study of these recordings. In the second, I discuss the evolution of the concept album and Roger Waters' contribution to that genre. From the remainder of the book, readers should gain further insight into the complexity of these art works than may have been previously apparent. It has been written under the assumption that its readers have a strong familiarity with the recordings in question; therefore they should familiarise themselves with them beforehand if they have not yet done so.

I hope the book also enables readers to achieve, if they do not already possess it, the state of consciousness which I suspect the artist initially required in order to allow him the composition of these pieces. For if there is any kind of summary that can be made from my study of the content of these works, it is that their words and sounds work together in order to communicate one fundamental concern, and one which is effectively articulated by the journalist Karl Dallas—these works are all characterised by their "affirmation of human values against everything that conspires against them in life". Although this comment was made in relation to *The Dark Side of the Moon,* it applies equally to the other works considered.

Aside from the distinction that I suspect they will continue to receive solely from their artistic merit, it is my prediction that the underlying ideas and sentiments that are presented in both these and his post Floydian works, will be the features that even moreso distinguish their author among the vast group of his contemporaries. I believe that his work will be perceived, in the future, as having made a seminal contribution to the positive changes which I am desperately hoping we shall witness across the globe. Clearly this depends both on their being given the proper critical attention, and to the subsequent inclusion of their concepts in the education of young people. If this book in any way helps to facilitate this process, it will have fulfilled its purpose.

> Phil Rose
> Hamilton, Canada

Introduction

"They talk about 'intervals' of sound, and listen as carefully as if they were trying to hear a conversation next door...They all prefer to use their ears instead of their minds...".

Plato

Methodological Background

The study of rock music is still in its infancy, but there are a couple of reasons for this. Perhaps the principal one is the great deal of resistance which it has faced from academic institutions over the years; most have refused to acknowledge any other types of music but those from the European "classical" music tradition as being *serious* and thus worthy of study. But, as this book attests to, this perception has begun to change.[1] The other primary impediment to the pursuit of such studies in the past has been the understandable confusion about what are the most suitable means which one should employ to approach rock music. It has been well illustrated that this confusion is clearly also the result of the underlying assumptions and ideologies of traditional musicology, and the inadequacy of its methods when confronted with other types of music *(see Middleton 1990: 103-107).*

Richard Middleton recounts that foremost among these characteristics is its terminology, which has been moulded by the needs and history of Western classical music. This terminology also always involves selective conceptions of what music *is*. Therefore when it is applied to other kinds of music, the results are problematical. As Middleton suggests:

> In many kinds of popular music, for example, harmony may not be the most important parameter; rhythm, pitch gradation, timbre and the whole ensemble of performance articulation techniques are often more important; 'dissonance' and 'resolution' may be produced by non-harmonic means (stop-time in rhythm and blues, for instance); 'motives' may be used not for 'development' but as 'hooks' or 'riffs'; drones may be an important and complex structural device (for instance, 'bottleneck' guitar variations on a single chord, in many blues songs). *(Middleton 1990: 104)*

The second aspect of the problem is that musicology is traditionally slanted by the characteristics of notation, which tends to foreground those parameters which can be easily notated. It is often the case that these particular parameters are the least important in rock music as Middleton suggests above in the case of harmony. Philip Tagg observes that music that is neither conceived nor designed to be distributed as notation is often characterised by a large number of important parameters of musical expression which are "either difficult or impossible to encode in traditional notation" *(Tagg 1982: 41)*. The implication of this tendency for notation-centric training to "foreground" certain parameters and neglect other, often more important, parameters is that it "induces particular forms of *listening,* and these then tend to be applied to all sorts of music, appropriately or not"; but, as Middleton goes on to say, "(i)t needs a considerable act of sociological sympathy to grasp that other listeners may actually hear different things, or hear them in different relationships" *(Middleton 1990: 105)*.

This leads to the third aspect of the problem which is the orthodox assumption that art works are autonomous, and that analysis therefore should be always text-centred. The underlying result is that musicology has had great difficulty relating musical discourse to the remainder of human existence in any way, the description of emotive aspects in music either occurring sporadically or being avoided altogether. Under such consideration, music has had the semblance of existing in a vacuum. As Tagg notes, this tendency has given rise to "a culture-centric fixation on certain 'notable' parameters of musical expression (mostly processual aspects such as 'form', thematic construction, etc.), which are particularly important to the Western art music tradition" *(Tagg 1982: 41)*. It is hardly surprising then that those musicologists whose musical experience is rooted in the traditional approach view other music styles as generally lacking.

As an alternative, rock music analysis has insisted on the priority of *meaning;* such studies, as the reader shall see, tend necessarily to be interdisciplinary. John Shepherd stresses that "music as opposed to its sounds can only be understood by references to the whole range of human activity: political, economic, religious, educational and so on" *(Shepherd 1994: 139)*.[2] With rock music in particular, McClary and Walser cite the importance of giving attention to many specific extra-musical characteristics in order that meanings can be construed. Included among these are verbal texts, performance styles, video imagery, modes of commercial production and distribution, the construction of band or star images, the history of a singer's career, and political issues (the positioning of the music with respect to class, race, gender). All of these must be analysed carefully in conjunction with musical components *(McClary and Walser 1990: 290)*.

Of course the assumption behind this viewpoint is that meaning arises from the mutual mediation of music and society. Many people will have difficulty with this notion, however, as most of us are not accustomed to thinking about music in this way. As Nicholas Cook suggests, in order for it to be considered as possessing meaning, music must be viewed as a form of communication:

> It is helpful at this point to contrast the concept of meaning with that of effect. Nobody could reasonably deny that music has effects, and in principle it is perfectly possible to discover what those effects are. With meaning, however, it is quite different; not only are there widely divergent explanations of musical meaning, but whole systems of musical aesthetics have been built on the premise that music simply does not have meaning. Now what distinguishes the concepts of meaning and effect is that the former is predicated on communication, on human agency, whereas the latter is not (that is why we talk about the effects of sunlight, not its meaning). It follows that any analysis of musical meaning needs to begin with a clear grasp of the communicative context within which this meaning is realised. But musical meaning is all too often discussed in the abstract rather than in terms of specific context, as if it were somehow inherent in 'the music itself' regardless of the context of its production and reception. *(Cook 1994: 27-8)*

Cook suggests that instead of asking "what music means", we should be talking always about "what the music means here", thereby making allowance for the context in which musical meaning emerges. No sooner has he established this when he finds it to be problematical also. In reference to the use of Mozart's *Marriage of Figaro* overture in a television commercial he says:

> [A]s my use of the word 'emerges' may suggest, even asking 'what the music means here' is problematic. Consider the grammar of the sen-

tence: 'means' is a transitive verb, with 'what' as its object. To pose the
question this way is to suggest that meaning is something that music
has. But that is not what the Citroen commercial seems to show. To be
sure, the music in the commercial - Mozart's music brings various attributes or qualities with it, attributes or qualities that enter into the discur-
sive structure of the commercial and become associated with the product. But the particular significance of these attributes or qualities - their
meaning in terms of the commercial emerges from their interaction with
the story line, the voice-over, and the pictures. If the music gives meaning to the images, then equally the images give meaning to the music.
(Cook 1994: 30)

Cook concludes that "meaning is constructed or negotiated within the context
of the commercial" and instead of "talking about meaning as something that
the music *has*", it makes more sense to talk about it as "something that the
music *does* (and has done to it) within a given context".

Many of the meanings that music brings to the commercials in Cook's analyses are, in his own words, "ready-made". An example of these are genre references. Different genres have different inherent connotations (eg. electronic
musics connote technology). But Cook stresses that "purely musical" relationships are equally capable of creating meanings through their emotive qualities:

In an attempt to formulate a general theory of musical meaning, Daniel
Putnam has described how 'the contour of instrumental music, with its
broad yet recognizable strokes, 'fits' the contour of those broad emotions
in life which, as feeling-states of the organism, can be independent of
particular situations and can be transferred to a variety of diverse
objects'. Now we do not experience emotions in the abstract; we experience them to the extent that (as Putnam puts it) they are transferred to
specific objects in specific contexts. And this provides an attractive
model of what happens in the commercials, where the broad expressive
potential of musical sounds acquires specific meaning by virtue of its
relationship to words and pictures - through its transfer, to repeat
Putnam's words, to a variety of diverse objects .... If this is valid, then
music in the abstract -'music alone', as Peter Kivy calls it - does not have
meaning. What it has is a *potential* for the construction or negotiation of
meaning in specific contexts. It is a bundle of generic attributes in search
of an object. Or it might be described as a structured semantic space, a
privileged site for the negotiation of meaning. And if, in the commercials,
meaning arises from the mutual interaction of music, words, and pictures, then at the same time it is meaning that forms the common cur-
rency between these elements - that makes the negotiation possible, so
to speak. But of course the commercials are just one arena for such
negotiation of meaning. Exactly the same applies to the relationship
between music and words in song. *(Cook 1994: 39)*

Cook's conclusions reinforce the necessary relationship between musical
hermeneutics and the need for an interdisciplinary approach to the study of
music. At the same time, he highlights the importance of the relationship in
songs between words and music; both work together in order to deliver mes-
sages to listeners.

Historically, nonetheless, song analyses generally have been merely interpretations of a song's text with little or no attention paid to the music. Simon Frith

has observed the inadequacy of this approach:

> In songs, words are the sign of a voice. A song is always a performance and song words are always spoken out, heard in someone's accent. Songs are more like plays than poems; song words work as speech and speech acts, bearing meaning not just semantically, but also as structures of sound that are direct signs of emotion and marks of character. Singers use non-verbal as well as verbal devices to make their points - emphases, sighs, hesitations, changes of tone; lyrics involve pleas, sneers and commands as well as statements and messages and stories
> ... *(Frith 1988: 120)*

Frith's suggestions are taken even further by Walser who recognises the importance of analysing the *music* of rock music "beyond the vocals", thereby grounding discussion in the history and significance of actual musical details and structures *(Walser 1993:26)*.[3] Through doing so, readers will likely be surprised how frequently additional insights into the works considered arise throughout this book.

There is one thing, however, that readers should keep in mind throughout their reading of this book. In my opinion, it is best stated by the musicologist Lawrence Kramer:

> Interpretation ... cannot be regimented, disciplined, or legislated-at least not successfully. As a practice, it is opportunistic, unruly, and contestatory, inescapably committed to both preserving and appropriating whatever it addresses.... An interpretation unhesitatingly seizes on any association, substitution, analogy, construction, or leap of inference that it requires to do its work. If it is guided by rules, then it partly makes up the rules as it goes along.... Unlike a true account of something, an interpretation can never exclude rival, incompatible accounts. For any given interpretation, an alternative always exists... [4] *(Kramer 1990: 14-15)*

Whether concerning lyrics, music, album covers or otherwise, my intention in this book is merely to attempt to support an interpretation of the concept albums arrived at through the information I have been able to gather about them.

Roger Waters and the Evolution of the Concept Album

The transition in rock music from dance compositions to music composed expressly for listening was realised in the work of progressive or "art" rock musicians in the 1960s and one result was the development of the record album as a genre. Alan Durant observes:

> It is only in the course of the later 1960s, particularly with the emergence of the 'concept album' and with experimentation in stereo following more widespread commercial availability of stereo equipment around 1968, that the album takes on its appearance as a distinct, compound musical form. Before this period, it is only in 'classical' music (and to some extent in jazz-particularly in its aspirations towards a scale of form and cultural influence along the lines of 'classical' music), that use of extended playing time is widely made. *(Durant 1984: 212)*

The work most commonly cited as initiating this trend is The Beatles' *Sergeant Pepper's Lonely Hearts Club Band* (1967), a recording which was to take seven hundred hours of studio time (in comparison with ten hours for the earliest

Beatles LP in 1963), a fact indicative of the greater sophistication that artists and producers began to display in their use of the recording studio. Along with its reprise of earlier material (the title song), *Sgt. Pepper* displays this tendency particularly by its fusing of certain songs together making them continuous and thereby suggesting that they are not to be perceived as separate entities.[5] Though it undoubtedly influenced the birth of the concept album, I would suggest that *Sgt. Pepper* itself is not a concept album in the accepted sense (though many have referred to it as such) due to the lack of cohesion present between the texts of its songs. The vast majority of albums both contemporary with and since this landmark recording have been, in fact, merely collections of unrelated songs. To differentiate the concept album from a regular album, then, is to say that it is a form in which the music and, perhaps more importantly, the texts are often thematically and conceptually linked.[6]

To my knowledge no other artist has been as dedicated to the concept album as Roger Waters. Pete Townshend for example, an artist who has contributed much to the development of the genre, has interspersed many of his conceptual works with albums which are collections of individual songs rather than extended unified works. This appears to be true of Waters' former bandmates also. His interest in concept albums was initially met with resistance by the other members of Pink Floyd. According to guitarist and singer David Gilmour in 1972:

> We've had huge arguments about what exactly to do on some of those soundtrack albums and other albums. Some of us thought we should just put songs on them, others thought we should turn the whole thing into one subject concept for the whole album .... Roger has certainly got a bit of an obsession about making the whole album into a one subject deal, into what you might call a concept album. *(Miles 1980)*

Beginning with *The Dark Side of the Moon* (1973) and continuing through to his third solo album *Amused to Death* (1992), all of Waters' recordings have taken this form. Gilmour's statement suggests that Waters may have been greatly influenced by Pink Floyd's involvement in the composition of film soundtracks particularly with regard to the linking of music to a narrative, and the increasing length of musical structures.[7]

It may be obvious to most readers, but nonetheless I shall attempt to clarify why I have been tempted to refer to all of these recordings as his works (when in fact the majority of the recordings to which I am referring were made with Pink Floyd). It is primarily as a result of their texts that these recordings can be defined as concept albums and it was with *The Dark Side of the Moon* that Waters assumed the responsibility for writing all the group's lyrics.[8] Even in their live performances, Waters appears to have been the member of Pink Floyd most concerned with the communication of ideas.[9] Pink Floyd were, of course, well known for the theatrical visual effects they employed during their concerts and, besides enhancing the presentation, these effects reinforced the material's meaning. As Dallas suggests:

> The special effects tended to be Roger Waters' ideas. ...At one of the Wembley rehearsals [1977], I heard him instructing the crew:'I want the smoke to begin at the words "all tight lips and cold feet" at the beginning of the second verse of "Pigs". And I want as much smoke as you can

give me. I don't want the audience to see the pig until the loud solo from Dave that comes after the verse'. *(Dallas 1987: 59)*

According to Nick Griffiths, an engineer who worked with the band, the film footage that accompanied Pink Floyd in concert was also Waters' domain:

> Roger edited it and oversaw it and made sure it fitted the bill ... He can walk into a film cutting room, sit down with the editor, and take control very knowledgeably of the whole proceedings. He knows the technology, doesn't really need to rely on anyone else to come up with the ideas. He has his own ideas. *(Schaffner 1991: 217-218)*

One need only look at the album credits, though, to see Waters' gradual creative domination of the group musically as well,[10] but by no means do I intend to belittle or suggest that the musical and production contributions made to these recordings by the other members of Pink Floyd are insignificant (particularly the compositional contributions made to *The Dark Side of the Moon* and *Wish You Were Here*); I merely suggest that Waters' work formed the basis for the communication of ideas and meanings.

People enjoy the works of Roger Waters and Pink Floyd for various reasons: some for the incredible care and sophistication apparent in the quality and precision of the recordings; some for the expressive nature of the songs; and some primarily for the complexity and seriousness of subject matter with which the albums deal. Although I must include myself a member of all of these camps, the ultimate concern of this book is to discuss the latter.

Chapter 1 — The Dark Side of the Moon

Sergeant Pepper is commonly taken in accounts of rock music to have initiated the musically or thematically cohesive rock album...*Dark Side of the Moon* is equally frequently considered perhaps the exemplary peak of that form and aspiration...'.

Alan Durant[1]

The name Phoebus means "brilliant" or "shining" and, in Greek mythology, Phoebus Apollo—who spoke no falsities and in whom no darkness existed—was often considered the Sun-god, but he became best known as the God of Light and Truth. His twin sister was the Moon-goddess Artemis (Diana in Roman mythology) who, on the other hand, represented inconstancy or uncertainty and became known as the "three-form goddess". She was often identified with Selene (Luna in Latin) and Hecate, the latter being associated with deeds of darkness and bearing the title Goddess of the Dark of the Moon. *(Hamilton 1942: 29-32)*

Whether due to religious orientation, for astrological reasons, or merely as a result of their use as tools for the measurement of time, it seems that as long as human beings have existed they have had a fascination with the sun and moon. Roger Waters draws on this fascination employing the sun and the moon as symbols throughout Pink Floyd's *The Dark Side of the Moon* (1973). He recognises the same basic qualities in these celestial bodies as did the Greeks before him, but extends their symbolic connotations to the fullest, suggesting, in his own words, their representation of "the light and the dark; the good and the bad; the life force as opposed to the death force". *(Dallas 1987: 107)*

Throughout the work Waters suggests that we, as human beings, are still aligned metaphorically with one or the other. More often than not, however, no matter how much we may aspire toward visualising the beauty of truth in life that can be achieved only through the illuminative powers of the sun, we are—due to certain "pressures which are anti-life" *(Waters in Miles: 1980)* and which help to bring out negative aspects of our nature—seemingly doomed to be aligned with what Waters sees as the inherent dark quality and uncertainty represented by the moon, an untrustworthy guide whose comparatively dim light leaves much in shadow and is merely a false reflection of the sun's luminous truth. This idea is confirmed by the spoken lines that are faintly heard during the fade at the end of the record:

"There is no dark side of the moon really...as a matter of fact it's all dark."

Many, but not all, of the "anti-life pressures" with which Waters deals are particular to life in an often alienating, twentieth century technological capitalist society. It is the frustration caused by these pressures, and by this seemingly forced alignment with the moon, which subsequently leads one to lunacy (taken from the Latin word *luna* meaning moon), or "the psychic state provoked to unpredictable and uncontrollable cyclic episodes of madness by the waxing and waning of the moon" *(Neaman 1978: 181)*. As guitarist David Gilmour recalls, before the group began recording the album, "[w]e sat in a rehearsal room...and Roger came up with the specific idea of dealing with all the things that drive people mad..." *(Miles: 1980)*, and it is these things which are dealt with throughout all of the songs on the album and which, at the end of side two, culminate in "Brain Damage".

The album begins with "Speak to Me" and the fade in of a heartbeat which suggests the gradual beginning of life; the period of gestation which eventuates in the climactic crescendo of birth portrayed by the screaming, child-bearing female who ushers in the first chords of "Breathe (in the Air)". It is significant that this scream is at the same time suggestive of a wail of madness, because the collage of sound effects superimposed over the prolonged crescendo represents, in part, the various elements of stress and strain which are responsible for the eventual madness apparent in "Brain Damage". The collage consists of the ticking clocks of "Time", the cash register sounds of "Money", the rumbling synthesizer present at the beginning of "On the Run", and the resultant maniacal laughter of "Brain Damage". As well as foreshadowing the effect of these elements on the new life, it is possible that the listener may hear the effect that they have already had on the life from which it emerges. The fact that Waters sees this outcome as being widespread in the modern condition is illustrated by the voices (from alternate speaker channels) which are heard alongside these sound effects saying "I've been mad for fucking years, absolutely years...over the edge...working...", and "I've always been mad...I know I've been mad like the most of us are...very hard to explain why you are mad, even if you're not mad...".

Although the melodic lines played on slide guitar in "Breathe" may to some listeners suggest a baby's cry (the upper legato slides almost seem to articulate the syllable 'wah'), the mother's hasty demand to "Speak to Me" is juxtaposed with the opening lyric of "Breathe (in the Air)" which, in its rapidly extensive look at life seems to suggest the fleeting years of youth. The mother figure says:

> Breathe, breathe in the air
> Don't be afraid to care
> Leave but don't leave me
> Look around and choose your own ground
> For long you live and high you fly
> And smiles you'll give and tears you'll cry
> And all you touch and all you see
> Is all your life will ever be.

After urging the child to breathe independently for the first time, the mother expresses warm sentiments and expounds humane and spiritual principles, but her tone suddenly becomes cold and impersonal after the sixth line when she suggests that all her child's life will amount to is material things (only those things which can be touched or seen). This shift in manner suggests her affiliation with the volatile tendencies of the moon, and it is interesting that Waters chose a female character to portray this. The female is associated with the moon through her menstrual cycle, which is well-known to occur at the same frequency as the lunar cycle, and, in the mythology of Western culture this is sometimes thought to create a volatility in women. The character's erratic shift of tone is best displayed by the odd means she uses to address her progeny ("rabbit"), and her preaching manner is supported by the gospel-like organ entry as the following lines are sung:

> Run rabbit run
> Dig that hole, forget the sun,
> And when at last the work is done

Don't sit down it's time to dig another one.

Rather than stressing the value of emotions and human relationships, the mother (representing the dominant voice of industrial ideology) displays her misguided sentiments by impelling her child to hurriedly work non-stop instead of striving for the truly enriching things that the sun has to offer in life. Waters almost seems to have in mind the rabbit working toward the purchase of a vacation home after paying off its permanent residence. His comments from 1971 are in tune with these lines:

> Many people are robbed of their whole lives because they are trapped in the system. They are used to produce Volkswagens. People are paid for their work, buy televisions and fridges and believe that this compensates for the fact that they spend their whole lives putting cars together. And they live in this rut for 48 weeks out of every 52. *(Wicke 1990: 108)*

The necessary alignment of this position with the moon is expressed in the next stanza, the first line of which has appeared before; but now it acquires a different meaning due to the lines which follow:

> For long you live and high you fly
> But only if you ride the tide
> And balanced on the biggest wave
> You race toward an early grave.

Whereas in its first appearance it seemed to be a wish for the character's well-being, this line now seems to have connotations of a blessing for prosperity or high economic status which is only achievable if one "rides the tide" which is, of course, controlled by the moon. The last two lines forecast the treacherous build-up of the character's ambition and his or her eventual premature demise due to the endless race that is necessary to achieve such "high" ideals; a scenario that is musically portrayed in the following selection "On the Run".

This instrumental piece, which commences immediately after the last word of "Breathe", begins with a low, ominous note over which is heard the sudden metamorphosis of the organ's timbre, its warm sustained chord transformed into a harsh mechanical texture. This sound is manipulated in order to give the impression that it is moving in circles. The effect of combining the short melodic figure (produced electronically using a VCS3), which is almost endlessly repeated, with the sounds of running footsteps moving back and forth from one speaker channel to the other, gives the piece an overall feeling of directionlessness and lack of progress. This is caused by the sense of alienation often created in the human being from living in a mechanistic, technological society; a connotation of the transformed organ sound (heard only at the beginning), the mechanical repetition of the high-hat cymbal, the sound of airport announcements, and the variety of unique electronic timbres; some of which, by musically achieving the Doppler effect, are used to suggest the passage of airplanes over the head of the runner.

The runner's gasps for breath are the result of his attempt to keep up with the incredibly fast electronic melodic figure (a figure which could not have been reproduced by a performer for such an extended time on an ordinary musical instrument), but this figure finally terminates with the sound of a plane crash (an event which was recreated during Pink Floyd's live performances with a plane crashing into the stage), and this represents the runner's burnout or "early grave". The mad laughter heard throughout the piece, symbolising the final outcome of the stress created by being "on the run", has a mocking quality that is turned back on the runner (especially when heard immediately preceding the explosion) almost as if it were in response to the runner's confident statement heard earlier: "Live for today, gone tomorrow, that's me...". The runner's persistent footsteps, representing all those who are slaves of the "rat race", still heard following the disastrous crash serve to usher in the next piece, which is launched by the sounds of various clocks first ticking and then ringing/chiming, a sound effect which serves as an excellent transitional device. Besides foreshadowing the tolling bell of the "Breathe Reprise", the alarm which likely wakes the runner in the morning to begin "digging his hole" also foreshadows the arousal from his reverie of the idle figure portrayed in "Time".

Anticipating its opening lyric, "Time" begins with a clever rhythm track which imitates the ticking of a clock. This is juxtaposed with a return of the heart beat (this time much slower, suggesting the idle individual). The low, ominous-sounding, timbre that began the previous track returns, and is soon heard alongside an innocent, high pitched, music-box sounding keyboard. This unlikely combination creates a sense of dramatic irony and unease further enhanced by the fact that the low, dark timbre sounds repeatedly back and forth between only single pitches (E and F-sharp) and not chords. The chord tones are provided by the abetting music-box keyboard which withholds the thirds of the chords (the pitch which designates a chord as major or minor) until the second appearance of the F-sharp (now heard as F-sharp minor). At this point the tonality is ambiguous as it is impossible to discern whether the song is in a major or minor key, the listener yet unaware of the quality of the "tonic" (the chord which defines the key). Immediately following, however, the keyboard designates the first chord as E major (giving the impression that this is the key of the piece), but the initial feeling of unease is further sustained when, after the fourth repetition of the E to F-sharp minor motif, the F-sharp is repeated rather than once again falling back to E, and this gives the impression that F-sharp has usurped E as the key-defining pitch. This is confirmed when the chord progression A-major, E-major, F-sharp minor is heard—outlining the tonality of F-sharp minor.

Comprising the harmony of the first and third verses, and used extensively by Waters/Pink Floyd, particularly in *The Wall*, this progression surrounds the tonic note of a minor pentatonic figure (flat third/flat seventh/tonic) and seems to help establish feelings of claustrophobia in whatever context it is used due to its narrow melodic range and circularity. Both this stifling figure and the initial static progression (E to F-sharp) are heard against heavily reverberated roto-toms. According to Philip Tagg:

> One of the main reasons for adding such "reverb" (apart from counteracting the invariably "dead" acoustics of recording studio environments) is to bring about an illusion of large space, imitating the acoustics of a large concert hall and giving the recording a broad or even "symphonic" dimension'. *(Tagg 1979: 96)*

This immense sense of space, in the midst of these feelings of claustrophobia, produces a sense of irony; this time due possibly to the startling paradox that these types of feeling can exist within the microcosm of the alienated individual who lives in the great expanse of the macrocosm.

The first verse, characterised by sharp percussive keyboards and a harsh distorted electric guitar timbre, is sung in an almost shouting manner which, in combination with the instrumental qualities, suggests a violent anger and frustration on behalf of the narrator which is directed toward the idle figure portrayed in the song:

> Ticking away the moments that make up a dull day
> You fritter and waste the hours in an off hand way
> Kicking around on a piece of ground in your home town
> Waiting for someone or something to show you the way.

This anger or frustration is also suggested by the rhythmically strong repeated accents which characterise the delivery of the words. These accents generally appear on the same pitch, and in the third line correspond to Waters' use of internal rhyme (around, ground, town). Both of these devices serve to heighten the effectiveness of conveying the overriding feeling of stress; an effect which is also achieved through the use of consonance (a repetition of the harsh/sharp consonants "k" and "t").

The idle figure, lacking any ambition or sense of direction whatsoever, appears to have stayed in his/her "home town" rather than ambitiously venturing out into the world, heeding perhaps too closely the initial words of the mother figure in "Breathe (in the air)" ("Leave but don't leave me"). This is suggested primarily because of the use of the word "ground" in both songs, while the use of the word "waiting" in the last line brings to mind Samuel Beckett's *Waiting for Godot* (1948), a work which similarly presents the uncertainty and aimlessness that is apparent, for some, in the modern condition.

The second verse, in which the lead vocal this time is sung by Richard Wright rather than David Gilmour, seems to represent another aspect of the narrator which displays sympathy towards the lost figure in the song. Wright's gentle singing seems to provide comfort for the listener or addressee; his melody fluctuating, for the most part between two notes, indicating that perhaps the narrator can relate to the addressee's undirected or claustrophobic state. Wright's voice is supported by passionately soothing female background vocals. Their appearance here (as well as throughout the album) seems to connote a positive motherly presence similar to that which characterised the narrator during the opening of "Breathe (in the air)".

This sudden gentleness is also achieved through Waters' use of assonance (the repetition of the long "i" sound, and to a lesser degree the repetition of the long "o") and consonance (with soft consonant sounds like "s", "l", "y", "n", "m", and "ng"); the disappearance of the "hammering" high-hat; as well as through the change of harmony which employs major-seventh chords—a harmony which typically provides a "bittersweet" quality, presumably because it contains both a minor and major triad. Like the figure in "Breathe (in the air)" and "On the Run" who has "forgot" or turned his back on the sun, so has this character, due to the boredom caused by his unproductive basking in the "sunshine". His alignment with the moon is also demonstrated by his conception of time:

> Tired of lying in the sunshine staying home to watch the rain
> You are young and life is long and there is time to kill today

> And then one day you find ten years have got behind you
> No one told you when to run, you missed the starting gun.

The character seems to measure time not by the sun, which defines it by the earth's daily rotation, but by the moon whose cycle measures a monthly period of time. This gives him/her the impression that there is "time to kill". Of course, due to this extended conception of time, it takes ten years to realise the error because, unlike the individual from the previous tracks whose mother initially told him/her to run, this character missed the beginning of the race and is trying desperately to catch up.

Not only do the words in the third verse make this apparent, but it also seems to be musically portrayed through the guitar solo which is played over the entire musical form of the piece (i.e. two different formal sections). As Walser suggests in the case of heavy metal songs:

> Musically, a dialectic is often set up between the potentially oppressive power of bass, drums, and rhythm guitar, and the liberating, empowering vehicle of the guitar solo.... The feeling of freedom created by the freedom of motion of the guitar solos and fills can be at various times supported, defended, or threatened by the physical power of the bass and the violence of the drums.... The solo positions the listener: he or she can identify with the controlling power without feeling threatened because the solo can transcend anything. *(Walser 1993: 53-54)*

The above observation is not limited to heavy metal music but can also be applied to much rock. In heavy metal, however, this association is enhanced by the technically virtuosic and improvisatory character that most solos in that genre tend to have. This is a crucial point in considering the music of Pink Floyd, whose guitarist David Gilmour's lead playing is almost always very slow and extremely melodic (each note appearing deliberate and reflective) so that it seems always to have been composed—even in the cases where it has not been. As a result, his solos give the impression of an *attempt* at transcendence or liberation (due to their typical position in the mix above the rest of the instruments), but a failed attempt when considered in the context of Waters' characteristically bleak texts. This is, perhaps, one of the reasons for the effectiveness of Waters' and Gilmour's collaborations.

In the first half of the solo from "Time", the guitar attempts to transcend the musically frustrating and claustrophobic character of the background, but its failure is signified when over the second set of harmonic changes (which were initially supposed to provide a kind of relief) Gilmour executes the solo confining himself almost exclusively to sliding up and down one string.

The details of the situation are, of course, more clearly expressed in the lyrics of the third verse, which is set over the "hectic" music of the first. This individual can now also be seen to be "on the run":

> And you run and you run to catch up with the sun, but it's sinking
> And racing around to come up behind you again
> The sun is the same in the relative way, but you're older
> Shorter of breath and one day closer to death.

The character's haste is reflected in the "non-stop" phrasing of the first line; there are no pauses in between the delivery of words as there are in the first verse. The frustration of the situation (also conveyed by the repetition of "and you run" in the first line) is caused by the inability to "seize the day" by "catching up" with the sun, also by the sun's apparent indifference. From the runner's perspective the sun appears to be "racing", but of course time merely marches on as it always has. Anxiety is created from the realisation that during the attempt to "achieve" the sun, the runner has gained nothing but "shortness of breath" (metaphorical psychological discomfort), and yet another wasted day. Suggested also is the inverse of this concern which is that the runner is "one day closer to death". This foreshadows another frustration that later inspires worry and fear in the individual, and which becomes the focus of "Breathe Reprise" and "The Great Gig in the Sky".

The last verse, returning to the same consoling music as the second, is even more reassuring than before. The female background vocalists display their sympathetic understanding, this time with soulful fills. Waters' adoption of the first person displays that he too feels the same frustrating pressures (suggesting that the anger in the first verse was not really directed at the character but at his condition):

> Every year is getting shorter, never seem to find the time
> Plans that either come to naught or half a page of scribbled lines
> Hanging on in quiet desperation is the English way
> The time is gone the song is over, thought I'd something more to say.

The implied relationship set up between unrealised plans and the "half page of scribbled lines" (this song) seems to betray Waters' doubt as to the value of what he has written. He seems to fear that the song may be flawed due either to its having been completed too hastily as a result of an imposed time restriction (implied by the lines having been "scribbled"), or because he's uncertain whether or not it is complete (the lines amount only to "half a page", and he suspected, in the end, that he had "something more to say").[2] Waters suggests that the typical "English" method of coping with these fears is to "hang on in quiet desperation", or simply to repress one's anxiety. This, of course, eventually leads only to feelings of frustration and eventually madness.

Richard Middleton has suggested that Eero Tarasti's "mythical" approach to music may be useful in the analysis of concept albums due to their reprises of previously heard musical materials. This situation appears in the case of this album with the reprise of "Breathe". Myth, according to Tarasti:

> ... always alludes to something earlier, in the distant past, to which the mythical message must be related. The mythical universe is based on the simple division: before/after (avant/après). We now detach this simple abstract relation from the temporal dimension of myth and transfer it to that of music. Thus, using purely morphological criteria, one could deem mythical any sign in musical discourse which refers to some *preceding* sign. Consider a composition where, for example, after a long development and many incidental passages a theme which is introduced at the beginning of the work, reappears at the end. Now, however, its meaning is completely different from what it was when it first occurred in the composition. What is important is precisely the distance between the theme's first appearance and its recapitulation. Everything that has happened meanwhile is in a certain sense present and immersed in the memory of the listener when he hears the theme a sec-

ond time. It is this temporal distance which gives the recurrence of the theme a mythical dimension. *(Tarasti 1979: 67-68)*

Tarasti suggests that this same principle applies both in the case of a transformed theme and a musical quotation from an outside work.

These ideas are very useful to adopt at this juncture. When one considers what has transpired since "Breathe (in the air)" (and even throughout the second half of that song), it amounts primarily to the expression of many feelings of anxiety or "running". But the first verse of "Breathe Reprise" is one which finally expresses relief and comfort:

> Home, home again
> I like to be here when I can
> When I come home cold and tired
> It's good to warm my bones beside the fire.

The narrator's relief (partly conveyed by the repetition of "home") is due to his finally having the opportunity to relax. Waters seems to be suggesting that a balance is necessary between ambition/productivity and idleness; this is suggested in the second line when the character says that he can't *always* be at home. The narrator's initial fatigue is now expressed by the harsh and detached "stumbling" or "plodding" of the guitar and electric piano, but the image of sitting at the fireside is one of comfort and rejuvenation. By utilizing the music of "Breathe (in the air)" which was first used to portray birth, during the singing of these lines, *rebirth* is suggested; a feeling of return to the presence of the consoling mother figure.

This contentedness does not last long, however, because the narrator's peace leads him to quiet reflection about the religious issue of death and resurrection. The image of death is primarily intimated by the tolling bell (a symbol for death at least since John Donne's *Meditations* [1624]):

> Far away across the field
> The tolling of the iron bell
> Calls the faithful to their knees
> To hear the softly spoken magic spells.

The narrator's view of death results in further feelings of anxiety and fear which, for him, are not relieved through faith in resurrection. He is not among the "faithful" who are "far away", but sits alone merely observing. These lines are ushered in with the entrance of an organ (an instrument connoting the Christian Church) whose melodic descent (C,B,A,G,F,D#,D) seems to express his falling spirits. His anxiety appears also to be portrayed harmonically in the cadence of the piece. At the end of the first appearance of the music of "Breathe (in the air)" the piece cadences on the tonic (D7#9, D# diminished 7th, E minor); but in the reprise, the ambiguous diminished-7th chord (which has four possible resolutions), cadences on the minor dominant (D7#9, D# diminished-7th, B minor), an unsettling effect on the listener's ear.

Waters also seems to imply that the "faithful" or religious are called to serve a higher power obediently because of their fear of death—merely responding to the sound of the bell. The unpleasant thought of death (or unpleasant sound of the tolling bell) is expressed through the harsh "t" at the beginning of "tolling". For the faithful the uneasiness caused by this "tolling" is relieved through "the softly spoken magic spells" which create an effect of soft alliteration and consonance. By referring to the "reassuring" scripture readings as incantations, Waters seems to be suggesting that religious belief is essentially superstition, like a belief in magic.

This derisory attitude toward religious thinking is also expressed in the title of the next piece, "The Great Gig in the Sky", which appears to be a mockery of the simplistic view of heaven as a place above the clouds or state of supreme *personal* bliss (i.e., all our heavens are custom made). The title poses an affinity between Waters and the narrator due to the word "gig"—a term used by musicians meaning a single engagement or performance. The title suggests that a musician's "heaven" is the ultimate performance.

The feelings of uncertainty caused by the narrator's apprehension about death reach apocalyptic dimensions in "The Great Gig in the Sky". This is initiated directly at the beginning (where the piece continues from the uncomfortable cadence on the dominant minor in "Breathe Reprise") as a result of the tritone relation that exists between the first two chords of the piece, the tritone (the interval of a diminished fifth or an augmented fourth) being the most unstable and jarring interval in tonal music.[3] This effect is sustained since no certainty of tonal centre exists in the piece until the fifth and sixth bars (a ii—V progression in F major). This sense of stability is supported by the entry of the bass and clean electric guitar which provide a sense of comfort to the lone acoustic piano, an instrument which now makes its first appearance on the album. The appearance of an acoustic instrument suggests nature, and the fact that the fear of death is not limited to twentieth-century human beings makes the piano's employment during this piece appropriate. This two-measure progression is repeated so that the sense of F major is strengthened, but no sooner has this occurred than the piece immediately shifts to B-flat major:

	F: I	IV	I	ii	V	ii	V	I	Bb:
Bm	F	Bb	F/A	Gm^7	C^9	Gm^7	C^9	FMA^7	

tritone

(IV)I	IV	ii	V	I	IV	I
BbMA^7	Eb	Cm^7	F	Bb	EbMA^7	Bb

The piece acquires stability at this point remaining in B-flat major until the end of this section, but the initial instability instills a sense of uncertainty and suspicion in the listener (especially after considering the piece as a whole) that is transferred to the narrator's upcoming statements (which enter during the transition from F to B-flat major) suggesting, perhaps, that these statements are not to be trusted:

> ...and I am not frightened of dying...anytime will do I don't mind.... Why should I be frightened of dying...? I see no reason for it...you've got to go some time....

The initial sense of harmonic uncertainty returns in the next section as we are suddenly thrust back into F (a repeated ii—V progression), justifying our doubt in the truth of the narrator's words.

Transformed into a female (demonstrating that the character is representative of all humankind), the narrator erupts into hysterical screaming (some of the pitches are literally screamed), but one is led to suspect that this outburst is not, in reality, outwardly observable. It takes place purely in her psyche, and we are now able to observe the horror that she truly experiences when she conceptualises her non-existence. This external / internal dichotomy is suggested by the apparently calm and confident spoken statements which appear at points before and after the outburst (the latter statement is "I never said I was frightened of dying") which is juxtaposed with the unrestrained, non-texted singing. Here the absence of words suggests that nothing is supposed to be communicated to an outside party. But we are able to view her mental landscape and witness the true torture within her state of "quiet desperation", or the repression of her fear, an idea first intimated during the conclusion of "Time".

The vocal techniques utilised by the singer are derived from blues and gospel music. They help to convey the character's compounding spiritual frustration as a result of achieving no resolution in her struggle. This frustration becomes ours as well during this section, as the ii—V chord progression begs for resolution to the I chord which would provide a feeling of rest or stability. This progression is repeated for a total of eighteen bars causing frustration to the ear because it continually anticipates a resolution to the tonic (F). Her frustration is also augmented by the expanded texture which is provided by the entry of multiple tracks of organ pad which become louder and more aggressive (an effect achieved by using tremolo) as do the drums which also enter at this point. Of course, the resolution to F which we expect never comes: the piece cleverly modulates back to the ambiguous and uncertain B minor chord with which the song began.

With the return of the first harmonic section the music reverts back to a much quieter dynamic level, suggesting our retreat from the depths of her psyche. Also, this is intimated by the placement of the vocals during this transition, in the back of the mix compared to the instruments. The drums and organ both drop out after this "outburst" and the texture returns to bass guitar and acoustic piano. The guitar is apparently displaced by the vocal.

The remainder of the piece seems to be devoted to the aftermath of the narrator's horrifying glimpse; an expression of sadness characterised by her impassioned voice which, at times, gasps and whimpers. That this piece is not merely about the fear of dying is implied after we are given the impression that the singer is still trying to hide her feelings, unaware that we are already witnesses to her suffering. This is suggested by her apparent denial of being afraid to die. Her withdrawal or distancing is portrayed musically with another occurrence of the voice retreating, away from the listener, to the back of the mix during the last bars of the piece. The feeling of discomfort generated by this musical portrayal of what is a typically twentieth-century characteristic—a retreat into the self (this later becomes Waters' primary focus with The Wall)—is intensified by the occurrence of a chromatic fluctuation in pitch which occurs during the fade-out on the final chord of the piece.

The next "anti-life" pressure with which the album deals is that of "Money". This pressure encompasses both the ill effects of an ideology engrained within capitalism that equates personal success and happiness with economic well-being, and the frustrating contradictions in our personalities to which it ultimately gives rise. The narrator of this song appears to be a symbol for the capitalist ideal: "Get a good job with more pay and you're O.K." (certainly the primary motive for attending universities nowadays). The character, foreseen earlier in "Breathe (in the air)", represents the pinnacle of success because he is wealthy. However his personal goals and ambitions consist merely of the acquisition of material possessions; his ambitions which, like the pursuit of power, are seemingly unending. For him a "new car" and "caviar" rate only as a "four star daydream" and are thus insufficient (five stars, of course, denote the best in our society), hence his solution: "Think I'll buy me a football team".

His endless discontent, as well as his arrogance and conceit ("I'm in the hi-fidelity first class travelling set"), are also portrayed musically. The harmonic scheme of "Money" is derived from the twelve bar blues format. This brings many associations with it. The blues (a Black American folk music often associated with slavery), in this context (a song sung by a wealthy white man who is a slave to money) provides the song with a bitter sense of irony. In what is largely an expression of discontent because of his need for "a football team" and "a Lear jet", the narrator uses a form of expression originally used to articulate the spiritual and emotional woes of an oppressed people. As if this weren't enough, the narrator's blues (a form normally in "common" time), as a reflection of his endless ambition, is in 7/4 time—making his more musically "sophisticated" and, therefore, seemingly superior.

This character's love of money ("it's a hit"/ "it's a gas") becomes an obsession ("Grab that cash with both hands and make a stash"), which makes him suspiciously defensive and unapproachable ("get away"/ "get back") in addition to being merely selfish ("I'm all right Jack keep your hands off my stack"). But after the second verse, which ends with the statement that most fully conveys his arrogance, the piece launches into a "growling" saxophone solo ostensibly representing the character's assertiveness, and *impression* of transcendence. Yet his discontent in having anything less than the best, in combination with his endless ambition, forces him to exchange this instrument after one chorus for a more powerful one—an amplified and distorted electric guitar *(on distortion and power see Walser 1993: 41-44)*. Besides being "adorned" with the effect of distortion, this guitar is double tracked (in both speaker channels) and characterised by its rich reverberation. However, it too plays one chorus only, after which it is suddenly "robbed" of its decorative attributes. Now single tracked, demoted to one speaker channel, and reduced to a "flat" (non reverberating) and raw distorted sound, this change suggests that our hero has fallen victim to the market forces and lost his position of power. This part of the solo receives a less bombastic support from the other instruments as well. Another guitar (similar in quality to the first) takes over the lead confirming this. The fallen narrator is consigned to a subsidiary role playing background rhythm guitar. Oddly enough, his fall is ironically foreshadowed at the first entry of solo guitar by the shift to "common" time.

The former characterisation of the narrator is suddenly lost when, in the last verse, it is made apparent that he has been satirizing the majority of us (foreshadowed in the second verse when he accuses the listener saying, "Don't give me that do goody good bullshit"):

> Money it's a crime
> Share it fairly but don't take a slice of my pie

Money so they say
Is the root of all evil today
But if you ask for a rise it's no surprise that they're giving none away.

Initially a "gas" or "hit", money is now soberly referred to as a "crime", presumably due to its potential to create an inconstancy in human beings just as the moon supposedly does. In this case there is a variability between what we know or say, and what we do. It is interesting that the moon and money have often both shared a similar reputation of being "the root of all evil".[4] The narrator admits that money is a crime since he recognises that it should be shared fairly but knows he would be unwilling to give up any of his own. It is this statement which erases the former irony created by an apparently unauthentic adaptation of the blues. He notes the absurdity of this paradox also in that "they" can tell you the same thing by using a clichéd expression ("Money is the root of all evil"), which states a truth about humanity not really apparent to most.

During the out chorus of "Money" and the transition to the beginning of "Us and Them", there is a montage of speaking voices which helps to bridge the two pieces. Roger Waters' general comments about voices on the album are helpful in establishing their relevance:

> I wanted to use human voices, looped or straight, in the background of the record because it was, generally speaking, supposed to be about human experience. So I came up with this idea...to write a series of questions on index cards. I wanted to interview people, but without being in the room so that all you got was (A) their voice recorded very clean, and (B) them responding to something.... So it was a series of cards which said things like "What is your favourite colour?"; "When was the last time you were violent?"; "Do you think that you were in the right?".
> *(Redbeard: 1993)*

It is the interviewees' answers to the last two questions that are heard at this juncture and which effectively serve to connect the concerns of the previous song to those of the next. Almost all of the responses heard (particularly "Yeah, absolutely in the right" and "I certainly was in the right") display the interviewees' confidence that they were all justified in their inflictions of violence, yet Waters seems to express a quality of doubt, by juxtaposing with these another's uncertain statement "I don't know ... I was really drunk at the time" (thrice repeated and the last comment heard before the fade of "Money"). "Us and Them", a common British working-class expression for the relationship between workers and bosses, is a song that explores the divisions that exist between human beings, or as Sheila Whiteley has suggested, "man's inhumanity to man" *(Whiteley 1992: 113)*. This transitional material implies that people are, perhaps, often too quick to believe that they are "in the right".[5]

"Us and Them" begins with a softly sustained organ chord (D major) whose suspensions and plagal qualities connote a feeling of "spiritual peace". The song's opening contrasts "Money" in every respect (much slower tempo, low dynamic range, more acoustic instruments, instrumental performance smoother and more sparse) which also helps to achieve this effect. The saxophone's reappearance (its tone less assertive, and more legato than in the previous song) and knowledge of its previous role in "Money" also brings to the song a "humble" quality which anticipates the song's opening lyric.

This feeling is prolonged when the other instruments enter, but a slight sense of ambiguity and confusion arises which seems to spoil the former sense of "self awareness". This effect is created by the harmonic ambiguity which is heard against the pedal point on D. The pedal point, sustained throughout the four-chord progression, connotes stasis or stability (a positive feeling in this context), but the chord progression which appears over it (Dsus2, Esus2/D, Dmin[maj]7, G/D), challenges this sense of confidence because of the ambiguous nature of its first three chords (the first two without 3rds and therefore neither major nor minor, and the third challenging the initial tonality established by the organ—as well as having a naturally ambiguous quality in itself). The musical portrayal of ambiguity is heightened when the voice enters, due both to its strange echo which is unnaturally slow, and to its approaching the listener at different points across the speaker channel spectrum. Although we are able to distinguish what is being said, there is a feeling of communicative division between the speaker and the addressee. The sonic image is not unlike that which Waters was to express lyrically six years later in *The Wall* (1979):

> There is no pain, you are receding,
> A distant ship smoke on the horizon,
> You are only coming through in waves....

(Comfortably Numb)

The oddness of the situation is augmented yet again when listeners realise that this strangely treated voice is not only directly addressing them, but also allying itself with them:

> Us, and them
> And after all we're only ordinary men
> Me, and you
> God only knows it's not what we would choose to do.

After the song creates division between the listener and the song's speaker through the music, the latter sarcastically suggests that a similar division exists between "us" and "them"; "we" being merely "ordinary" men and "them" being somehow "extraordinary" or superior, as a result of their rank or position of authority within the establishment (this implied by mention of the "General" in the following lines).[6] The last line of this section with its natural stress on "we" (it is placed on the downbeat and is, in fact, the only word in this line— besides "do"—that falls on beat one) suggests that "we" would not choose to harm people who may have a lower status than ourselves (the way the General does in the following lines); but it also ironically foreshadows the speaker's own guilty actions which take place at the end of the song *(see below)*.

The next section of the song accentuates the division between the speaker and listener even further. Musically there is a shift of harmony (to B minor) and a powerful increase in dynamic intensity (more erratic drumming, distorted electric guitar, much fuller texture) as the speaker's formerly gentle and conversational tone erupts into an outburst which is sympathetically supported by background voices. The initial affinity created between speaker and listener disappears. The speaker suddenly adopts a narrative role which refers to a situation outside his direct relation to us:

> Forward he cried from the rear
> and the front rank died

And the General sat, and the lines on the map
moved from side to side.

Through Waters' portrayal of war as a game of chess *(noted also in Dallas 1987: 78)*, the speaker's burst of passion becomes a response to the high ranking individual in the rear (the back row in chess—the King, Queen, bishops, knights and castles) who orders the front rank or "ordinary men" (the front row in chess—the pawns who are the pieces of the smallest size and value) onward to sacrifice. Meanwhile "the General", who is likely not even on the battle field, *sits* and plays this "game of war, oblivious that '*the lines on the map [which are] moved from side to side*' are comprised of fellow human beings" *(Nicholas Schaffner 1991: 160)*.

With a return to the music of the first section, the listener half expects to be addressed by the speaker again directly, but nothing in his address suggests this, amplifying the division we have already come to feel:

Black and blue
And who knows which is which and who is who
Up and Down
And in the end it's only round and round and round.

Rather than following the oppositions that we have come to expect (us/them, me/you), Waters breaks this pattern, and in doing so, challenges the chess comparison. Commonly black and white in the game (a clear distinction between sides), the pieces on the chess board referred to here are figuratively wearing "black and blue" uniforms, suggesting the underlying difficulty in distinguishing which side is the enemy, both being composed of human beings.[7] The remaining portion of this section describes first the movements of pieces "up and down" the board (complementing the earlier "side to side"), and then the situation which commonly occurs towards the end of a game when one player launches an attempt to capture the other's king. The result can be an endless circling as the player under attack tries to escape checkmate. This image suggests that violence or the activity of war is not a means to progress, but an endless circling in which nothing is achieved.

In response to this view comes the image of the protester in the following section:

Haven't you heard it's a battle of words
the poster bearer cried
Listen son, said the man with the gun
There's room for you inside.[8]

The protester's well-being is also threatened by an authority figure (a riot policeman). The latter's position of power depends on the fact that he "bears" a gun rather than words, however, and his hostility threatens the former's freedom.

The last section of lyric begins with a clever transitional phrase which, besides implying the loser of the chess game, introduces the destitute figure at the end of the song who is victim of another type of competition:

Down and Out
It can't be helped but there's a lot of it about
With, without

And who'll deny it's what the fighting's all about
Out of the way, it's a busy day
I've got things on my mind
For want of the price of tea and a slice
The old man died.

Waters superimposes over the scenes of war and violence an individual who represents a casualty of the capitalist economic situation. At the same time, he suggests that the individual's circumstances symbolise the origin of all division and hostile conflicts whether they be rooted in the desire for (or protection of) wealth, power or property. His comments from 1993 are illuminating:

> ...[I]t's that fundamental attempt to connect with somebody else...and it's something that we all have to learn. Now most of us learn it the hard way [but] it would be good if we could produce a society in which we helped our children learn it the easy way. It's interesting that the Archbishop of York yesterday, it was reported on the front page of the London Times, has finally come to the conclusion that what's largely creating the problems that we face socially in England now, is the fact that our politics foster a competitive society where we encourage our children to believe in a "dog eat dog" philosophy; and then we wonder why they A) commit crimes, and B) grow up rather unhappy. It is the great question that needs unravelling, before the millenium hopefully, and that is; "What lies in the gap between the high ideals enshrined and embodied in the American Constitution and in the reality of life in the United States?". What is in that chasm? We need to find what it is and somehow bridge it. *(Redbeard: 1993)*

The "down and out" individual in "Us and Them" becomes a victim of the narrator (apparently a member of a higher economic class) in whom an individualistic sense of division is strongly engrained. This division ironically causes him to be unaware of his own inhumane actions despite the conclusions which preoccupy him. This irony, in combination with the impression of division created between the speaker and listener, seems to convey Waters' suspicion that there is an innate "darkness" present within human beings that sometimes asserts itself even against our best intentions. As well as casting an irony on the narrator's earlier declaration that "it's not what we would choose to do", this idea leads to a reinterpretation of the lyric as implying that sometimes, because such characteristics may be perceived as being a part of human nature, perhaps we are not even free to choose. In addition to being implied by the phrase "it can't be helped" (from the final stanza), this idea is conveyed by Waters' comparison of war to the game of chess, the uncomfortable irony being that human beings can find amusement in an activity which simulates war. It is these suspicions or realisations that help lead people to a belief that they may at times be mad, or, in other words, controlled by the moon rather than being in control of themselves.

According to Waters, the title of the next piece, "Any Colour You Like", is related to this idea of not being free to choose:

> ...[I]t comes from...it's a Cockney thing, and maybe regional as well. At cattle markets and street markets..., it's a street trader thing. In Cambridge where I lived, people would come from London in a van—a truck—open the back, and stand on the tailboard of the truck, and the

truck's full of stuff that they're trying to sell. They have a very quick and slick patter, and they're selling things like crockery, china, sets of knives and forks. All kinds of different things, and they sell it very cheap with a patter. They tell you what it is, and say, "It's ten plates, lady, and it's this that and the other, and eight cups and saucers, and for the lot I'm asking NOT ten pounds, NOT five pounds, NOT two pounds...fifty bob to you!" you see, and they get rid of the stuff like this....If they had sets of china and they were all the same colour, they would say, "You can 'ave 'em ten bob to you, love. Any colour you like, they're all blue." And that was just part of that patter. So, metaphorically, "Any Colour You Like" is interesting in that sense, because it denotes offering a choice where there is none. And it's also interesting that in the phrase—if you go "any colour you like, they're all blue"—I don't know why, but in my mind it's always they're all blue, which...if you think about it, relates very much to the light and dark, sun and moon, good and evil. You make your choice but its always blue. *(Personal Interview: February 28, 1995)*

The idea of "offering a choice where there is none" appears to be presented musically in this instrumental piece. The track is divided into two main sections, the first of which features the synthesizer as the lead instrument, and the second the electric guitar. The synthesizer's melodic material is presented in contrapuntal layers. But this thick texture, rather than being composed of a variety of melodic material, is actually only a single melody—repeated each time beginning on the next beat. The ear believes that there is an assortment of melodic ideas, whereas there is, in effect, only one.

During the guitar solo, the chord progression is played by another electric guitar whose timbre is identical to that playing the solo. At first, the listener is relieved by the duality established between rhythm and lead guitar, but is frustrated by the lead guitar's tendency, at times, to become simply another rhythm guitar. Much of Gilmour's solo is, in fact, constructed out of rhythmic, chordal ideas. The synthesizer reasserts itself over the guitar towards the end of the second section. Characterised by the same qualities it had initially, it threatens any possibility of transcendence that the guitar may have achieved. During the transition to "Brain Damage", the guitar is, once again, featured by itself, but this time its sense of freedom is thwarted harmonically.

The harmonic construction of the piece features, almost entirely, the back-and-forth repetition between a Dmin7 chord and a G7 (a ii–V progression in the key of C). This movement is similar to that observed earlier in "The Great Gig in the Sky", and has the same effect. The chord sequence continually leads the listener to expect resolution to a C modality, but this expectation is not fulfilled. Instead, the aforementioned transition to "Brain Damage" features the following sequence of chords, which serve as modulatory material to the "D major" modality of that piece: B-flat Ma7, Am, E-flat Ma7, F, C, C-sharp (flat 5) add sharp nine.

This idea of frustrated expectations is portrayed on the album's cover also. On its front is a transparent prism, which separates a beam of white light into a spectrum of colours. This spectrum runs through the middle of the sleeve (in its original vinyl form, where one of the colours becomes a cardiogram) and leads back to an inverted prism, re-fusing the colours into the original single beam of white light. The album cover's cyclical character reflects that of the recording itself *(see below)*. According to Storm Thorgerson, a member of the firm Hipgnosis that designed the album's sleeve:

> The idea of the prism came from a series of conversations with the band, especially with Roger and Rick. Roger spoke about the pressures of touring, the madness of ambition...and the triangle is a symbol of ambition....It was Roger's idea to incorporate the heartbeat, on the inner spread, as part of the design. *(Thorgerson 1992: 51)*

If the equilateral triangle is a symbol of ambition (because, when sitting flat, its sides converge to a single point which forms the triangle's peak), then the inverted triangle is a symbol of frustrated ambition. Relating the white light's component colours to life itself (as represented by the heartbeat), this array seems to represent the illusion that there is a choice of "colours", when, in fact, there is not. Every "colour", or choice, ultimately leads to frustrated ambitions, and consequently madness.

The position of "Any Colour You Like" on the album is also significant. It acts as a bridge between "all the things that drive people mad", which are represented in each of the previous songs, and "Brain Damage"—the actual fear of becoming mad. The title, "Brain Damage" is related to the image of lobotomy (a surgical procedure that destroys parts of the brain) in the third verse of the song, and suggests that this is actually less a fear of going mad, than a fear of being perceived by others as mad.

The Dark Side of the Moon, and "Brain Damage" in particular, alludes to a serious social concern current with the album's release: the general distrust of psychiatry and its questionable therapeutics, and the confused nature of what constitutes its views of mental illness. Studies of this phenomenon began to appear with some regularity almost simultaneously with the release of the album. One such study was *Brain Control* (1973), in the foreword of which Walle Nauta states:

> In this time of anguished reappraisal of the human society it is little wonder that the subject of this book, the control of human behaviour by electrically stimulating or surgically destroying parts of the brain, has aroused intense public interest and anxiety. Emotions engendered by psychosurgery (perhaps better called psychiatric neurosurgery) have come to run high enough to frustrate meaningful discussions between those who disagree on the use of this practice....An important conclusion that suggests itself from these chapters is that the current conflicts over psychosurgery have their origin not only in the largely pragmatic nature of psychiatric-neurosurgical practices and in the great difficulty of measuring accurately the functional losses associated with their benefits, but also in a surprising absence of legal statutes stating and safeguarding the civil rights of prisoners and other institutionalised human beings. *(Valenstein 1973: vii-viii)*

Valenstein, who overall seems to offer a balanced and objective account of these issues, gives the reader an idea of the careless, and possibly biased, nature of historical research into the technique of psychiatric neurosurgery, and "its overly optimistic and, in retrospect, excess ridden heydays of the 1940s and early 1950s" *(Valenstein 1973: viii)*. The author also documents the drastic reduction of such operations in the second half of the 1950s, but notes that at the time he was writing "approximately 600 brain operations are [still] performed each year in the United States":

> The problem of evaluation of the newer psychosurgical techniques remains difficult, since many of the shortcomings of the earlier lobotomy studies are still evident. It is also necessary to recognise that there has been a clear shift in the type of patients selected for psychosurgery....Today the patients considered to be the best candidates are those with tensions, anxieties, phobias, obsessions, compulsions, and severe hypochondriacal symptoms. As a group the patients are not nearly as deteriorated as the earlier lobotomy patients, but this does not mean that their symptoms are mild. The patients may be constantly anxious or depressed and suicide attempts are not uncommon. *(Valenstein 1973: 317)*

It is interesting that among the symptoms displayed by some of those who were selected for psychosurgery circa 1973 are those which Waters suggests are caused by characteristic "pressures which are anti-life". It is no surprise, then, that the narrator of "Brain Damage" harbours "dark forebodings" for the simple reason that the anxiety and sadness caused by reflection on the modern condition could be interpreted by society as mental illness or abnormality.

This is not an absurd possibility. In 1974 the U.S. Department of Health, Education, and Welfare published a document called *Psychosurgery: Perspective on a Current Issue* which attempted to elucidate the issue. Certain portions of the pamphlet are very disturbing:

> Psychosurgery was recommended for curing or ameliorating schizophrenia (Sankar 1969), depression (Knight 1969), homosexuality (*Medical World News* 1970), childhood behavior disorders (Andy 1970), criminal behavior (Vaernet and Madsen 1970; Koskoff and Goldhurst 1968; Hirose 1968) and a variety of narcotic addiction (Smolik 1950; Scarff 1950; Wikler et al. 1952) and other psychiatric problems. *(Brown, Wienckowski and Bivens 1974: 1)*

The range of "psychiatric problems" included here is shocking, moreso when one understands that some of the above, and particularly homosexuality, are no longer considered behaviour disorders.

Besides the threat of psychiatry's continued misconception of what constitutes mental illness is that of the potential it has to abuse its powerful means of controlling behaviour. The uneasiness this causes is enhanced when someone like Valenstein says regarding electroconvulsive therapy:

> To induce convulsions by passing an electric current through the brain conjures up images of "electric chairs" and medieval tortures. In Ken Kesey's novel *One Flew Over the Cuckoo's Nest*, there is a very dramatic representation of electroshock as a device to control and punish patients, having no therapeutic value. The novel may be an effective allegory for attacking authoritarianism, but it certainly does not present electroshock treatment accurately. *(Valenstein 1973: 148)*

Valenstein may be correct in saying that Kesey does not portray this treatment accurately, but this was not necessarily Kesey's intention, which instead, I would suggest, was to portray the gross misuse of the procedure *(see Fuller Torey 1974: 72-73 and Chavkin 1978: 9-10 for instances of this)*; Valenstein seems to down play this threat.

Samuel Chavkin, in his book *The Mind Stealers: Psychosurgery and Mind Control*, cites an article, "Criminals Can Be Brainwashed—Now" (1970) written by James McConnell, professor of psychology at the University of Michigan:

> ...the day has come when...it should be possible...to achieve a very rapid and highly effective type of positive brainwashing that would allow us to make dramatic changes in a person's behavior and personality...We should reshape our society so that we all would be trained from birth to want to do what society wants us to do. We have the techniques now to do it...No one owns his own personality...You had no say about what kind of personality you acquired, and there is no reason to believe that you should have the right to refuse to acquire a new personality if your old one is antisocial...Today's behavioral psychologists are the architects and engineers of the Brave New World. *(Chavkin 1978: 10)*

Chavkin sees this view not as an attempt to cure criminals, but to force them into submitting to whoever wields authority. He notes:

> There is much concern about the growing acceptance of behaviorist and psychosurgical remedies for what basically are socioeconomic problems requiring political solutions....The tendency in dealing with crime and delinquency is to bypass the social roots of violence (the nation's economic upheavals, unemployment, etc.) and to focus instead on the "pathology," genetic or otherwise, of the culprit who fails to "shape up"....[T]he emphasis made in terms of money and planning is to improve the efficiency of the law enforcement agencies in subduing the culprit and recycling him or her into a conforming individual, one who will accept the very conditions (drug traffic, unemployment, slum housing) that precipitated his or her criminal acts to begin with. *(Chavkin 1978: 3, 5 and 9)*

Chavkin's argument about the need for concern culminates with his reference to the 1977 scandal in the United States where "the nation was stunned to learn that a large-scale behaviour control experimentation program had been going on in the [country][9] for upward of twenty-five years":

> These CIA activities were clearly illegal and were carried out with the participation of at least 185 scientists and some eighty institutions: prisons, pharmaceutical companies, hospitals, and forty-four medical colleges and universities.... The main idea of this mammoth...effort, which cost the taxpayers at least $25 million, was to program an individual to do one's bidding even if it would lead to his own destruction. As quoted by the *New York Times*, a CIA memorandum of January 25, 1952, asked "whether it was possible to 'get control of an individual to the point where he will do our [CIA's] bidding against his will and even against such fundamental laws of nature as self-preservation. *(Chavkin 1978: 12-13)*

The initial idea about the lack of choice presented in the phrase "any colour you like" appears, obviously, to have further significance when explored in the album's contemporary social context. The idea seems even more disturbing in the light of a situation like the following. Ten years after the release of *The Dark Side of the Moon*—in a Canadian weekly news magazine called *Maclean's*—there appeared a story called "The fight to refuse treatment" *(Goldman 1983: 36)*, about a woman who lost her fight in court for the right to refuse electroconvulsive therapy.

In the song "Brain Damage", the connection between the moon and lunacy is made explicit. Waters returns to the album's first half to confirm the mental states of the initial two characters (the ambitious "runner" and the unambitious "idle" figure), this time dealing with the latter first:

> The lunatic is on the grass
> The lunatic is on the grass
> Remembering games and daisy chains and laughs
> Got to keep the loonies on the path.

This figure, who sits idly thinking about past amusements, appears to be a portrait of the late 1960s hippies who were often portrayed as "...sitting on the grass with flowers in their hair...".[10] The hippies were representatives of a counter-culture whose "heady optimism" was apparent in the belief, "'change the mode of consciousness and you change the world'"—this "change of mode" was sought through a "retreat into Eastern mysticism [and a reliance] on drugs" *(Whiteley 1992: 104 and 110)*. Waters appears not to have subscribed to this belief, which is hardly surprising after having witnessed the deterioration of Syd Barrett (Pink Floyd's original guitarist whose prolonged use of LSD contributed to his mental breakdown). It is this counter-culture's belief to which Whiteley suggests the entire album was, in part, a reaction *(Whiteley 1992: 104)*.

The second verse documents the mental states of the ambitious "runners" whose high-profiles ensure their regular appearance in the newspapers:

> The lunatic is in the hall
> The lunatics are in my hall
> The paper holds their folded faces to the floor
> And every day the paper boy brings more.

However, the success of these individuals appears to be the result of their having "folded faces" or in other words, to their being "two-faced". Appropriately, when Pink Floyd performed the song live, a film was projected of Edward Heath, England's Prime Minister during the years 1970-1974, "apparently singing along" *(Dallas 1987: 51)*. Heath seems an appropriate representative of the "runner". Aside from the fact that he was a politician, he was "generally regarded as new-style Conservative in that he had none of the usual aristocratic background and connections..." *(Roud 1966: 137)*.

The first appearance of the "chorus" section of the song has the narrator, the same character who had seemingly achieved a balance between ambition and idleness in the "Breathe Reprise", documenting his own condition. This character, whose feelings of relief and repose were disturbed by his thoughts on death, again has premonitions, but this time of his own premature demise by drowning. This was the predicted fate of the "runner" portrayed in "Breathe (in the air)", but it is not the narrator's destiny because he has a desire to "ride the tide", or align himself with the moon by choice; it is because of circumstances (or metaphorically, some force) beyond his control:

> And if the dam breaks open many years too soon
> And if there is no room upon the hill
> And if your head explodes with dark forebodings too
> I'll see you on the dark side of the moon.

The narrator envisages a situation in which he will be unable to escape the dam's torrents of water. The anxiety created by this "dark foreboding" leads him to feeling an association not merely with the moon, but with its dark side in particular which represents the mysterious or unknown. It is important to observe, however, that this "darkness" is affecting the narrator from within and not from without. This reflects Waters' view of the mysterious complexity inherent in humankind (already portrayed in "The Great Gig in the Sky", "Money" and "Us and Them"). The next verse displays the narrator's feelings of madness which result from this "darkness" within; but these feelings have been musically conveyed long before this point of the song is reached.

The verses of the song, from the beginning, contain many qualities that suggest madness or alienation. Among these is the excessively chromatic melodic line (quite rare in rock songs of this type) which is, for the most part, reinforced by the arpeggiating guitar's chord voicings. Also, the vocal harmony (which enters on the third line of every verse) appears predominantly a tritone above the lead voice; the tritone, as mentioned earlier, is the most unstable and jarring interval in tonal music. These feelings of alienation are combined with an instability or "unrootedness" which is supported by the bass guitar's sudden retreat into the mix (the bass guitar most often playing the roots of chords) and the comparatively "thin" tone it adopts in comparison to that which characterised it in "Any Colour You Like". This sudden "thinness" is enhanced by the insecure sounding vocals (both lead and background) which are also characterised by a "high", "thin" quality. This overwhelming lack of "foundation" is, in addition, portrayed through the "clean" guitar fills which ignore the roots of the chords over which they are played, always resolving on the third or the seventh of a chord instead.

The third verse conveys the narrator's suspicions of his own madness, which is highlighted by maniacal laughter. It also communicates the understandable paranoia which accompanies these suspicions, augmented by the sense of distrust suggested by his addressing the listener as a member of society who may possibly view him as insane also, and may subsequently try to *cure* him through one of the popular "therapeutic" techniques of the day:

> The lunatic is in my head
> The lunatic is in my head
> You raise the blade, you make the change
> You re-arrange me 'till I'm sane

> You lock the door
> And throw away the key
> There's someone in my head but it's not me.

This portrayal of lobotomy illustrates, in the last three lines, the frightening irreversibility of the operation and its rather undesirable effects—i.e. destroying the person who existed before.

The first line of the chorus section's return seems now to recall the idle figure in "Time" who withdrew from the sun, and due to boredom stayed home "to watch the rain". But the narrator, as before, experiences "the rain" first hand to a traumatic degree, again apparently not by choice. He anticipates that the listener may also experience this "rain":

And if the cloud bursts, thunder in your ear
You shout and no one seems to hear
And if the band you're in starts playing different tunes
I'll see you on the dark side of the moon.

The third line of this section seems to allude to Syd Barrett, who was permanently replaced by David Gilmour in March 1968 due to the former's mental deterioration,[11] and the storm imagery suggests his unstable condition. The storm is internal and the attempt to "shout" above it is an attempt to explain the subsequent fears to, or identify with, an outsider about the "din" within. But the "dark foreboding" this time is that no one else will understand (the word "hear" as in "I hear what you're saying" or "I understand"). According to Waters:

> The line *I'll see you on the dark side of the moon* is me speaking to the listener saying: I know you have these bad feelings and impulses because I do too and one of the ways I can make direct contact with you is to share with you the fact that I feel bad sometimes. *(Dallas 1987: 107)*

The comfort which the last line of this section brings is also conveyed musically, partially a result of the relief achieved from all of the unsettling musical effects of the verses, beginning with a change of key to the subdominant. The melody of the chorus contains none of the excessive chromaticism of the verse. The tritone vocal harmonies are altered to the interval of a third, perhaps the most consonant of intervals, and in rock, certainly the most frequently used in vocal harmonies. The texture is now filled (the full band enters) with a powerful bass which clearly outlines the chordal roots, and the addition of organ and gospel-like female background voices (first singing merely syllables, but then singing the lyric), in combination with the strong plagal movement (C-G), convey a feeling of "spiritual ease".

This sense is conveyed to an even greater extent throughout "Eclipse", the last piece on the album, which is positioned so that it seems to replace the chorus of "Brain Damage". This piece, like the aforementioned chorus, provides relief from the instrumental verse music which appears at the end of the previous song, but it also evokes a mood of celebration. This is achieved by the energetic entry of all the instruments, which gives an impression of unity, and the sudden adaption of a very rhythmic 6/4 meter. The lead vocal, which begins alone, is immediately joined on the second "verse" by the female background vocalists, who punctuate with passionate fills the lead vocalist's statements throughout the song while also providing support by occasionally echoing one of the lines after him ("all that you give" and "everyone you meet")—a direct allusion to gospel music techniques. About half way through the song, other group members begin to sing along with the lead voice and this enhances the original sense of unity. Interestingly, on each appearance of the third chord of the progression (B-flat), the guitar plays its open E string (creating the interval of a tritone), but the jarring effect which is felt is continuously resolved, the E becoming the fifth of the next chord (A). This suggests that although these feelings of unease will consistently arise, some relief will always arise in the knowledge that we are never alone.

The lyrics list a wide variety of human experience, partially drawing on the other songs of the album (for example the first two lines are taken from "Breathe (in the air)"), to present many of the positive and negative facets of existence. In the last section all these are grouped together to represent their occurrence through the entire spectrum of time, or that which humankind commonly perceives as eternity ("All that is now / All that is gone / All that's to come"). This is followed by the record's penultimate statement:

> and everything under the sun is in tune
> but the sun is eclipsed by the moon.

The image is a strong one because of its various implications. The line, in part, suggests that the truth or beauty which we as human beings strive for (so apparent and harmonious in the clarity of the sun) is overshadowed by the darkness or uncertainty created by our seemingly more natural alignment with the moon, just as life itself is eventually overshadowed by death (hence the fade out of the heart beat at the end of the album). The constant repetition of these frustrations in the lives of succeeding generations is portrayed through the album's cyclical character (it faded in with a heart beat at the beginning). Waters says of the lyric:

> I think it's a very simple statement saying that all the good things life can offer are there for us to grasp, but that the influence of some dark force in our natures prevents us from seizing them. The song addresses the listener and says that if you, the listener, are affected by that force, and if that force is a worry to you, well I feel exactly the same too. *(Dallas 1987: 107)*

This comfort or sense of relief provided for the listener through the connection made with another person, and the knowledge that someone else experiences these feelings, is conveyed almost purely musically as I discussed above.

Equally intriguing is the nature of the "dark force" to which Waters refers, and which he symbolically represents by the moon; a force whose existence was suspected by another twentieth-century thinker as Terry Eagleton describes:

> His estimate of human capacities is on the whole conservative and pessimistic: we are dominated by a desire for gratification and an aversion to anything which might frustrate it. In his later work, he comes to see the human race as languishing in the grip of a terrifying death drive, a primary masochism which the ego unleashes on itself. The final goal of life is death, a return to that blissful inanimate state where the ego cannot be injured. Eros, or sexual energy, is the force which builds up history, but it is locked in tragic contradiction with Thanatos or the death drive. We strive onwards only to be constantly driven backwards, struggling to return to a state before we were even conscious.[12] *(Eagleton 1983: 161)*

Waters' suspicions, as well as coinciding with and reinforcing those of Freud, suggest a serious issue. The album ends with a voice saying, "[t]here is no dark side of the moon really... as a matter of fact it's all dark". This appears to be the album's overriding emphasis—a concern for our failure to build on Freud's postulations, or come any closer to illuminating a remedy for the human condition. Freud once said, "[t]he motive of human society is in the last resort an economic one" *(Eagleton 1983: 151)*. As Waters intimated above, and seems also to conclude later in *The Wall*, perhaps our difficulties are less rooted in psychology than they are in sociology. As he suggests, this appears to be the great question that requires unravelling before the millenium. Until then, "I'll see you on the dark side of the moon".

Chapter 2 — Wish You Were Here

...the divisions that always existed between popular music and serious music are no longer there. You can't get any more serious than Lennon at his most serious. If you get any more serious than *that* you fucking throw yourself under a train!'

Roger Waters[1]

Coinciding with the rise of mass media in the twentieth century has been the phenomenon of superstardom, a reality which, for many, has been a difficult one to face. For some—Judy Garland, Marilyn Monroe, Jack Kerouac, Jim Morrison and most recently Kurt Cobain, to name only a few—it has brought an untimely end; the frequency of testaments such as John Lennon's display the dilemma in which such individuals often find themselves:

The idea of being a rock and roll musician sort of suited my talents and mentality. The freedom was great, but then I found out I wasn't free. I'd got boxed in.... The whole Beatle thing was just beyond comprehension. And I was eating and drinking like a pig, and I was fat as a pig, dissatisfied with myself, and subconsciously was crying for help... *(Solt and Egan 1988: 76)*

Pink Floyd's *Wish You Were Here* (1975) deals with the common tendency to crumble under the pressures of this situation. Having attained "megaband" status "on the order of The Rolling Stones or The Who" *(Schaffner 1990: 166)* owing to the enormous success of *The Dark Side of the Moon*, the members of Pink Floyd found themselves facing such a condition. Waters recalls:

At that point all our ambitions were realized. When you're fifteen and you think, "Right, I'm gonna start a group," the pinnacle that you see (apart from very vague thoughts about rather smart bachelor flats and not having to get up till four in the afternoon)...is the Big Album. The number one in *Billboard*. And once you've done that, a lot of your ambitions have been achieved....Yes, it does feel wonderful for a month or something...and then you begin to start coping with [the realisation] that it's not going to make any difference really to how you feel about anything, and—it doesn't work. It doesn't mean changes. If you're a happy person, you were before and you will be afterwards, and if you're not, you weren't before and you won't be afterwards. And that kind of thing doesn't make a blind bit of difference to how you feel about anything. But even though you know that, it still takes you a long time to assimilate it. *(Schaffner 1990: 172)*

One of the pressures applied to anyone involved with mass media culture is the frustrating paradox of creating art in the context of a multi-million dollar industry. Immediately following the release of *Wish You Were Here*, Waters remarked:

The name 'Pink Floyd',...not the individuals in the band, but the name Pink Floyd is worth millions of pounds. The name is probably worth one million sales of an album, any album we put out. Even if we just coughed a million people will have ordered it simply because of the name. ...[H]aving become very successful...having made it, if we could all have accepted that's what we were in it for, we could then have all split up gracefully at that point. But we can't... *(Sedgewick 1975: 15-16)*

Of the group's members, Waters appears to have felt the pressures of these contraditions between art and rock 'n roll the most:

> I've been through a period when I've not wished to do any concerts with the Floyd ever again. I felt that very strongly, but...I've had vague kind of flickerings, feeling that I could maybe have a play. But when those flickerings hit the front of my mind I cast myself back into how fucking dreadful I felt on the last American Tour with all those thousands and thousands and thousands of drunken kids smashing each other to pieces. I felt dreadful because it had nothing to do with us—I didn't think there was any contact between us and them. There was no more contact between us and them than them and...I was just about to say the Rolling Stones and them. There obviously is contact of a kind between Mick Jagger and the public but it's weird and it's not the kind of contact that I want to be involved with really. I don't like it. I don't like all that Superstar hysteria. I don't like the idea of selling that kind of dream 'cos I know its unreal 'cos I'm there. I'm at the top...I am the dream and it ain't worth dreaming about. Not in the way they think it is anyway. It's all that "I want to be a rock 'n roll singer" number which rock 'n roll sells on. It sells partly on the music but it sells a hell of a lot on the fact that it pushes that dream. *(Sedgewick 1975: 20-21)*

After spending a good deal of 1974 in a state of semi-retirement, the group set themselves back to work; but "the pressures inherent in following up such a blockbuster were so intense that they found themselves locked in a state of creative paralysis" (Schaffner 1990; 174). In conjunction with this there arose a "communication trough" due to the artistic differences present within the group which, according to Waters, were the result of "a divergence of opinion about what we should be doing, what records should be about" *(Dallas 1987: 109)*. Waters summarised the situation for Nick Sedgewick:

> When we got into the studio January '75, we started recording and it got very laborious and tortured, and everybody seemed to be very bored by the whole thing. We pressed on regardless of the general ennui for a few weeks and then things came to a bit of a head. I felt that the only way I could retain interest in the project was to try to make the album relate to what was going on there and then *i.e.* the fact that no one was really looking each other in the eye, and that it was all very mechanical...most of what was going on....The interesting thing is that when we finally did do an album [it was] actually about not coming up with anything, because the album is about none of us really being *there*, or being *there* only marginally. About our non-presence in the situation we had clung to through habit, and are still clinging to through habit—being Pink Floyd....I definitely think that at the beginning of [the] 'Wish You Were Here' recording sessions most of us didn't wish we were there at all, we wished we were somewhere else. I wasn't happy being there because I got the feeling we weren't *together*... *(Sedgewick 1975: 11-12)*

For Waters, the fragmented character of Pink Floyd was symbolised by the mental state of the band's original leader Syd Barrett who, in Waters' opinion, seemed to have "[succumbed] to the pressures of life in general and rock 'n roll in particular" *(Sedgewick 1975: 13)*. This view was supported by Peter Jenner, one of the group's original managers, who suggested, "it's tragic that the music business may well have a lot to do with doing him in..." *(Schaffner 1990: 118)*. William Ruhlmann suggests that when the group began, "[a]s far as the band's managers and most of its fans were concerned, Pink Floyd was Barrett and some backup musicians" *(Ruhlmann 1993: 26)*. It was, perhaps, partially this pressure of becoming the group's star figure that forced Barrett into his later condition of apparent mental illness.

Although *Wish You Were Here* is not overtly dedicated to Barrett, he is the figure who is addressed in the song "Shine On You Crazy Diamond", the piece of which the majority of the record is comprised. Primarily an instrumental work, "Shine On" is divided into nine parts, the first half separated from the second by "Welcome to the Machine", "Have a Cigar" and "Wish You Were Here". These songs, according to Waters, each "had some kind of relevance to the state we were all in at the time" *(Sedgewick 1975: 13)*, but the album as a whole, naturally, seems to document its author's own premonitions of succumbing to the "pressures of life". This is reinforced by statements like that of Richard Wright, the group's keyboardist who remarked, "Roger's preoccupation with things such as madness and the Business is something that I didn't feel nearly so strongly about" *(Schaffner 1990: 186)*.

Around the time of this album's release Waters submitted that "[t]he quality of life is full of stress and pain in most of the people I meet...and in myself" (Miles 1980). When Sedgewick commented to Waters about the remarks that people had made regarding the album's sadness, Waters replied:

> I'm glad about that...I think the world is a very, very sad fucking place...I find myself at the moment, backing away from it all...I'm very sad about Syd.... 'Shine On's' not really about [him]—he's just a symbol for all the extremes of absence some people have to indulge in because it's the only way they can cope with how fucking sad it is—modern life, to withdraw completely. *(Sedgewick 1975: 21)*

Seen in this light, the album can be regarded conceptually as a sequel to *The Dark Side of the Moon* in that it documents an individual's long term reaction to frustrations and "pressures which are anti-life" (Waters quoted in Miles 1980).

With regard to the album as a whole, Waters suggested, "...I think we made a basic error in not arranging it in a different way so that some of the ideas were expounded lyrically before they were developed musically". This displays his concern that the work's meanings may have been diluted by "the very drawn-out nature of the overture bits that go on and on and on and on..." *(Schaffner 1993: 186)*. I would suggest that Waters' fears are unwarranted, however, as it is necessary that one hear the work in its entirety anyway in order to comprehend its overall meaning. After one has experienced the piece as a whole, meanings can be fairly easily construed.

Throughout "Shine On You Crazy Diamond", an opposition is set up between synthesizer and guitar. That the piece begins and ends with a synth solo seems to establish this instrument as the work's leading "character" or protagonist, who is, of course, Barrett. Part I consists of a melody which, as Dallas comments, is softly played by a "trumpet-like synthesizer" *(Dallas 1987: 111)* over a keyboard pad which imitates a string orchestra. Harmonically, Part I remains on a sustained G-minor chord, and this, in combination with its rhythmically fluid melody, establishes a modal sound reminiscent of the beautiful simplicity which characterised the music of the Western world in its early stages of development, particularly Gregorian Chant. This modality, in combination with the pure sounding timbre of the lead synthesizer and its "straight" articulation of the "chant-like" melody, connotes a sense of "musical innocence" while, at the same time, suggesting "art" music because of the imitation of orchestral instruments.

It is with the electric guitar entry that Part II of the work begins, and the dichotomy between instruments is established. The electric guitar immediately connotes rock 'n roll partly due to its long association with this popular music genre, and because of Gilmour's bending of strings to attain pitches—a technique associated with the blues and one that separates rock electric guitar playing from jazz. This technique also makes it possible to play "blue notes" and their presence here, in combination with the guitar's irregular melodic phrasing, serves to establish a contrast with the "art" music connotation of the first section.[2] The guitar also "corrupts" the initial modal innocence bringing with it harmonic change shortly after its entry. It has an unintimidating quality, however, as a result of its quiet tone and purely clean, "unadulterated" timbre which is untouched by any effects.

This quality is lost at the beginning of Part III, however, when the guitar plays a repeated four-note motif

which is highly ornamented with electronic effects—a typical stylistic quality of rock guitar timbres. This shift of character seems to foreshadow the initially deceptive nature of the narrators in both "Welcome to the Machine" and "Have a Cigar". This four-note motif held particular significance for Waters. According to him, it "inspired the whole piece":

> It was very strange. The lyrics were written—and the lyrics are the bit of the song about Syd, the rest of it could be about anything—I don't know why I started writing those lyrics about Syd... I think because that phrase of Dave's was an extremely mournful kind of sound and it just...I haven't a clue... *(Miles 1980)*

Rather than saying "the rest of it could be about anything", I would suggest that, judging by his comments quoted above, Waters means "the rest of it could be about *anybody*". The four-note motif is comprised of four large, disjunct intervallic leaps, and connotes the mental condition of Barrett because of its disjointedness. Its first and last notes outline a tritone—the first harsh dissonance of the piece. This dissonance, in combination with the guitar's aforementioned characteristics, seems, for Waters, to conjure up a memory of "the machinery of a music industry that made and helped break Syd Barrett" *(Edmunds 1975: 63-64)*. The figure first functions as a signal for the full band to enter, which they do following a subtle two-bar crescendo, and then it becomes a repeated motif, punctuated each time by a guitar chord which is aggressively executed by Gilmour's consistent use of the tremolo bar.

The orchestral-like background synthesizer is replaced by an organ upon the full band's entry, leaving behind the former "art" music connotations. Immediately before the lead guitar returns for a solo, the original lead synth subserviently takes over the four-note motif suggesting, perhaps, its joining the "machine". The lead guitar is noticeably both louder and brighter than before, allowing it to stand out more strongly above the accompanying instruments. Towards the end of this solo section (eight bars before), the guitar powerfully erupts into a seemingly hostile attack with a notable increase in distortion and volume. This hostility becomes very significant when the listener realises that the accompanying chord progression appears later in the texted portions of the work which are addressed to Barrett (first heard behind "You were caught in the crossfire..."). Here it serves to foreshadow the lyrical account of Barrett's demise, the antagonistic electric guitar seemingly aiming its attack at him.

Part IV begins with a reduction in volume and a return to the lead synth, "more French horn-like this time" *(Dallas 1987: 111)*, which continues to employ a regular phrasing compared to the guitar. These qualities bring back the original connotations of both "art" music and Barrett. They imply the paradox of an artist attempting to express himself in the context of the rock music industry. In contrast to the powerful sound of the guitar, the synthesizer's timbre is rather impotent, foreshadowing Waters' expression of Barrett's vulnerability lyrically in Part V. The addition of acoustic piano evokes a sense of naturalness. This serves to contrast the former section which, with the exception of drums, is entirely played on electric instruments, supporting its representation of the "mechanised" music business. The guitar now takes the accompaniment role, sharply "observing" the synth with its percussive attacks on the back beat. The piano drops out to re-establish the lead guitar's mechanised background when it returns halfway through Part IV to reassert itself yet more powerfully than before.

The vocal entry marks the beginning of the next section and Waters' direct address to Barrett. It is interesting that although the group uses female background voices during this piece, they do not achieve the reassuring effect which they did in *The Dark Side of the Moon* because they are mixed in so much in the background, and almost inaudible unless one listens especially for them. Lyrically, Part V's structuring of meaning parallels that of its musical construction. Following the first two lines of each verse is a hopeful refrain ("Shine on you crazy diamond") which is set off from the other lines in a variety of ways; first of all with the sense of group unity conveyed when all the voices join Waters in paying tribute to Barrett. The importance of this line's message is conveyed through its constant repetition, and its hopefulness is reflected in the accompanying tonal shift to the relative major (B-flat) each time. The dissonant harmonic and melodic material of the other portions also serves to illustrate this, creating an extreme contrast to the consonance of the refrain:

The jarring effect of the tritone relations present in the initial lines, in combination with the extensive use of chromaticism, assists in conveying the harsh truth about Barrett's story. It is also significant that the lead guitar constantly appears in these "dissonant" segments with fills, confirming the presence of the rock music industry's spectre. The guitar does not, however, interrupt the singing of the optimistic refrain. This suggests that the music industry has not yet posed any threat to Waters and the other members of Pink Floyd.

The second half of the verse sets up a similar contrast both lyrically and musically:

The music here is entirely characterised by chromaticism, and the first half continues to document Barrett's downfall. This is musically portrayed by the descending melody and bass line. The second portion which, once again, urges Barrett to "shine", counters this descent with a reversal of the melody in an upward direction. This provides a sense of striving for transcendence which eventuates in a perfect (V—I) cadence, and subsequent, albeit momentary, feelings of satisfaction and ease.

The initial line of the opening verse in Part V employs one of the primary symbols used in *The Dark Side of the Moon*. The first half of the verse reads:

> Remember when you were young, you shone like the sun.
> Shine on you crazy diamond.
> Now there's a look in your eyes, like black holes in the sky.
> Shine on you crazy diamond.

These lines establish a contrast between the time preceding and that following Barrett's collapse. Waters indicates that, as a youth, Barrett was a source of brilliance and splendour comparable to the magnificent radiance of the sun. The image, with its previous associations *(see page 16)*, suggests also that Barrett, once full of life, is now in a metaphorical state of death, his eyes being "like black holes" suggesting a blank stare or void. The image is an appropriate one because nothing that enters a black hole, not even a light ray, can escape. This proposes that, in Waters' view, the real Syd Barrett appears to be permanently lost. The comments of Joe Boyd, producer of the band's first single, bring a harsh truth to the image:

> ...the great thing about Syd was that if there was anything about him that you really remembered it was that he had a twinkle in his eye. I mean he was a real eye-twinkler. He had this impish look about him, this mischievous glint and he came by and I said "Hi Syd" and he just kind of looked at me. I looked right in his eye and there was no twinkle. No glint. And it was like somebody had pulled the blinds, you know, nobody home. *(Miles 1980)*

Waters' portrayal of Barrett as a diamond is, appropriately, multi-faceted. Besides the obvious connotation that diamonds are objects of great worth, they are transformed from one state (graphite) to another due to intense pressure in the crust and mantle of the earth, much like Barrett whose altered state, in Waters' view, owes to those extreme pressures "which are anti-life". The word diamond is a corruption of the Greek word *adamas* which means "unconquerable", and this association suggests that Barrett's present state may protect him entirely from the world's pressures; but this is exposed as a fallacy in the last line of the verse when he is referred to as a "martyr".[3] Also significant is that a diamond, like the moon, is not itself a source of light, but is, nonetheless, one of the most effective reflectors of light. This also supports the idea that Barrett is no longer as he was when he "shone like the sun". The appeal made by Waters and the group for Barrett to continue to "shine" seems to be an attempt to enable him to reflect some of their "light" by immortalizing him through the tribute which they pay in the song.

In the second portion of the verse, Waters elucidates some of the factors that led to Barrett's transformation:

> You were caught in the crossfire of childhood and stardom,
> blown on the steel breeze.

Waters proposes that Barrett was under attack from two sources at once. Besides being harmed by the pressures of stardom, Barrett was simultaneously dealing with many of the difficulties of youth as he was only twenty-one years of age at the time when his deterioration began. The "steel breeze" is a powerful image because it suggests some invisible force in the universe or life which, as cold and sharp as steel, presents resistance to the aspirations of human beings, or is even capable of "blowing" them entirely "off course", as in Barrett's case. It also effectively connotes, through its use of the word steel, the music industry which is later in the album portrayed as the "machine".

In the last line of the verse, Waters urges Barrett to "shine" once again:

> Come on you target for faraway laughter, come on you stranger,
> you legend, you martyr, and shine!

With the first image, Waters appears to imagine a malevolent entity in the cosmos that mockingly laughs at human suffering. This is a fairly common image and forms the first half of Thomas Hardy's poem *Hap (1866)*:

> If but some vengeful god would call to me
> From up the sky, and laugh: "Thou suffering thing,
> Know that thy sorrow is my ecstasy,
> That thy love's loss is my hate's profiting!"

> Then would I bear it, clench myself, and die,
> Steeled by the sense of ire unmerited....

This mention of laughter is foreshadowed by the actual laughter which interrupts the first line of the song. It apparently mocks both the memory of the promising young Barrett, and his present condition as a tormented "stranger" who is no longer the same person that Waters and the other members of Pink Floyd once knew. Barrett is also referred to as a "legend". Waters' comments are illuminating:

> ...there are no facts involved in the Barrett story so you can make up any story you like—and [journalists] do. ...it's all hearsay and none of them *know* anything... *(Sedgewick 1975: 21)*

Because of the lack of knowledge about Barrett's situation, he has become an enigmatic character who has inspired a host of "legends" *(see Schaffner 1991: 116-120)*.

Bridging the first and second verses is a lead guitar interlude (triple tracked and harmonised). It is, significantly, at this point that the lead guitar comes into contact with the music of the refrain, suggesting that the rock music industry also affects the other group members. This is supported during the second occurrence of the refrain in the next verse (also in the entire third verse from Part VII), where the voices are no longer in unison. This seems symbolically to represent the band's fragmented condition during the recording of the album.

Barrett's extensive drug use is generally well known. As Richard Wright, the group's keyboardist, suggests with regard to his breakdown:

> Certainly acid [LSD] had something to do with it....The point is, you don't know whether the acid accelerated this process that was happening in his brain, or was the cause of it. No one knows. I'm sure the drugs had a lot to do with it. *(Schaffner 1991: 76)*

Waters also seems to allow that drugs played a major role in Barrett's deterioration. The second verse begins:

> You reached for the secret too soon, you cried for the moon.
> Shine on you crazy diamond.

The secret to which Waters refers is evidently that of Barrett's quest for mind expansion. Nicholas Schaffner suggests that Barrett felt "...obliged to seek his enlightenment...through artistic expression, and through chemicals" *(Schaffner 1991: 29-30)* after his request to be initiated into an Indian-based religious cult called Sant Mat was rejected by its Master—the Maharaji Charan Singh Ji. Later, according to Schaffner, "Barrett...could hardly have been more unequivocal in his embrace of both the underground's ideals and its excesses" *(Schaffner 1991: 51)*. The line above, like the opening line of the first verse, alludes to *The Dark Side of the Moon* through its use of that album's other major symbol. Barrett's association with the moon and lunacy is extended to the next line also:

> Threatened by shadows at night, and exposed in the light.
> Shine on you crazy diamond.

Barrett is "threatened" because his ability properly to perceive reality is hampered by the "dim light" or uncertainty which the moon presents. Sadly enough, however, Waters seems to suggest that Barrett is left completely unprotected or "exposed" in the daylight (i.e. sunlight), where he is even more "threatened" by reality.

According to Waters, "[Syd] had become completely incapable of working in the group" (Miles 1980), and as a result of his "random precision" (an effective oxymoron), Barrett "wore out his welcome". A good example of this "random precision" (acts of apparent precision which were, in fact, random) occured when, towards the end of his time with Pink Floyd, Barrett brought in a new song for the band which went "Have You Got It Yet", and kept changing it so that no one could learn it. Waters recounts the story:

> It was a real act of mad genius. The interesting thing about it was that I didn't suss it out at all. I stood there for about an hour while he was singing "Have you got it yet?" trying to explain that he was changing it all the time so I couldn't follow it. He'd sing "Have you got it yet?" and I'd sing "No, no." Terrific! *(Miles 1980)*

Aside from having "worn out his welcome" with Pink Floyd, Barrett did the same with "the machine" of the rock music industry, and eventually with the world in general. As Barrett archivist Mark Patress suggests, "...the adult world appeared too gruesome, too corrupt, and altogether too unreal for Syd Barrett" *(Schaffner 1991: 118)*, who now "rode on the steel breeze", succumbing to all its pressures. Now a "raver" and "seer of visions", Barrett's mental state resulted in his reclusive withdrawal which was, for the most part, indefinite. A "painter" *(Watts 1971: 34)* and a "piper" (he wrote almost all of the material on the debut Pink Floyd album *The Piper at the Gates of Dawn* [1967]), Barrett was ultimately to become a "prisoner" of his own body as a result of the imaginary protective layers with which he, like the lead character who was to appear later in *The Wall*, surrounded himself.

After the singing of these verses, and Waters' final plea for the band's ex-leader to shine, he seemingly does, but this time through the solo of a baritone saxophone. This instrument, because of its long time association with jazz, appropriately represents the transformed Barrett because this style of music had finally, after an extremely long period of time, begun to achieve the status of an art form; though, especially after Charlie Parker, its innocence, like Barrett's, was gone. The four-note motif is heard almost immediately behind the solo and serves as a reminder of Barrett's demise. Tension is created when this phrase is transformed by the guitar into an arpeggiating figure which adopts a 12/8 feel while the rest of the band continues to play in 6/4. Fourteen bars later the band, unable to withstand the tension, follows the guitar by "succumbing" to double time. This surrender to the "machine" results in the band's fall, signalled by the five-note descending bass line; its collapse is finally complete as the rhythm section (the "back bone" of the band) drops out, and the rumbling sound effects of the machine slowly fade-in over the saxophone cadenza. As the memory of Barrett and the saxophone both slowly begin to retreat or fade-out, the solo furiously attempts to assert itself, becoming more "bebop-like" (more technically difficult) but to no avail.

According to Waters, "'Welcome to the Machine' is about 'them and us', and anyone who gets involved in the media process" *(Sedgewick 1975: 13)*. "[A] scorching indictment of the Music Biz", this piece "begins with the opening of a door—which Waters has described as an ironic symbol of the sense of musical discovery and progress that is ultimately betrayed by a 'Rock Machine' driven far less by artistic considerations than by greed and empty dreams of 'success'" *(Schaffner 1991: 187)*. Waters compares the alienation which he feels from the economic "machine" of the rock music business which has little to do with "human" values, to that which many people feel from the increasing mechanisation of twentieth-century life. Besides being apparent in the lyrics, this theme is conveyed musically through electronic innovation. The piece is not a traditional type of rock song (guitar, bass and drum format); it is, rather, purely a composition for tape. David Gilmour explains:

> It's...a made-up-in-the-studio thing...which was all built up from a basic throbbing made on a VCS3, with a repeat echo to give the throb. With a number like that, you don't start off with a regular concept of group structure or anything, and there's no backing track either. Really, it is just a studio proposition where we're using tape for its own end, a form of collage using sound. *(Dallas 1987: 111)*

In the midst of this electronic recording is an acoustic guitar which seems to represent nature or, more specifically, humanity caught in the grips of this "machine". The melody of the piece is also "mechanised". It is performed by two voices singing, for the most part, in octaves; their phrasing and melodic fluctuations are absolutely identical, giving the vocals a "mechanical" quality. This melody is also characterised by a narrow range which evokes feelings of claustrophobia similar to those in "Time" from *The Dark Side of the Moon*. The guitar's initial strums are arranged in the mix so that they alternately appear in opposite speaker channels, and this foreshadows its eventual converging with the machine (the pulsating sound effects of the machine move back and forth between speaker channels). Tension is created by the added second in the E minor chord with which the guitar makes its entry, and this feeling of tension also seems to act as a foreboding of the acoustic guitar's joining the machine permanently following the first verse. After the initial strums, however, the guitar drops out as the vocals enter with the song's opening lines:

> Welcome my son, welcome to the machine.
> Where have you been? It's alright we know where you've been.

The deceptive cordial greeting of the narrators (the "moguls" who run the music business) recalls the deceptive innocence of the clean guitar entry in Part II of "Shine On". The narrators' use of "my son", may initially suggest a wise father figure, but it is revealed as condescending when after asking, "where have you been?", the narrators do not wait for an answer but respond assumptively with "it's alright we know...". Aside from being conveyed by the shouting quality of the vocals, the harsh, abrupt tone of the narrators' condescension is expressed musically by the insertion of a bar of 3/4 time within this melodic phrase (also at the same point in the second verse) which causes a premature strong beat to occur when the next bar appears on the last word of the line.

The narrators know the powerful attraction that the addressee initially has for stardom. They suggest, in their business-like manner, that he fits the stereotype of the "rock 'n roll rebel" who has been wasting time in the system while awaiting the end of his formation (the expression "in the pipeline" means "awaiting completion or processing"). In the mean time, he has been "provided with toys and [Robert Baden-Powell's] 'Scouting for Boys'". According to the narrators, the addressee "bought a guitar", not because he enjoyed music, but "to punish [his] ma", who presumably hoped her son would attend school, and then settle down to a secure job. But the narrators "know" that the addressee "didn't like school", and, in order to win his trust, ironically suggest that he's "nobody's fool".

The return of the acoustic guitar corresponds with the narrators' repetition of the line "welcome to the machine", representing the addressee's joining the workings of the "mechanised" music industry (the acoustic guitar is heard throughout the rest of the song). Meanwhile the electric guitar makes a somewhat insignificant appearance in the transitional material which leads to the "middle section", confirming its previous connection to the "machine".

The "middle section" of the song is characterised by its shift to 6/4 time, the dominant meter of "Shine On", and this evokes a memory of the group as it was before being "transformed" by the machine. In conjunction with its strumming of the rhythm, the acoustic guitar (the real musician or artist in this mechanical soundscape) picks out a very slow, rising sequence of notes up a minor scale from E to A, each note sliding to the next suggesting a "limping" or "crippled" movement; this movement is not fluid, but a very deliberate change from one pitch to the next. The acoustic guitar never reaches its apparent goal of B, however, because it is "overwhelmed" by the "machine"; the transformed synthesizer (originally soft, subtle timbres representing Barrett's innocence and art music), now loud and penetrating, drowns out the guitar, "overshadowing" its honest intentions. The synth's original "artistic" intent is displaced by a "mechanical" adulteration which is portrayed by its now "cold", "buzzing" timbre, and its characteristically electronic melodic fluctuations. Very much toward the back of the recording mix can be heard tympani (an instrument which has had a long association with art music), supporting the idea that artistic intentions are now demoted to the background.

Lyrically, the second verse is similar in structure to the first. It begins:

Welcome my son, welcome to the machine.
What did you dream? It's alright we told you what to dream.

Beneath the last line is heard an A major chord, altered from the minor in the first verse. This creates a sense of irony, almost as if the narrators are smiling mockingly while they deliver their lines. The song's addressee, once again, is cut off before he is allowed to answer. This too supports the idea of the "machine's" silencing of the artistic voice as a result of its underlying "dream" of fame and fortune:

You dreamed of a big star, he played a mean guitar,
He always ate in the Steak Bar. He loved to drive in his Jaguar.

During the coda of the piece there is an attempt to create some "musical interest", to provide some relief from the continuous pulsations of the machine by turning the beat around. It seems insincere because of its short duration and because it is played on an electronic keyboard instrument. This display leads to another example of what Waters characterises as a portrayal of insincerity at the end of the piece—the sounds of a party. He explained:

That was put there...because of the complete emptiness inherent in that way of behaving—celebrations, gatherings of people who drink and talk together. To me that epitomizes the lack of contact and real feelings between people. *(Schaffner 1991: 187)*

In this superficial kind of human interaction Waters proposes that there is something innately "mechanical" or inhuman also. The original vinyl album used another powerful symbol to represent this idea: on a sticker which adorned its cover there appeared two mechanical hands locked in a handshake symbolising "a physical presence and an ostensibly friendly gesture that often amounts to little more than an empty and meaningless ritual". This sticker, which appeared against "a backdrop quartered into the elements of fire, air, water, and earth...[representing] the sun signs of the four astrologically well-balanced band-members", suggested an association with the band's physical presence, yet psychological absence that had been observed by Waters during this time. The handshake motif is also present in the photo on the front cover of the album, "a businessman consumed by flames, obliviously shaking hands with his lookalike", intimating that "people withdraw their presence from others, concealing their true feelings, out of fear of 'getting burned'" *(Schaffner 1991: 191)*. Schaffner also notes the association of the phrase "getting burned" with the idea of being swindled, an important element in the album's next piece.

The song "Have a Cigar" incorporates many of the "traditional" rock music characteristics, including its "bluesy" main riff and 4/4 groove, and a recurring guitar "lick" which is composed of a descending blues scale that first appears during the eighth bar of the introduction. The piece has many qualities which display that it is not an authentic rock 'n roll tune, however, and its spuriousness anticipates the insincere nature of the song's narrator. The first characteristic which conveys this is Gilmour's use of a phase shifter, which endows the guitar with a somewhat "mechanical" sound; but it is primarily with the synthesizer's appearance that this is communicated. The synthesizer is, of course, an instrument which was originally the sole domain of progressive or "art" rock groups such as Pink Floyd, and these groups were often charged with being unauthentic because of their artistic claims.[4] The synthesizer now has completely joined the guitar or "machine" as demonstrated by its playing of the same melodic line. Another trait which marks the song as "untraditional" is its frequent interruption of the 4/4 meter with the addition of a 5/4 bar.

"Have a Cigar" acts as a continuation to "Welcome to the Machine". Besides sharing its key, the song initially limits itself to nearly the same chord progression (E minor to C major). Lyrically it makes even more explicit the ideas that were presented in its predecessor, but this song, cutting directly to the source, is a scathing parody of the "record-biz fat cat" *(Schaffner 1991: 187)*. The narrator, who opens the song with the same condescension and deceptively cordial greeting that we have come to expect, attempts to fill the addressee's head with the stereotypical "rock 'n roll dreams":

> Come in here, dear boy, have a cigar.
> You're gonna go far, fly high,
> You're never gonna die, you're gonna make it if you try;
> they're gonna love you.

The narrator's insincerity is exposed, however, when he betrays his intention to find out who the marketable star of the group is:

> Well I've always had a deep respect,
> and I mean that most sincerely.
> The band is just fantastic, that is really what I think.
> Oh by the way which one's Pink?

The narrator pretends to have had a long time appreciation for the group, but displays his dishonesty through his ignorance of the fact that none of its members are named "Pink Floyd".

The narrator's true intentions are fully revealed in the second verse:

> We're just knocked out. We heard about the sell out.
> You gotta get an album out, You owe it to the people.
> We're so happy we can hardly count.
> Everybody else is just green, have you seen the chart?
> Its a helluva start, it could be made into a monster
> if we all pull together as a team.

After hearing about the sold out concert and the high charting single, the narrator tells the group that everybody else is envious of their "success". Now is the perfect time to release an album. According to Waters:

> When you record a single, you are not interested in showing the public how far you've advanced [artistically] since the last record. You've got to please the recording company, apart from any other consideration, otherwise they won't release it. *(Miles 1980)*.

It was generally the practice during the late 1950s and early 1960s to introduce new recording artists through the now defunct "single" or 45 r.p.m. disk, which contained only one song per side. As Dallas suggests regarding Pink Floyd:

> "...their attitude to singles...made them one of the first of the 'album bands' and laid the basis for later rock groups like Led Zeppelin, who were able to build a whole career without ever recording a single" *(Dallas 1987: 63)*.

During the group's live concerts, a film of animated graphics was projected during the song "Welcome to the Machine", depicting a mechanical, reptilian "monster" scrambling across "a lunar landscape" *(Dallas 1987: 15)*. The lunar landscape changes into "a sea of blood that becomes an ocean of grasping hands and arms" *(Dallas 1987: 112)*. The film effectively connects "Welcome to the Machine" to "Have a Cigar", from where the "monster" image comes—the monster of course being Pink Floyd—while the grasping hands represent the dreams of stardom that are accompanied by such a "mechanical monster".

At the end of "Have a Cigar", it is the nature of what the narrator refers to as "team work" which is the source of frustration for one involved in the rock recording industry; the irony being that a work of art, in order to reach people, must be turned into a commodity. This frustration is augmented by the realisation that the industry is more concerned with its product than it is with art works:

> And did we tell you the name of the game, boy,
> we call it Riding the Gravy Train.

The final image of the song, a slang expression implying that the industry views a "monster" such as Pink Floyd merely as a source of easy financial gain, best represents what Waters sees as the relationship between the artist and the "machine" of the mass media. The harmonic progression during these lines leads to a perfect cadence (V—I), suggesting the "fat cat's" smug satisfaction, and this is followed by a rhythmically-abrupt chromatic chord sequence back to the original E minor modality. This rhythmic figure appears to represent the frustrated response of the artist to this "game". The song's narrator is portrayed on the album's back cover as a faceless "Floyd salesman" (flogging a copy of the album) whose "lack of genuine presence is emphasized by the absence of wrists and ankles: he is, after all, little more than an empty suit" *(Schaffner 1991: 191)*.

Guitar fills are interspersed throughout "Have a Cigar", and a long solo is heard after the second verse until the end of the song. The feelings of transcendence achieved by the guitar (narrator) are abruptly terminated at the end of the piece as the group appears to have the last laugh, "pulling the plug" on the narrator:

> I wonder how many first-time buyers have anxiously checked their system during Gilmour's solo at the end of the track, which sounds as if their output stage has suddenly blown. Its all part of the sound mix, however. *(Dallas 1987: 112)*

The sense of satisfaction achieved from this effect is mixed with the dissatisfaction caused by the suddenly inferior sound quality, and by the subsequent search through various radio stations—apparently in the hope of finding something preferable to listen to. This transition represents a shift from the concerns of the music industry to those of the individual, or artist.[5] Eventually, the dial stops on what becomes the next song "Wish You Were Here", a song very much in the singer/songwriter vein which is associated with "confessional intimacy" *(Middleton 1990: 232)*. It is at this juncture that the listener is finally given the opportunity to observe the effects that all of this "mechanisation" has had on the alienated individual.

"Wish You Were Here" musically represents a retreat from the machine, suggesting that Waters and the group, like Barrett, have been forced to withdraw. Almost completely performed with acoustic instruments, the piece establishes a sense of honesty and sincerity, in contrast to the musical portraits of the previous two pieces. It is an assertion of humanity or "natural" values, displayed particularly by the humble guitar solo which precedes the vocal entry. This humbleness is conveyed by the solo's brevity, and by the fact that it is performed on an acoustic guitar. The lead vocal is very much at the front of the mix, especially in comparison with its position throughout the rest of the album. This feeling of "closeness", aside from contributing to the impression of honesty and intimacy, also adds to the song's sense of ambiguity; musically it creates an impression of intimacy, while the lyrics express, apparent already from the title, a sense of absence.

The song's lyric begins with the juxtaposition of positive and negative images, but these are not simple opposites; their contrasts are complex. The narrator seems to question the addressee's ability properly to perceive reality, or to discern between these contrasts, suggesting that, in his own case, things do not seem to present themselves so clearly:

So, so you think you can tell Heaven from Hell,
blue skies from pain.
Can you tell a green field from a cold steel rail?
A smile from a veil? Do you think you can tell?

The last couplet (smile / veil) supports the narrator's concern. Using an image which alludes to the album's common motif of deception, the narrator seems to have good reason for questioning one's ability to distinguish reality (a smile) from false appearances (a veil). It seems significant that this final image deals specifically with the difficulty of making a distinction between the positive and negative aspects of human beings from whom, of course, all notions of understanding (including that of reality) arise.

This theme of appearance versus reality is also significant in the album's packaging. The record originally came with a postcard, appropriate because of the album's title, which is often used as a meaningless postcard cliché. The card depicted a man diving into a lake without making a splash, or disturbing the water at all. On the album's inner sleeve appeared a photo depicting "a veil in a windswept Norfolk grove" *(Schaffner 1991: 192)*. The veil, which relates the photo directly to this song, appears to be suspended of its own accord in this windy environment, and the parallel rows of trees look as if they converge in the distance due to the camera's perspective.

In the second verse of "Wish You Were Here", the narrator asks if "they" (the music industry) deceived the addressee into "trading" one thing, for another, presumably inferior, thing. Waters continues to juxtapose images as before, but, after the first line, the clarity of the possible distinctions between positive and negative images seems to become confused, or to actually break down:

And did they get you to trade your heroes for ghosts?
Hot ashes for trees?
Hot air for a cool breeze? Cold comfort for change?
And did you exchange a walk on part in the war for a lead role in a cage?

The first juxtaposition entails the substitution of a negative, unsubstantial image ("ghosts") for a positive, substantial one ("heroes"). The listener is taken aback when, directly following this, the relationship appears to have been reversed; the negative, unsubstantial image ("hot ashes") is now replaced by a seemingly positive, substantial one ("trees"). This confusion manifests itself further in the apparent absence of any concrete distinction between the images that ensue. "Hot air", a common slang expression for words that lack substance, is traded for a "cool breeze" (an allusion to the "steel breeze")—both seemingly negative images. Similarly, "cold comfort" (an expression meaning poor or inadequate consolation) is replaced by what, in the context of the album, appears to be a predominantly *uncomfortable* "change", but one which is here unspecified. This ambiguity culminates in the final juxtaposition; borrowing terms from the theatre, Waters suggests that the addressee "exchanged" a subsidiary or minor role ("walk on part") in the "battle" of life, for a major or starring role "in a cage", an image which conjures the memory of Barrett—a "prisoner" in the cage of his own body and mind.

The connection to Barrett is suggested by the apparent allusion to the "steel breeze", and also by the "ghosts" in the first line of this verse which allude to the "seer of visions". His presence is also suggested by the subtle addition of the "innocent" synthesizer timbre in the instrumental section between the second and third verses. The song laments Barrett's absence:

> How I wish, how I wish you were here.
> We're just two lost souls swimming in a fish bowl,
> year after year,
> Running over the same old ground. What have we found?
> The same old fears. Wish you were here.

That the song is not entirely meant to be about Barrett can be deduced from the last verse of "Shine On" *(see below)*, but also from the musical retreat *(see above)* which suggests that Barrett continues to function merely as a symbol for the fragmentation within Pink Floyd—or, ultimately, within Waters himself. This is supported by Waters' statement:

> In a way it's a schizophrenic song. It's directed at my other half, if you like, the battling elements within myself. There's the bit that's concerned with other people, the bit that one applauds in oneself, then there's the grasping, avaricious, selfish little kid who wants to get his hand on the sweets and have them all. The song slips in and out of both personae so the bit that always wants to win is feeling upset and plaintively saying to the other side, *wish you were here. (Dallas 1987: 112)*

Waters' explanation sheds some light on the confusion and ambiguity present between the first two verses which, purportedly, attempt to portray the somewhat unrelated thoughts of a schizoid. Schizophrenia—a mental disease marked by a breakdown in the relation between thought, feelings, and actions, which is frequently accompanied by delusions and a retreat from social life—in E. Fuller Torrey's words, is a condition in which people have "problems with reality" *(Fuller Torrey 1974: 156)*. R.D. Laing's account is also helpful:

> If the individual cannot take the realness, aliveness, autonomy, and identity of himself and others for granted, then he has to become absorbed in contriving ways of trying to be real, of keeping himself or others alive, of preserving his identity, in efforts, as he will often put it, to prevent himself losing his self. What are to most people everyday happenings, which are hardly noticed because they have no special significance, may become deeply significant in so far as they either contribute to the sustenance of the individual's being or threaten him with non-being. Such an individual, for whom the elements of the world are coming to have, or have come to have, a different hierarchy of significance from that of the ordinary person, is beginning, as we say, to 'live in a world of his own', or has already come to do so. It is not true to say, however, without careful qualification, that he is losing 'contact with' reality, and withdrawing into himself. External events no longer affect him in the same way as they do others: it is not that they affect him less; on the contrary, frequently they affect him more. It is frequently not the case that he is becoming 'indifferent' and 'withdrawn'. It may, however, be that the world of his experience comes to be one he can no longer share with other people. *(Laing 1965: 42-43)*

Laing's statements elucidate the figurative mental condition which Waters describes. Through his exposure to the machine, Waters' self has become fragmented because of the deceptive "dream", based on glory and greed, that the music industry sells; the "machine" has driven away the favourable aspects of his character, leaving behind only the naturally unfavourable part of him which coincides with the predominant interests of the music industry. This reality, which Waters feels unable to share with others, drives him to retreat into himself because he is unable to secure a feeling, or state, of integration. As Waters suggests above, the song expresses the desire for his various personae once again to amalgamate, but the addition of a background harmony vocal, during the last verse, musically portrays his continued fragmentation.

The song fades into an aural representation of the "steel breeze", which metaphorically illustrates Waters' confrontation with the same forces which he sees to have caused Barrett's demise. Significantly, Stephane Grappelly, a respected, virtuoso jazz violinist, played on the album, but his playing can be barely heard beneath the wind sound effects. According to Waters:

> You can just hear him if you listen very, very, very hard right at the end of "Wish You Were Here," you can just hear a violin come in after all the wind stuff starts—just! We decided not to give him a credit, 'cos we thought it might be a bit of an insult. *(Miles 1980)*

Here the "steel breeze" once again overwhelms the artistic voice which is made practically inaudible in its midst.

The bass guitar (Waters' instrument) can be heard emerging from the wind. Its entry is ominous because it is initially heard a great distance away, and its approach to the foreground of the mix is very gradual. Its pulsations, the intermittence of which contributes to their ominous character, are taken over by an eighth-note rhythmic figure produced by an overdubbed bass guitar. This second bass guitar part is characterised by a high, thin sounding tone, and this rare practice (overdubbing bass parts) also serves musically to illustrate Waters' continued fragmentation. Ushering in Part VI of "Shine On", this rhythmic figure becomes an ostinato pedal point on G, reminiscent of that which began the album, yet this one seems to represent the "cage", alluded to in the lyrics of the previous song. Repeated attempts to break out from this "cage", or pedal point, are implied by the simple B-flat which is continuously heard above the pedal during every fourth bar of the ostinato; but each attempt fails—the pedal returning every time. The 12/8 time signature reminds the listener of the original portrayal of the group's transformation at the hands of the machine *(see p. 48)*. The abrupt and seemingly threatening guitar entry (first appearing as a menacing slide and then as forceful, rhythmically off-beat chords) ushers in the drums, which establish a "plodding" 4/4 time against the 12/8 feel of the bass, representing the group's reaction to, and impending collapse from, the pressure caused by its transformation at the hands of the machine. Like the footsteps in "On the Run" from *The Dark Side of the Moon*, the group appears unable to keep up with the machine.

The synthesizer enters, now fully transformed, having very much the same qualities already displayed by the guitar (a symbol of the rock music industry): its phrasing is now very irregular; it is adorned with an echo effect; and it employs the same type of "blue" notes that the guitar characteristically produces—achieved through Richard Wright's use of the synthesizer's pitch bender. Its incredible similarity to a guitar is displayed when the lead guitar (played with a slide) finally enters, doubling the synthesizer; the two are practically indiscernible. The guitar enters eight measures before the harmony changes, suggesting a connection between an escape from the "cage", and a return to the "machine". The guitar plays in unison with the synthesizer for thirteen bars, but after this, begins to play an independent line which, three bars later, leads to the guitar's reassertion of its overpowering character (achieved through its tremendous volume). At this point the meter changes back to the strong 12/8 and the guitar overwhelms the lead synth, which can be heard attempting to assert itself beneath—but to little avail. At the first turn-around of the harmony during the guitar solo, the descending bass guitar run (from the dominant down to the tonic) which initially signalled the downfall of the group *(see p. 48)*, returns apparently to confirm the group's demise. The lead guitar becomes progressively more furious as it moves higher and higher towards the top of its range (Gilmour actually slides off the fingerboard at times). This increased furiousness is conveyed when the lead guitar doubles itself eight bars before the recapitulation of the music from Part V, and also by the increasing violent "pounding" of the rhythm guitar.

The transition to Part VII is signalled by the reappearance of the melodic figure in the guitar which, before, served as an interlude between the first and second verses of Part V. This figure also initiates a change back to the 6/4 meter which characterised the group before it was transformed by the "machine": this change coincides with the music of the "hopeful" refrain, and suggests a possibility of the group returning to its former state.

The lyrics of the third verse, once again, are addressed to Syd Barrett:

> Nobody knows where you are, how near or how far.
> Shine on you crazy diamond.
> Pile on many more layers and I'll be joining you there.
> Shine on you crazy diamond.

The first line alludes both to Barrett's physical and mental absence. During the 1970s and up to the present, Barrett has had a mystique similar to the legendary "Bigfoot"; his extremely occasional emergences from seclusion are nicknamed "Syd sightings" *(Schaffner 1991: 116)*. Similarly, no one knows to where the original healthy personality of Barrett has disappeared. As is now apparent, Waters seems to forecast his own permanent withdrawal into the self. In fact, the image of "layers" seems to suggest the "piling up of bricks" which was to take place two albums later in *The Wall*. The group's continued fragmentation is suggested by the background voices during the singing of the refrain, as they have not returned to their original unison.

The second half of the last verse creates a disturbing sense of ironic ambiguity:

> And we'll bask in the shadow of yesterday's triumph,
> and sail on the steel breeze.
> Come on you boy child, you winner and loser,
> come on you miner for truth and delusion, and shine!

Waters' choice of the word "bask", a pleasant image which literally means to lie in the sunlight, becomes ironic when used with the word "shadow"; Waters now appears to surrender willingly to the "anti-life pressures", and paints a pleasant view of withdrawing from the "sun" or life, to become a "diamond" himself. This pleasant image is reinforced by the suggestion that he will "sail", or be carried pleasantly, with Barrett on the "steel breeze". Waters does not altogether appear to believe this picture however; he continues, as he did before, to encourage the memory of Barrett as "boy child", to "shine", rather than leaving him in darkness. At the same time, Waters displays his own safe return to "reality" through his repetition of clear opposites in the last two lines (something he seemed incapable of during the previous song). He recognises Barrett's ambiguous fragmentation or division; he is both "winner and loser", and a "miner" for both "truth and delusion". By referring to Barrett as a "miner", the darkness/shadow imagery is cleverly sustained; miners generally work in the dark caverns of the earth, in comparison to Barrett's location within the "dark caverns" of the mind. The doublet of truth/delusion is a connotation of the light/dark imagery, and Waters' appeal for Barrett to "shine" seems to be a supplication for Barrett to find his way through the dark "diamond mine" toward the light of truth—or reality.

The ambiguity between hopeful endurance and tragic surrender is sustained at the beginning of Part VIII with the return of the arpeggiating figure (originally a transformation of the sad, four-note motif—*see p. 43*), which seemed to force the band's surrender to the machine. Its appearance now invites the listener to enquire whether or not the group will again succumb to the pressures of the media process; the band's establishing of a driving 4/4 meter against the 12/8 feel of this guitar, however, suggests that they will not. The absence of a distorted guitar in this section, in combination with its now purely rhythmic function, suggests that the threat of this happening has considerably diminished. Uncertainty is still present, however, as a result of the listener not yet having heard a return to the synthesizer's original state. Instead, it seems to become first an electric piano, and then a clavinet; this uncertainty is augmented when the "mechanised" or guitar-like synthesizer appears first behind the clavinet, but then comes to the foreground of the recording.

Part IX provides some reassurance to the listener with its return of the lead synthesizer's previous identity, characterised by its "French-horn timbre" and regular articulation. This is also achieved through the almost complete absence of guitar, and the acoustic piano's return during this section. Part IX seems to suggest some dissatisfaction for the listener, however, and this is primarily because of its intense sadness. This portrayal of sadness is achieved by the "dragging" half time feel (the music appears to progress with great effort), the preponderance of minor chords, and by the initial entry of repeated backwards-recorded cymbals; the latter effect results in an uncomfortable reversal of the attack / decay relationship which occurs under normal aural conditions. The dissonances that are created by the harmonic progression of the piece, and its notable absence of "comfortable" resolutions also contributes to the discomfort portrayed by this music:

Gm		Bbm	
Fm		Fm/Eb	
Cm		Cm/A	Cm/G
D	D/F#	D	D/A

The first chord change from G minor to B-flat minor achieves a dissonant effect because it features an internal tritone movement, while the occurrence of chords over bass notes which are non-chord tones (Fm / E-flat and Cm / A), and their either non-existent, or weak, resolutions also conveys a great deal of dissonance. This effect is most successfully created by the denial of the V—I root motion which the listener expects at the end of the progression before it is repeated each time. The impression of sadness is, perhaps, a result of the realisation that the synthesizer (protagonist) has not entirely escaped the machine; it appears to have been "scarred". This is illustrated by the background keyboard pad which plays the chords beneath the lead synth's melody. Identified by its distinctive "buzzing" timbre (quite unlike the original keyboard timbre which imitated strings), its position in the back of the mix is seemingly symbolic of the sub-conscious.

At the end, this sadness is displaced when Part IX cadences on a G major chord. This device, very common in baroque music and referred to by musicologists as a *picardy* third, brings an incredible sense of satisfaction to the ear, especially after such an extended time in the parallel minor. The G major chord is sustained and the lead synth is still present, as it was at the beginning of the album, suggesting a return to a state of artistic innocence. Although the background synthesizers are still characterised by a "mechanical" timbre, the sustained major chord provides a positive contrast to the sustained minor at the beginning. This positiveness seems to reflect the realisations about both the music industry and himself that Waters has gained throughout his experience. The reminder of Barrett's apparently permanent loss to the machine is ever present in his mind, but the feelings of relief achieved from his own safe return to reality—which, fortunately, has thus far been maintained—is portrayed musically.

Chapter 3 — ANIMALS

[A] society's ideology...that complex structure of social perception which ensures that the situation in which one social class has power over the others is either seen by most members of the society as 'natural', or not seen at all...'.

Terry Eagleton[1]

In *A Contribution to the Critique of Political Economy* (1859), Karl Marx and Frederick Engels state, "[t]he mode of production of material life conditions the social, political and intellectual life process in general", and from this premise Marx formulated the concepts 'infrastructure' and 'superstructure'. Infrastructure, for Marx, is "the economic structure of society"—the social relations established by a society's organisation of material production. In the capitalist system this relation is characterised by a ruling capitalist class which owns the means of economic production, and a proletarian class whose labour-power the capitalist buys for profit. From the infrastructure (economic "base"), emerges a superstructure which consists of "certain forms of law and politics", and what Marxism designates as *ideology*—"'definite forms of social consciousness' (political, religious, ethical, aesthetic and so on)". The essential function of this superstructure, as Marx sees it, is "to legitimate the power of the social class which owns the means of economic production". *(Eagleton 1976: 4-5)*

Animals (1977) is a critique of the capitalist economic system. Roger Waters documents his own recognition of superstructure and, like Marx, attempts to illuminate the masses about their exploitation and oppression. It would appear that his primary concern, however, is to reveal the effects that capitalism has on the nature of human beings, and the divisions that it creates between them as individuals.

Like George Orwell, in his political allegory *Animal Farm* (1945) based on the events following the Russian Revolution in 1917 *(see Lee 1986: 39-52)*, Waters anthropomorphically divides human beings into different "classes" of animals. For Waters, however, three species suffice—pigs, dogs, and sheep. His hierarchy of animals coincides with that established by Orwell, where the pigs, protected by the dogs, are the ruling "class"; the sheep, of all the "lower" animals, are those who are most mindlessly unquestioning of their oppressed condition, continuously attempting to convince themselves of their contentedness by repeating, in times of doubt, the maxim "Four legs good, two legs bad!" *(Orwell 1983: 49)*. Although this is the fundamental social hierarchy established on the album, Waters' characterisation of each animal is developed in more subtle and complex ways, as shall be seen.

Animals primarily portrays as pigs the capitalist class "which owns the means of economic production", and who are, as a consequence of this, the ruling class. They represent the pinnacle of materialistic progress, the symbols of ambition that the capitalist system, by its very nature, promotes. This is depicted on the album's cover, the huge, inflatable pig suspended high above London's Battersea Power Station—itself a symbol of tremendous power as it was once the primary source for London's industrial and commercial interests. It is significant, however, that in every photo depicting this scene (the album's sleeve boasts numerous shots of this scene taken from various angles), the view is either from behind some type of barrier (barbed wire, tall iron gate), or seen from an incredible distance away, suggesting that, for the average person, this goal is virtually unattainable.

The album portrays as dogs those who are not pigs, yet aspire to become pigs. The dogs represent those who ruthlessly pursue the ideal of material prosperity, so much promoted by the "American Dream", to the detriment of their fellow man—engaging in the "dog-eat-dog" tactics to which this "dream" gives rise. By virtue of their position above the sheep, the dogs can be seen to represent the bourgeoisie, while the sheep are, of course, the unsuspecting proletariat, oblivious both to the threat posed to them by the dogs, and to their continued exploitation by the pigs.

Animals opens with "Pigs on the Wing (Part I)", a piece which, as we find out lyrically at the end of the album in Part II, provides the narrator with a "shelter" from pigs. Musically, however, this impression is conveyed directly at the beginning of the album. The piece is performed with solo acoustic guitar and vocal in the singer/songwriter format, which, as we saw in the song "Wish You Were Here", is associated with "confessional intimacy" *(Middleton 1990: 232)*, or honesty. The acoustic guitar becomes a pastoral symbol, which contrasts the mechanical, or inhuman associations which arise from the use of electronic timbres or textures. Its use here, as in the song "Wish You Were Here", represents a retreat from the technological alienation we often experience from mechanistic modern life.[2] At the beginning of the album, listeners are in this state of retreat too; but during the body of the work they are exposed to the "machine" of modern life, which is portrayed by the album's predominant use of electronic instruments, as was the case with *Wish You Were Here*. It is significant that the machine on that record symbolised the "monster" of the music business, an incarnation of the capitalist industry which is driven by greed, because the pigs are, of course, a more generalised manifestation of this same greed.

The first song immediately expresses the album's primary concern—the importance of human relationships:

> If you didn't care what happened to me,
> And I didn't care for you,
> We would zig zag our way through the boredom and pain,
> Occasionally glancing up through the rain,
> Wondering which of the buggers to blame
> And watching for pigs on the wing.

The narrator suggests that the only means of escaping what he sees as the directionless or meaningless modern condition is through human affection. Waters' portrayal of modern life as "boredom and pain" seems to align him, once again, with Samuel Beckett and the views of the 'Theatre of the Absurd'; but as the album progresses, the listener realises that this perspective is primarily a result of the narrator's lack of interest in the greedy, competitive nature of his society and the tendency that it has to create barriers between people. The narrator displays his lack of interest in attaining material success by his only "occasionally" glancing up at the pigs. He does not strive to become one, but questions which of them may be most responsible for creating the bleak situation he sees. It is clear that the narrator believes the pigs to pose some type of threat, conveyed through the last line of the song where he seems to be warily looking out for them.

Just as the song which begins side two of the record bears the title "Pigs (three different ones)", the next song "Dogs" could easily have been called "Dogs (two different ones)", because the song portrays two quite different dogs. The first, whose part is sung by David Gilmour, is representative of the stereotypical "cut throat", dog who aspires to reach pig status—a character who symbolises, in Waters' view, the voice of capitalism that fosters a competitive society. The second dog, whose part is sung by Waters, appears to be the narrator who was introduced in "Pigs on the Wing (Part I)"—a dog who seems to have been initially conditioned by his society into playing the capitalist "game", yet begins to question it, recognizing the problems this way of life engenders.

The song begins with a faded in, double-tracked acoustic guitar, which moves from the background of the sound mix to the foreground. This subtle approach, in combination with the unrelaxed, syncopated rhythm, conveys a sense of apprehension, which—as the listener soon realises—accompanies the stealthy advance of the first dog. The fade in, combined with the move from background to foreground, gives the impression that the dog has traversed a great distance in his approach, as if crossing the "barren wasteland" of his ever-expanding "territory". This provides an effective contrast from the sense of intimacy conveyed in the first track where the vocal and guitar are positioned in the foreground of the mix. The opening harmonic progression (D minor 9, B-flat (add 4), A sus 4, B-flat / A-flat), of which much of the piece is comprised, also serves to establish a sense of unease. A great deal of tension is created throughout the progression, initially by the dissonance of the E-flat which is heard against the D in the second chord, but also by the ambiguity of the third chord (the dominant), which is neither major nor minor. The tension-filled, overall effect of the chord progression culminates in the last chord's return to the first, an event characterised by its disturbing tritone root movement. The use of the acoustic guitar again initially connotes a sense of honesty, but this merely foreshadows the deceptive character of this dog, which is exposed almost immediately when the listener hears the entry of a synthesizer, suggesting the obtrusive technological world. The synthesizer's subtle crescendo is similar in character to that of the guitar entry. Its gradual attack contrasts its comparatively swift decay, which occurs on a different note that suddenly appears in the opposite speaker channel. This is also a musical portrayal of the dog's predatory furtiveness; he begins his assault by sneaking up on his victim, and after a sudden attack quickly appears elsewhere. This dog, addressing the second, offers advice on what must be done in order to achieve pig status:

> You gotta be crazy, you gotta have a real need.
> You gotta sleep on your toes, and when you're on the street,
> You gotta be able to pick out the easy meat with your eyes closed.
> And then moving in silently, down wind and out of sight,
> You gotta strike when the moment is right without thinking.

The dog suggests that in order to be "successful", one must be fanatically obsessed, or have "a real need" for power and possessions. He warns about the ever-present fears of being attacked by the competition, recommending that the second dog must sleep very lightly while, at the same time, giving the impression that he is not asleep at all. Conversely, when the dog is in public, he must learn to "pick out", without fail if he is to survive, who the weak targets are (most often sheep, of course). Until the dog learns the art of deception (forecasted in the second verse), he must rely on his instinctual stealth and predatorial hunting prowess, striking at the most opportune moment.

The intimidating nature of this dog is portrayed musically in a variety of ways, but initially through his sharp enunciation of the "t" sound in "toes" and "street". The use of echo on the latter word endows the character with a tremendous sense of power, as does the sudden entry of the bass and drums after "eyes closed". This entry is made even more threatening as a result of the gradual cymbal crescendo which precedes it; the crescendo of this cymbal, and the momentary band entry seems, once again, to suggest the dog's stealthy approach, and sudden attack. The confident pause which follows the shouted words "eyes closed", and the dramatic reduction of volume in Gilmour's vocal during the next line, lends the character a demented, menacing aspect, which is further enhanced by the implication that this character is smiling: over the ambiguous A sus 4 chord Gilmour sings the major third (C-sharp)—a feature notably missing in Waters' rebuttal during the recapitulation of this material later in the piece. The staggered entry of the organ suggests a staggering victim, whose fall is intimated by the organ's adopting a position in the background as a supporting instrument. The full band enters permanently at the end of this verse, providing the dog with additional strength and support that anticipates his prediction of oncoming adeptness in the next verse.

The second verse begins with the dog's proposition that the attacker's tactics of destroying the competition can become more "sophisticated" in time:

> And after a while, you can work on points for style.
> Like the club tie, and the firm handshake,
> A certain look in the eye and an easy smile.
> You have to be trusted by the people that you lie to,
> So that when they turn their backs on you,
> You'll get the chance to put the knife in.

The dog suggests that eventually the attacker can adopt a deceitful, businesslike persona—characterised by a deceptively friendly "look in the eye", and a fraudulent smile that can be called upon whenever necessary. He recommends that trust must be established in the victim whom the attacker intends to deceive for the furthering of his own interests, in order that the victim can be easily conquered, and thus removed from the competition by "a stab in the back". The addition of a background vocal in the last line of the verse brings the speaker extra clout, suggesting to the addressee that this dog is not alone in possessing these horrific "ideals". This thought attacks the mind of the second dog with incredible intensity, portrayed by the distorted, electric guitar solo in the next section, which is supported by aggressive drum fills, and forceful china cymbal crashes that appear on the first beat of every bar during the solo. The disturbing effect of this instrumental interlude is augmented by the excessive chromaticism in Gilmour's solo, and by the first dog's scream and maniacal laughter; the character's outburst suggests that this "killer" approaches his work (the ruining of other people's lives) with a frightening sense of glee.

Immediately after the first line of the next verse (marked by the absence of "you gotta" and "you have to"), the first dog seems to realise that he is giving advice to a potential competitor. He subsequently attempts to discourage the second dog by forecasting a sorry end to anyone who becomes involved in the competition:

> You gotta keep one eye looking over your shoulder.
> You know its going to get harder,
> and harder and harder as you get older.
> And in the end you'll pack up and fly down south,
> Hide your head in the sand,
> Just another sad old man,
> All alone and dying of cancer.

The dog forecasts that the stress caused by the competition—the constant threat posed by other dogs—will eventually wear the attacker down to the stage where he will have to flee. Both the adoption of a strong pulsating rhythm by the bass guitar, and the thrice repeated "harder" (the latter in combination with the echo used on Gilmour's voice), enhances the effectiveness of the speaker's attempt to discourage the addressee. The first dog's intimidating character is portrayed through Gilmour's confident "yeah" which occurs after the word "older", and is reinforced by the use of echo on his voice again during the words "south" and "sand" in the following lines. The speaker predicts that the attacker, for his own protection, will have to relocate "down south"; due to his age, the only defence mechanism he will have at his disposal will be that of the ostrich (ostriches are often thought to hide their heads in the sand when they fear an attack). This image also suggests that the only way the attacker will be able to cope with his condition is by refusing to accept that he is "sad", "alone" and "dying of cancer".

During the singing of the word "cancer", the drums begin to play in half time, implying that the first dog's onslaught is beginning to weaken. The reason for this is that the second dog begins to reflect melancholically on what has been said, the alienating content of which is apparently represented by the synthesizer solo that follows. Eventually, the acoustic guitar also ceases its persistent rhythm, leading to a slow instrumental section which is characterised by its multiple overdubs of electric guitar parts—a section which seems to be a musical portrayal of the second dog's sadness and resignation. This effect is communicated by the "staggering" drum fills, and Gilmour's technique of bending the guitar's strings. Often when a guitarist bends strings upward to attain a certain pitch (a technique used almost exclusively by rock guitarists), the effect is that of an ecstatic striving. Here, for the most part, Gilmour uses a technique that is generally less common; that is, he bends the strings upward to the desired note, but lets them slowly fall to the next note—creating the opposite effect. The affect of this melodic display is compounded as a result of the many overdubbed guitars during this section.

After this interlude, the bass and drums drop out suggesting that the second dog is momentarily left alone in his thoughts; the memory of the first dog's disturbing words are translated into aggressive barking and chilling howls (taped sound effects). His isolation is also implied by the prolonged harmonic stasis (the D minor 9 chord is sustained for eight bars). The addressee's solitude is, once again, disturbed by the first dog who reasserts his attack—portrayed by the disappearance of the recorded sound effects, which coincide with the re-entry of bass and drums, and the return of the solo electric guitar. The tempo is greatly reduced from the first dog's initial onslaught, but his continued intimidation is portrayed by the dissonances of the guitar solo, particularly at the point when Gilmour bends two strings together, but also when he repetitively bends a low tone in conjunction with the use of artificial harmonics (probably executed near the bridge of the guitar), which produces a harsh, metallic tone. This lick also terminates in a power chord, adding to the solo's forcefulness.

The still menacing character of the first dog is confirmed by the now double-tracked lead vocal entry, but also by the return of the supportive background vocals. He describes the frightening condition caused by the second dog's eventual, increasing paranoia—the final consequence of his past actions:

> And when you loose control, you'll reap the harvest you have sown.
> And as the fear grows, the bad blood slows and turns to stone.
> And it's too late to loose the weight you used to need to throw around.
> So have a good drown, as you go down, alone.
> Dragged down by the stone.

The imagery presented in the second line is a terrifying poetical representation of coronary thrombosis, and this anticipates the "heart attack" which the first pig has in "Pigs (Three different ones)" *(see below)*. The relationship established between the two songs implies that the speaker is describing the state of a dog who is no longer a dog, because he has achieved pig status. This is hinted at also by the image of being overweight, another characteristic of the first pig. The "pig's" blood is contaminated by his bad qualities, which are portrayed as the origin of his downfall. His coronary arteries become blocked as this blood coagulates into stone, and his demise is symbolically portrayed as a horrific vision of drowning,[3] caused by the weight of the stone which it is "too late to loose". Once again, the character is sadly portrayed as being "alone".

The word "stone" is given special musical consideration during these lines to stress the horror of the image. The first occurrence of the word is strengthened through its being set up, in the preceding bar, by sixteenth notes played in the electric guitar and bass (enhanced further because the electric guitar has been absent since the beginning of the verse), which contrasts the quarter note feel established by the drums throughout the verse thus far. With the singing of "stone" (a pushed beat and the highest note in an ascending phrase), the instruments drop out and give way to a prolonged melisma in the vocal. A series of strong accents lead to the next line, which is not segmented like the first two, but executed continuously with the accompaniment of a strongly rhythmic electric guitar part. The rhythmic momentum gained is enhanced further by Waters' clever use of internal rhyme in the line ("too late to loose the weight you used"); each rhymed word occurs on the same note. The next line also features internal rhyme (down/drown), and these words are accompanied by strong accents which are realised by the full band. These musical events all prepare the listener for the dramatic ending of the verse, which is characterised by a descending melodic line that accompanies the last line of lyric, and musically portrays the fate of the "pig" who, according to the first dog, is eventually "dragged down by the stone".

The most disturbing aspect of the image, for the addressee, is that it is a prediction of *his own* fate according to the first dog. His trauma is portrayed by the repeated echoing of the image of the stone—drilled into his mind with the help of the penetrative bass drum's appearance on the first beat of each bar. Dallas hints at this character's "dehumanisation" suggesting, "the human overtones of the voice are filtered out, till at the end it becomes little more than a high-pitched howl, like a cry heard through deep water" *(Dallas 1987: 114)*. The instrumental section which follows, apparently represents the second dog's stream of consciousness, and this shift in perspective is signalled by the music's shift to a 6/4 meter, and its complete change in texture. It is significant that this section is entirely synth-dominated (connoting technology) as it provides an enormous contrast to the humanistic, pastoral state in which the album began, conveying the character's intense feelings of alienation. His estrangement is also conveyed through his thoughts about the first dog's "barking", which is, at times, heard over the echoing of "stone". This time, however, the dog sound effects are heard through a vocoder, giving them an "electronic" quality that confirms, for the second dog, the first's "inhumanity". The character slowly begins to develop confidence, as portrayed in the increased activity of the drums; first the ride cymbal and bass drum, but then through the snare drum entry also. His confidence results from his suspicion that both he and the first dog are slaves of a system, set up by the pigs, which equates success to money and power. This suspicion is conveyed by the sounds of whistling heard towards the end of this section, which suggest that, as in *Animal Farm*, the dogs are merely "trained" by the pigs to protect their own interests. In this case, however, the pigs' power is maintained as a result of the fact that the dogs continue "killing" each other off. The renewed strength of the second dog, displayed through the return of the acoustic guitar which launches his counter-attack on the first, results from the mental liberation which he suspects he may have achieved through his recognition of the existence of what Marx termed "superstructure".

This character's continued apprehension, however, is conveyed in Waters' voice and is apparent also in his rebuttal:

> I gotta admit that I'm a little bit confused.
> Sometimes it seems to me as if I'm just being used.
> Gotta stay awake, gotta try and shake off this creeping malaise.
> If I don't stand my own ground,
> how can I find my own way out of this maze?

The second dog realises that his opponent was correct when, in the first verse, he stated that one has to "sleep on his toes". But the fact that this dog says he must "stay awake", intimates his reluctance to fall back into a "brainwashed" state. In other words, he must "stand his own ground" so that he does not fall under the influence of the first dog's individualistic espousal once again.[4] His disorientation is typical of one who has just "awakened".

His counter-attack, which is strongly supported by the full band's re-entry, begins in the next verse as he starts to elucidate the situation:

> Deaf, dumb and blind you just keep on pretending
> That everyone's expendable and no one has a real friend.
> And it seems to you the thing to do would be to isolate the winner.
> And everything's done under the sun,
> And you believe at heart, everyone's a killer.

The character explains that the first dog has been unable to perceive his pig-imposed, yet self-imposed, paranoid condition due to his closed-off senses—a state contributing, of course, to his loneliness which is suggested by the word "isolate" in the third line. The word also suggests the dog's belief that the "winner" of the competition (the pigs) should be identified and separated for attention because of their status; it is, in his belief, a goal for which to strive, and one worth doing "everything under the sun" in order to achieve. This belief results in his "dehumanisation", which is exacerbated by the division he creates between himself and others because he fears everyone is like him.

That the second dog's rebuttal is just as powerful as the initial attack launched by the first is illustrated by the presence of many of the same musical qualities which began the piece *(see above)*. The verse is followed by a retaliative guitar solo, but this one overwhelms with the dissonance of its last phrase, which is composed of a B-flat whole tone scale whose harmonisation forms parallel augmented chords. The return of the "sad" instrumental section suggests that the second dog recognises the first one as truly a "cry", just as he does later in his attack on the pigs in "Pigs (Three different ones)".

As Nicholas Schaffner observes, the last verse seems to allude to Allen Ginsberg's poem *Howl (1956)* because of the adoption of its technique of "beginning each unrhymed line with the word 'who'" *(Schaffner 1991: 200)*. Just as the poem is, in Richard Eberhart's words, "a howl against everything in our mechanistic civilisation which kills the spirit" *(Miles 1986: 155)*, so too is *Animals*. It is appropriate, therefore, that Waters portrays himself as a dog throughout the album.[5] The repetition of the beginning of each line, in conjunction with the repeated riff and aggressive drumming, helps to strengthen the second dog's final onslaught. This is also achieved by the repetition of each line of lyric beginning with "breaking away from the pack", the addition of background vocals in the last three lines, and the last line's repetition which fully restates the frightening image of being "dragged down by the stone".

Waters, in the first line, suggests that the other dog must have had a painful childhood, perhaps due to a divided family; his character has been possibly determined, in part, by his unfortunate psychological grounding. The rest of the verse illuminates that although the first dog was merely trying to scare off the second, all that he said was ultimately correct:

> Who was born in a house full of pain.
> Who was trained not to spit in the fan.
> Who was told what to do by the man.
> Who was broken by trained personnel.
> Who was fitted with collar and chain.
> Who was given a pat on the back.
> Who was breaking away from the pack.
> Who was only a stranger at home.
> Who was ground down in the end.
> Who was found dead on the phone.
> Who was dragged down by the stone.

Waters suggests that the first dog is "fitted with collar and chain" and, therefore, just as much a slave of the system as are the sheep; yet his slavery causes him to be "breaking away from the pack", and "only a stranger at home", unlike the sheep who still, at least, have the comfort of the "flock". The dog was "trained" not to disrupt the system, and subsequently "broken in", then reduced to a state of despair, by personnel who were themselves "trained". Conditioned by "pats on the back"—an "animalistic" translation for the original line "seats in the stand" (commonly rewarded by bosses for good work)—the dog obeys what he is "told to do" by the "big man, pig man", who is portrayed in the first verse of the next song saying "keep on digging".[6] As is apparent in the last three lines, the sorry end which was forecast for the second dog by his attacker, was really the latter's own. It is clear, also, that the extensive periods of time he spent on the telephone were not the result of "personal" calls.

Side two of the album opens with "Pigs (Three different ones)", which features the now confident, newly-awakened dog launching a verbal attack on the pigs. It becomes apparent in this song that the album's portrayal of pigs is not simply limited to the capitalist class; it is expanded to include two other figures who both somehow pose a threat to the rest of society because they are in self-established positions of power, and in some way responsible for promoting divisions between people. Each pig is a symbol of loneliness.

The song begins with an ominous pig sound effect followed by a short, piercing synthesized sound, both of which echo and quickly recede into the distance (the rear of the mix) creating a sense of apprehension for the listener. This is enhanced by the keyboard synthesizer's entry, which obscures the roots of the chords (the Em to C root movement is heard only *very* faintly in the background). The melodic figure, besides confining itself to the narrow range of a minor third, accentuates the claustrophobic character of the limited harmonic movement—the chords are identical except for the chromatic shift back and forth from B to C which is heard as the root movement in this figure. When the bass guitar enters, it too contributes to this unease. Playing abnormally high in its range, it first enters playing a B against the keyboard's C, which creates confusion because it challenges the established root movement. This effect is sustained when the bass ends its first phrase, not on a C but on an E. After outlining the B to C root movement momentarily, the bass continues to challenge it by playing an E beneath the Em, and then subsequently outlining both first and second inversions of these chords creating a great sense of instability. When it finally begins consistently to play an E to C movement, the bass forebodingly slides down from these notes to a pitch which is indefinite each time. The guitar entry achieves the same effect as the sounds which open the piece, though Gilmour creates it without actually using echo. Cymbal crashes accompany the entrance of another high-sounding synthesizer, which twice begins to play the melodic figure, but disappears as the harmony changes to Cmaj7. The combination of all of these musical features serves to establish a threatening and discomforting portrayal of the pigs.

Waters powerfully launches his attack with short, sharply accented syllables, receiving added support from the drum kit entry, his own double-tracked vocal, and the chorus of background vocals which join the lead each time in mockingly exposing the pathetic nature of each pig with the cry—"ha ha charade you are". The regular appearance of these background voices suggests that the first dog has recruited other dogs for his mission, an idea which is supported lyrically in the last verse when the narrator uses the pronoun "our". The escape from the repeated, claustrophobic chord progression to a G major chord helps to dispel the initial threat of the pig, which is also communicated by the confident "whew" that is heard in the lead vocal after the progression returns to the E minor chord.

The first pig represents the ruling class symbol of achievement—the "big man, pig man", alluded to in the previous song. This pig tells the dogs to "keep on digging", creating for both them and himself an unhappy, lonely state. He is the only character that is actually referred to as a pig, supporting the idea that he is the primary pig caricature in the work. Unlike the novice dogs who must "sleep on their toes", this pig is a "well heeled big wheel". With "pig stain on his fat chin", he is characterised by his never-ending greed. The narrating dog mocks the pig for his self-imposed heart condition:

> And when your hand is on your heart,
> You're nearly a good laugh.
> Almost a joker,
> With your head down in the pig bin.

The musical transition that occurs after "heart", lends further strength to the lower-classed dog's taunting assault. Until the end of the verse the harmony remains on an A minor chord, which is continuously struck with great force after being approached chromatically from below. The vocal is now almost spoken rather than shouted; its altered timbre, which results from the absence of reverb, gives the impression that the dog is speaking, not publicly, but privately in the ear of the pig. This is also conveyed by the absence of background voices until near the end of this section. The use of acoustic piano during this section contrasts the alienating, "technological" portrayal of the pig at the beginning of the piece that was achieved through the use of synthesizers. Another strong pastoral symbol—the cow bell—is appropriately used here also, its steady drive supporting the dog's onslaught. As he does with all the pigs, the narrator, displaying his own humanity, points out that the pigs are almost comic, but ultimately tragic:

> You're nearly a laugh,
> But you're really a cry.

The dog's sincerity seems to be displayed by the special musical treatment of the word "cry". The melody, during the singing of this word, features a striving octave jump which is followed by a decorative melisma. The word's appearance also coincides with a return to the E minor chord, an inserted 3/4 bar in the strongly established 4/4 meter, and the temporary absence of the cow-bell.

The pig portrayed in the second verse is at the opposite end of the economic scale. It is significant that she is "sandwiched" in by two socially powerful pigs. She is a victim of the capitalist system, poverty-stricken and living in a bus shelter. She is old and alone because she is devoid of humane feelings; she "radiates cold shafts of broken glass":

> Bus stop rat bag, ha ha charade you are.
> You fucked up old hag, ha ha charade you are.

It is clear that this character is a criminal because she is "hot stuff with a hat pin", and "good fun with a hand gun". That she, too, has a potential for power through her willingness to commit violence (she "likes the feel of steel"), makes her not only capable of exploiting others, but a physical threat to them also. The divisions she creates between people are permanent.

Between the second and third verses is a long instrumental interlude. Pig sound effects are heard first naturally, but then through a talk box—a device usually used by electric guitarists which enables them to speak through their guitar.[7] No matter how hard the pigs try, however, they are unable to articulate words. They continually fail in their attempts to assert their humanity, seemingly because they attempt to do it unauthentically, which is conveyed through their use of technological "tricks". Their lack of authenticity is exposed about halfway through the interlude when the listener hears the return of the synthe- sizer in the background, while the return of the introductory keyboard part also confirms this. Rather than being harmonised at the interval of a sixth this time, the keyboard part is now a single line melody. Because the sixth is a consonant interval, this alteration suggests that the pigs initially attempted to appear "in harmony" with their environment, but their detrimental characters are now fully exposed.

The third verse is aimed at Mary Whitehouse—"the self-appointed guardian of British morals" *(Schaffner 1991: 199)*, who played a major role in the censorship of both television and art works in the 1970s, particularly when they seemed blasphemous *(Tracey and Morrison 1979: 3-4)*:

> Hey you, Whitehouse, ha ha charade you are.
> You house proud town mouse, ha ha charade you are.
> You're trying to keep our feelings off the street.

Waters' use of assonance in the second line effectively contrasts the former attacks on the other pigs. The use of this device, in combination with the decreased occurrence of harsh consonants, makes his attack seem less vicious than ridiculing. Whitehouse is seen as a threat, in Waters' view, because of her desire for collective repression. As the verse progresses, she is portrayed as ner- vously censoring everything that comes out of her mouth. The dog taunts her with the threat of using profanities:

> You're nearly a real treat,
> All tight lips and cold feet,
> And do you feel abused?
> ....! ....! ....! ....!
> You gotta stem the evil tide,
> And keep it all on the inside.

Whitehouse's transferral of her own personal repression to society through the form of censorship became a serious issue in England. She is portrayed here as a hypocrite who hides her own, "evil" qualities, while attacking those she is allowed to observe in others. Waters suggests that she threatens to divide human beings by not having them communicate their thoughts and feelings. It is not surprising that Whitehouse, at times, "felt, as she put it, 'dreadfully iso- lated'" *(Tracey and Morrison 1979: 16)*.

The song ends with a guitar solo which is played over the E minor/Cmaj7 chord progression. Gilmour's technique of playing a note on the first string while bending the second string upward towards the same pitch, in combination with the use of distortion, volume and reverb, results in an extremely powerful effect. That the song fades out during this solo, however, suggests that the dog's confrontation could go on forever, never achieving an escape from the oppressive feelings caused by the eternally repeating, "claustrophobic" progression.

It is significant, therefore, that in the next song "Sheep", the dog tries to rouse the proletariat from its slumber, in order to incite a revolution against the pigs. While the sheep represent the masses, they are also used to represent the Christian populace. It is at this juncture that Waters addresses the influence of religion as superstructure. Seen in this light, the previous song's attack on Mary Whitehouse acts as an extremely effective transition to the present song, because Whitehouse's political successes make her an excellent example of how close the relationship is, at times, between political power and organised religion.

In 1977, Whitehouse, appealing to the common law offence of blasphemy, launched a private prosecution against the newspaper "Gay News", and its editor Denis Lemon, for printing James Kirkup's poem *The Love That Dares To Speak Its Name*—"a poem [which] used the imagery of [homosexual] physical love to convey [the poet's] feeling of union with his God" *(Boyle 1989: 20)*. Whitehouse won the case—the first successful prosecution for the offense of blasphemy in over fifty years *(Boyle 1989: 20)*. According to the trial judge in the case, the offense was defined as follows:

> Blasphemous libel is committed if there is published any writing concerning God or Christ, the Christian religion, the Bible, or some sacred subject, using words which are scurrilous, abusive or offensive and which tend to vilify the Christian religion (and therefore have a tendency to lead to a breach of the peace)... *(Boyle 1989: 3)*

It was ten years later, after the Ayatollah pronounced a death-threat against Salman Rushdie for the blasphemy against Islam contained in his book *The Satanic Verses*, that the British Muslim community discovered that this law did not protect its interests. In its pamphlet "The Crime Of Blasphemy—Why It Should Be Abolished", the International Committee for the Defence of Salman Rushdie and his publishers state:

> Such discrimination in the law is unacceptable in a democratic society which should guarantee freedom for all religions as well as systems of humanist belief, atheistic or agnostic. But the proper course is not to extend the blasphemy laws to other faiths rather as this pamphlet argues, it is to abolish the offences of blasphemy and blasphemous libel outright. Freedom of religion can only be fully ensured if all faiths are treated equally before the law and if none may invoke the power of the state to deter criticism or challenge to their beliefs. *(Boyle 1989: title page)*

Waters appears to have felt the same way about the issue of blasphemy, attacking Whitehouse again in "Sheep" with his grim parody of the twenty-third psalm—a representation which she likely would have labelled blasphemous.

Mullins, commenting in 1978, hints at the overriding difficulty apparent in Whitehouse's character:

> [Whitehouse] had become Britain's major symbol of repressive and guilt ridden attitudes towards sex. Her fundamentalist Christianity and her association with Moral Rearmament were responsible for some of her anti-intellectualism and proneness to equate personal unconscious wishes with the will of God... *(Mullins 1978: 112)*

The danger of someone like Whitehouse achieving political power is apparent—especially when one considers what Michael Tracey and David Morrison considered to be her ultimate objectives:

> In short, there is to all her work—all her speeches, lectures, lawsuits, controversies and books—one specific and clear leitmotiv, that man once more needs to have all his actions and thoughts guided by Christian principles. It was and is nothing less than the call for *the creation of a theocratic state. (Tracey and Morrison 1979: 188)*

The danger of a theocratic state, obviously, is the possibility of one "equating personal wishes with the will of God", but a theocracy is not the only form of government in which this happens. It is hardly necessary to recount the frequent historical abuses of the name of God. We can allow just one example to suffice, from the leader of the world's primary capitalist country. Waters remarked that this statement was the impetus behind the song "What God Wants (Part I)" from *Amused to Death* (1992):

> 'What God Wants' derives at least in part from George Bush's statements during what came to be known as Desert Storm—all that crap about God being on the side of the American people, which is always crass, but within the context of what was going on there, a 'holy war,' is ludicrous and obscene. The idea of whose side God is on is 600 years old.... It's good smokescreen material for the powers that be, but it doesn't help us ordinary people one little bit. It's no help to anybody, except him, of course. *(Resnicoff 1992: 40)*

With regard to the comment Waters makes in the last sentence, it is interesting to consider the statements of Garry Willis, who further illuminates the relation between religion and politics:

> About 40 percent of the American population attends church in a typical week (as opposed to 14 percent in Great Britain and 12 percent in France). More people go to church, in any week, than to all sports events combined. Over 90 percent of Americans say they pray some time in the week. Internationally, "Americans rank at the top in rating the importance of God in their lives. On a scale of 1 to 10, with 10 the highest, Americans average a rating of 8.21, behind only tiny Malta (9.58)." ...One would expect that something so important to Americans would affect their behavior as voters. And as a matter of fact, no non-Christian has ever been elected president of the United States. *(Willis 1990: 16-17)*

"Sheep" cleverly explores the relation between political and religious oppression. The song begins peacefully with the sounds of sheep grazing and birds singing, but this sense of peace is interrupted by the electric piano, which creates a feeling of unease with its sporadic playing and tremolo effect. The inconspicuous bass guitar entry also serves this purpose, providing a pedal point on D for the keyboard's dissonant chordings against the established Dorian modality. The tension is released momentarily when the bass shifts to an A (much of the tension was due to the keyboard's insinuated movement towards A minor), but returns when the harmony changes, oddly, to B minor. Four bars later, the harmony shifts back to A minor, and the backwards-recorded cymbal prepares the way for a delayed percussion entry, initially just bass and snare drum. This climactically builds to a full band entry which sets in motion the dog's arousal of the sheep. The gradual development of tension seems to convey, again, the dog's stealthful approach, his aim clearly being to startle the sheep into aware-ness. This is also effectively achieved by the sudden harmonic rise of the piece into E minor. It is interesting to note one reviewer's comments about a Pink Floyd performance at New York's Madison Square Garden during the 1977 'In the Flesh' tour:

> ...never have I seen such an extravagantly creepy show. Their set includes two caterpillar-like light towers which, when not providing spot-lights, act as eyes that search the audience for God-knows-what; a liv-ing-room full of inflatable people and furniture which rise, blow out, light up, and float aimlessly across the ceiling of the grand arena until they are deflated and drop as though dead; and a giant, air-filled pig that passes ominously over the entire arena... *(Mieses 1977: 18)*

It is obvious that Pink Floyd, in customary avant-garde fashion, attempted to communicate Waters' message to audiences by using shock tactics, just as the narrator does.

The melody of the vocal is comprised almost entirely of the back and forth movement between two notes; its similarity to the siren sounds of old-style British emergency vehicles is startling. Tension is also established by the melody's quarter note triplets (they establish a 4/4 feel), which are heard against the urgent 12/8 feel played by the band. At the end of each of the first two lines of lyric, Waters' voice is transformed into a long, sustained synthe-sizer note. The sustain of the synthesizer, supported by a sustained organ chord beneath it, strengthens his words. It becomes apparent that this is also a shock tactic. He has brought with him to the pastoral setting the reality of the alien-ating technological world. Each time, the sustained note ends with a power chord on the electric guitar, which adds additional force to his words. The long, fluid melodic lines contrast the short, sharply accented notes of the previous song's melody. This seems to help confirm that this piece is not an attack on the sheep, but merely the raising of an alarm.

Unlike the threatening first dog who was characterised earlier in "Dogs", this one (the second in "Dogs") is a sheep dog who tries to herd the flock in order to convey his message of the impending threat of other dogs:

> Harmlessly passing your time in the grassland away;
> Only dimly aware of a certain unease in the air.
> You better watch out,
> There may be dogs about.
> I've looked over Jordan and I have seen
> Things are not what they seem.

The dog hints at his new-found realisation (acquired during "Dogs") that the system set up by the pigs, seemingly legitimate because of superstructure, is actually not. Ultimately it enslaves everybody in one form or another, but the sheep, of course, are those most exploited by the system. The anxiety that char-acterises his delivery is communicated by the abrupt harmonic changes which comprise the remainder of the verse after the initial two lines (F-sharp major to A major). It is also sustained between the verses by the accented off beats played by the guitar. Interestingly, Waters alludes to a piece representative of another historically oppressed people with his reference to the anonymous negro spiritual *Swing Low Sweet Chariot (itself an allusion to Deuteronomy 3:26-27)*:

> I looked over Jordan, and what did I see?
> A band of angels coming after me,
> Coming for to carry me home.

By using the image of sheep, which in the Bible represent the faithful, in combination with this allusion to the slavery of blacks in the United States, Waters makes an observation about the ideology of Christianity: that the doctrine of passivity encourages oppression. The oppressed singer of the spiritual is able to receive comfort from his belief that his troubles will end because he is destined to return to heaven. David Chidester talks about the laws that were passed in the United States in the eighteenth century, which restricted any religious gatherings of slaves:

> These restrictive laws were clearly designed to maintain control over slaves by diffusing any possibility that religious gatherings might result in revolt against the slave masters. But they were also part of a larger pattern of religiopolitical power which used Christian religion to protect the property interests of slaveholders. Religious leaders in the established Christian churches presented a form of Christianity designed to make slaves more docile in their station in life. *(Chidester 1988: 143)*

The Christian tendency toward passivity is effectively portrayed in this excerpt from the poem *Patient Joe* (1795) by the English romantic poet Hannah More:

> He praised his Creator whatever befell;
> How thankful was Joseph when matters went well!
> How sincere were his carols of praise for good health,
> And how grateful for any increase in his wealth!
>
> In trouble he bowed him to God's holy will;
> How contented was Joseph when matters went ill!
> When rich and when poor he alike understood
> That all things together were working for good.
>
> If the land was afflicted with war, he declared
> 'Twas a needful correction for sins which *he* shared;
> And when merciful Heaven bid slaughter to cease,
> How thankful was Joe for the blessing of peace!
>
> When taxes ran high, and provisions were dear,
> Still Joseph declared he had nothing to fear;
> It was but a trial he well understood
> From Him who made all work together for good.
>
> Though his wife was but sickly, his gettings but small,
> A mind so submissive prepared him for all;
> He lived on his gains, were they greater or less,
> And the Giver he ceased not each moment to bless.
> (9-28)

According to Dudley Dillard, Christian ideology, specifically that of Protestantism, encouraged the early expansion of capitalism:

> The Protestant Reformation of the 16th and 17th centuries developed alongside economic changes which resulted in the spread of capitalism

in northern Europe, especially in the Netherlands and England. This chronological and geographical correlation between the new religion and economic development has led to the suggestion that Protestantism had causal significance for the rise of modern capitalism. Without in any sense being the "cause" of capitalism, which already existed on a wide and expanding horizon, the Protestant ethic proved a bracing stimulant to the new economic order. Doctrinal revision or interpretation seemed not only to exonerate capitalists from the sin of avarice but even to give divine sanction to their way of life. In the ordinary conduct of life, a new type of worldly asceticism emerged, one that meant hard work, frugality, sobriety and efficiency in one's calling in the market place similar to that of the monastery. Applied in the environment of expanding trade and industry, the Protestant creed taught that accumulated wealth should be used to produce more wealth....Acceptance of the Protestant ethic also eased the way to systematic organisation of free labour. By definition, free labourers could not be compelled by force to work in the service of others. Moreover, the use of force would have violated the freedom of one's calling. Psychological compulsion arising from religious belief was the answer to the paradox. Every occupation was said to be noble in God's eyes. For those with limited talents, Christian conscience demanded unstinting labour even at low wages in the service of God— and, incidentally, of employers. It was an easy step to justify economic inequality because it would hasten the accumulation of wealth by placing it under the guardianship of the most virtuous (who were, incidentally, the wealthiest) and remove temptation from weaker persons who could not withstand the allurements associated with wealth. After all, it did not much matter who held legal title to wealth, for it was not for enjoyment. The rich like the poor were to live frugally all the days of their lives. Thus the capitalist system found a justification that was intended to make inequality tolerable to the working classes. *(Dillard 1963: 840)*

After notifying the sheep about the dangers posed by the dogs, and illuminating the fact of their oppression, the "sheepdog" chides them for their passivity:

What do you get for pretending the danger's not real.
Meek and obedient you follow the leader
Down well trodden corridors, into the valley of steel.
What a surprise!
A look of terminal shock in your eyes.
Now things are really what they seem.
No, this is no bad dream.

The image of "the valley of steel" anticipates Waters' parody of the twenty-third psalm. The original version speaks of the inevitable "valley of death", but in Waters' parody, the sheep arrive at this unpleasant place because they are led there by "the leader". The "valley of steel" seems to be a symbol for what Waters regards as the alienating mechanisation of modern society. This is confirmed, at the end of the verse, when the sound of a factory machine is heard, which can be associated, appropriately, with the working class. The sheep, with a look of "terminal shock", finally recognise the reality of their situation.

In the ensuing instrumental section, the sense of urgency disappears as the drums and distorted electric guitar drop out. Rather than returning to the usual E minor, this section begins with an E major chord. In fact, the first portion of this section, with a pedal point on E, ambiguously alternates between the modality of E minor and E major, complementing the mixture of both positivity and negativity which is conveyed by the return of the image of the "stone". This echoing image from "Dogs" initially plagued the dog, but eventually led him to a feeling of liberation. The dog now seems to be calmly recounting his unsettling experience in the hope of further sharing his knowledge with the sheep, so that they too can benefit from his new-found knowledge. Immediately preceding the lead synthesizer's return, unease is created by the dissonance of an F-sharp major chord which appears over the continuing pedal point on E. The synthesizer, in combination with the drum kit entry and the bass guitar's adoption of a slow 4/4 feel (it formerly continued the 12/8 feel), conveys the changing temperament of the sheep. They appear to become infuriated. Slowly ascending an E dorian scale in parallel thirds (the pedal point remains), the synthesizer portrays their rising irritation, which culminates with the return of the urgent 12/8 feel and the distorted electric guitar.

The piece descends to the original D modality with which it began and the texture is once again reduced to bass guitar and synthesizer. In conjunction with the reduction in dynamics, this appears to convey that the dog has brought order to the sheep, or calmed them *down*. The disturbing nature of this section is depicted musically. First, by the ominous synthesizer figure (comprised of a D diminished seventh chord), which, instead of resolving to one of its four "natural" resolutions, falls to a D minor chord creating a feeling of unrest. This repeated figure is then complemented by the guitar, which plays a descending, arpeggiated diminished seventh chord also. The prolongation of this chord (composed of two simultaneously played tritone intervals) assists in creating the effect of unrest. The chord is reiterated by an organ and repeated a number of times, before it fades into the background of the mix. During this process, the agitated sheep can be heard congregating to organise their plan of revolt. The scene is similar to that in which Orwell's animals, during their initial meeting, establish the spirit of rebellion with the revolutionary song "Beasts of England" (Orwell 1983: 13).

The sheep recite, with the dog, the parody of the twenty-third psalm, but the dog's voice is heard through a vocoder. As Middleton suggests:

> ...[V]ocalizing is the most intimate, flexible and complex mode of articulation of the body, and also is closely connected with the breath (continuity of life: periodicity of organic processes). Significantly, technological distortion of voice-sounds (through use of a vocoder, for example) is far more disturbing than similar treatment of instrumental playing...
> *(Middleton 1990: 262)*

Apparent through the use of the vocoder, as well as through the text of the parody, is the disturbing aspect of the fierce hatred which is spawned by the characters' realisation of their exploitation and oppression. The shepherd is, of course, primarily a symbol for the pigs, but by using a biblical text, Waters seems to suggest that the sheep have lost their religious faith, and are also angered by the system of thought which may have contributed to their initial passivity. The shepherd is portrayed as a tyrant with "great power" who, by merely feeding on the sheep to appease his own "great hunger", removes their souls with "bright knives":

THE LORD IS MY SHEPHERD, I SHALL NOT WANT;

HE MAKES ME DOWN TO LIE.
THROUGH PASTURES GREEN HE LEADETH ME
THE SILENT WATERS BY.
WITH BRIGHT KNIVES HE RELEASETH MY SOUL.
HE MAKETH ME TO HANG ON HOOKS IN HIGH PLACES.
HE CONVERTETH ME TO LAMB CUTLETS.
FOR LO, HE HATH GREAT POWER, AND GREAT HUNGER.
WHEN COMETH THE DAY WE LOWLY ONES,
THROUGH QUIET REFLECTION, AND GREAT DEDICATION,
MASTER THE ART OF KARATE,
LO, WE SHALL RISE UP.
AND THEN WE'LL MAKE THE BUGGERS EYES WATER.

The characters refer to the pigs as "the buggers", as did the dog (or narrator) previously in "Pigs on the Wing (Part One)". Towards the end of the recitation, the agitated sheep are heard uniting in uprise. The backwards-recorded cymbal, which before initiated the sudden crescendo that startled the sheep, now returns to prepare the sheep's sudden explosion of violence. Foreshadowed by their previous vociferation, "LO, WE SHALL RISE UP", the piece rises by a tone— back to an E minor modality as the sheep revolt in the next verse:

Bleating and babbling we fell on his neck with a scream.
Wave upon wave of demented avengers
March cheerfully out of obscurity into the dream.

The narrating dog, feeling very much a part of the rebellion, becomes one with the sheep - "bleating and babbling". The disturbing feeling which was initially spawned by musical elements is now communicated by Waters' biblical allusion *(Acts 20: 36)*.

From Miletus, before his journey to Jerusalem, Paul sends to Ephesus for the elders of the church, to warn them against "grievous wolves" who will enter among them, "not sparing the flock" *(v. 29)*. Knowing that they "shall see [his] face no more" *(v. 25)* following his departure, the elders are saddened:

...And when he had thus spoken, he kneeled down, and prayed with them all./ And they all wept sore, and fell on Paul's neck, and kissed him... *(Acts 20: 36-37)*

This image, used also by Alfred Lord Tennyson in his poem *In Memoriam A.H.H* (1850),[8] is one of love and admiration towards the leader, but Waters distorts the image into a violent attack on the pigs which is spurred by hatred. The scream and mad laughter, which is heard after the first line, recalls that which was heard before the third verse of "Dogs". This suggests that the sheep, through their violence, have acquired something of the "demented" character of the cut-throat dogs who were negatively portrayed approaching their work with glee; "marching cheerfully", waves of sheep and conformed dogs join the hostilities. The possibility that this is merely a dream, however, is hinted at in the last line above, and reinforced by the "dream-like" repetition of the word "dream".

The dream takes an unexpected twist however:

Have you heard the news?
The dogs are dead!
You better stay home

> And do as you're told.
> Get out of the road if you want to grow old.

The death of the conformed "sheep dogs" ensures the failure of the revolution. Waters appears to suggest that the pigs are too powerful, portrayed by the overwhelming character of the repeated guitar riff which ends the piece (it is at least double tracked). Originally responsible for encouraging the rebellion, the narrator now warns the sheep to take shelter in the safety of their homes. He advises them, for their well-being, to return to their original obedient nature. Waters' comments about the song, from 1977, are informative:

> It was my sense of what was to come down in England and it did last summer with the riots...in Brixton and Toxteth...it had happened before in Notting Hill in the early Sixties. And it will happen again. It will always happen. There are too many of us in the world and we treat each other badly. We get obsessed with things and there aren't enough things, products, to go round. If we're persuaded it's important to have them, that we're nothing without them, and there aren't enough of them to go round, the people without them are going to get angry. Content and discontent follow very closely the rise and fall on the graph of world recession and expansion. *(Dallas 1987: 117)*

Waters' remark, "it will always happen", suggests his belief that the conditions imposed by the capitalist society as it is, appear to be unalterable. After short periods of change, the same conditions inevitably return.[9] The song implies that the risk of causing or suffering personal injury—too late for the dogs in the dream—is a price not worth paying. Rather than attempting to change these conditions through violent means, the song intimates the conclusion that was discussed earlier in relation to "Us and Them", and articulated by Waters in 1993—that we must discover the answer to what really is, as he calls it, the "great question" *(see p. 50)*. Of course, in the supposedly democratic age what might possibly accelerate this question's solution is if "the sheep" did not remain blind to the fact of their oppression. That Waters believes that the majority of them remain so, is illustrated by the return of the sound effects of the sheep grazing in the fields—much as they were before the narrating dog had intervened—confirming that the "dog's" arousal was, in fact, merely a dream. In the meantime, *Animals* proposes, to those of us who have been able to see through our society's ideological smokescreen, that we can take comfort in the fact that we are able to make honest and intimate connections with other people, just as the narrator does at the end of the album in "Pigs on the Wing (Part II)":

> You know that I care what happens to you.
> And I know that you care for me too,
> So I don't feel alone,
> Or the weight of the stone,
> Now that I've found somewhere safe
> To bury my bone.
> And any fool knows a dog needs a home
> A shelter from pigs on the wing.

Unlike the dehumanised pigs and dogs who have sadly isolated themselves, this dog has not allowed the system to crush his spirit. He is still capable of communicating his feelings. The comfort that he derives from the closeness of his relationship with another person acts as "a shelter" from the conditions of "boredom and pain" that are created by the desensitised pigs.

His renewed confidence is displayed musically. In the first part of the song, instead of embellishing the acoustic guitar's initial strummed G and C chords with suspended fourths as he did in "Pigs on the Wing (Part I), Waters assertively plays the actual IV chord (C in the first case, and F in the second). That he is not alone is also clear; instead of a solo acoustic guitar, now there are two.

Chapter 4 — The Wall

'According to Freud's surmise, as a result of the ceaseless impact of external stimuli upon the living organism, a surface or protective shield is gradually formed upon the organism. This surface, or vesicle, develops a permanent and unchangeable crust through which to receive external stimuli in small quantities by means of the sensory organs, and through which to be protected at the same time from too great an impact of external stimuli. Freud considered this shield to be effective in relation to outer stimuli only...'.

Sylvia Brody and Sidney Axelrad[1]

In the post-Freudian phase of psychoanalytic thought there arose what has come to be known as psychodynamic object relations theory. Essentially a British revision of Freud's teachings, its primary exponents have been Melanie Klein, Michael Balint, W. Ronald D. Fairbairn, D. W. Winnicott and Harry Guntrip. Object relations theory, as the name suggests, is primarily concerned with the individual's ability or inability to establish mature, healthy relationships with others. This is also the primary concern of *The Wall*. The work's central image is that of a barrier, or "protective shield", which is erected by its main character—aptly named Pink Floyd—in response to the ceaseless impact of negative, external stimuli. Pink's wall, however, eventually becomes such an effective barrier to external stimuli that it serves to impede his ability both to form and to maintain meaningful and mature personal relationships. As a consequence Pink eventually finds himself devoid of any contact with the external world or reality. Haunted by his excessive internal stimuli, he becomes mad.

In my view object relations theory can provide a deeper understanding of the various elements of *The Wall*. Thus, I shall have recourse to it throughout my analysis. For this reason, I will expound its primary concepts.

Object Relations Theory

The fundamental tenet of the object relations theorists is, as stated by Andrew Brink, that "[s]uccessive attachments to persons and to associated objects elaborate the forms by which a sense of significance in life is acquired and maintained". In relation to this principle, the underlying emphasis of these theorists has been on the importance of the formative relationships, those which individuals establish with their parents:

> Every psychoanalytic, and much psychiatric, interpretation of human nature rests on findings about the long dependency of the infant on the mother, and since she is supported by her husband, on the father.... The basic human tie, as Bowlby explains..., a tie comparable to that of sub-human primate infants and mothers, is so binding in humans as to continue almost to the end of the third year. So nearly absolute is this dependence that trustful acceptance of others than mother begins to develop only then. Thereafter, by slow gradations into adolescence, the unconditional maternal (or parental) tie lessens, and as we know, ties to persons outside the family are formed... *(Brink 1977: 16-17)*

Due to the incredible significance of these primary early "attachments" or "object relations", their influence on personality formation and socialisation is obvious. As Brink suggests, paraphrasing John Bowlby, "the individual's actual experiences of the earliest attachment figures are reflected in their expectations about attachments in subsequent life" *(Brink 1977: 14)*. In other words, any distortions of care during this period can have serious implications for the individual's maturational development.

Fairbairn states that the course of maturational development is characteristically "a process whereby infantile dependence upon the object gradually gives place to mature dependence upon the object":

> The gradual change which thus occurs in the nature of the object-relationship is accompanied by a gradual change in libidinal aim, whereby an original oral, sucking, incorporating and predominantly 'taking' aim comes to be replaced by a mature, non-incorporating and predominantly 'giving' aim compatible with developed genital sexuality.... Between these two stages of infantile and mature dependence is a transition stage characterized by an increasing tendency to adopt the attitude of mature dependence. *(Fairbairn 1962: 34-5)*

The course towards mature dependence, Winnicott suggests, is one of "development of the self towards its becoming a subject in relationship with objects"; failure to achieve this sense "means restricted or distorted development" *(Sutherland 1980: 839)*. The idea of mature dependence implies that subjects have successfully differentiated themselves from their "primary objects" or parents. According to David Holbrook:

> To be able to relate to a real person or a real world one needs to be a whole subject, an identity: only a *me* can recognize the *not-me*. There is a stage before this is possible: at the other extreme maturity is that independence which fully recognises the distinction between the self and the not-self, while yet accepting the human need for dependence upon an object. *(Holbrook 1971: 96-7)*

Fairbairn suggests that "it is to disturbances in the object-relationships of the developing ego that we must look for the ultimate origin of all pathological conditions" *(Fairbairn 1962: 82)*. I will illustrate in my study of *The Wall* that the character Pink never fully achieves the stage of mature dependence necessary for "normal" healthy relationships, but remains in a state of infantile object dependency due to the disturbances he experienced in his early attachments, primarily because of the unsatisfactory mothering he received and the loss of his father.

Psychologists, borrowing the term *adaptation* from biology, suggest that just as there is a tendency for organisms to repair themselves after experiencing physical damage, they are inclined to do likewise following psychological damage:

> As we know, all organisms are capable of repairing or replacing when there is tissue damage, while some of the lower orders of animals can actually regenerate lost parts as a means of maintaining function. Much harm to the body can be compensated for in nature, though the exact mechanisms of tissue maintenance and repair are yet to be explained. ...[W]e are perhaps not misled to think that...imaginative functions...are related to the organism's basic programme of reaching its maturational destiny, despite even the most serious setbacks, including damage to tissue and psychological damage. *(Brink 1977:6-7)*

Related to this idea is the concept of internal objects. It was Fairbairn's belief that when inadequacies of parenting occur, the parents become "bad objects" and are thus internalised:

When someone we need and love ceases to love us, or behaves in such a way that we interpret it as a cessation of love...when his mother refuses the breast, weans the baby, or is cross, impatient or punitive or is absent temporarily or for a longer period (these may be experienced as) rejection or desertion, or else as persecution or attack. Then the lost (or hostile) object, now become a bad object, is mentally internalised in a much more vital and fundamental sense than memory. An inner psychic world has been set up, duplicating the original situation....But it is an unhappy world in which one is tied to bad objects and feeling therefore always frustrated, hungry, angry, and guilty and profoundly anxious. It is bad objects which are internalised because we cannot accept their badness and yet cannot give them up, cannot leave them alone, cannot master and control them in outer reality and so keep on struggling to possess them, alter them and compel them to change into good objects, in our inner psychic world. They never do change. In our inner unconscious world where we repress and lock away very early in life our original bad objects, they remain always rejecting, indifferent, or hostile to us according to our actual outer experience. *(in Holbrook 1971: 115-116)*

Fairbairn suggests that during the transitional period of the individual's maturational development the great task "comes to be one, not only of establishing relationships with differentiated external objects, but also of coming to terms with objects which have already been internalized" *(Fairbairn 1962: 146)*. When this process is unsuccessful, the ultimate psychopathological issue becomes, as Guntrip states, "How do people deal with their internalised bad objects, to what extent do they feel identified with them, and how do they complicate relations with external objects" *(in Holbrook 1971: 99-100)*?

It was Fairbairn's belief that the ultimate goal of libido is the object. This, of course, carries certain implications with regard to internal objects:

...there is a general tendency on the part of individuals with a schizoid component to heap up their values in the inner world. Not only do their objects tend to belong to the inner rather than to the outer world, but they tend to identify themselves very strongly with their internal objects. This fact contributes materially to the difficulty which they experience in giving emotionally. In the case of individuals whose object-relationships are predominantly in the outer world, giving has the effect of creating and enhancing values, and of promoting self-respect; but, in the case of individuals whose object-relationships are predominantly in the inner world, giving has the effect of depreciating values, and of lowering self-respect. When such individuals give, they tend to feel impoverished, because, when they give, they give at the expense of their inner world. *(Fairbairn 1962: 18)*

Such individuals tend to be "preoccupied" with the self or withdrawn, a condition commonly referred to as narcissism. As Guntrip states, "narcissism is a characteristic that arises out of the predominantly interior life the schizoid lives. His love-objects are all inside him, and moreover he is greatly identified with them, so that his libidinal attachments appear to be to himself". To this Brink adds, "in 'normalcy' the attachment to the inner narcissistic object is readily given up in transfer of interest to persons with whom satisfactory relationships are formed" *(Brink 1977: 20)*. Narcissism, which is comparable to Pink's construction of a wall, "is an emergency measure and a second best to actual restored relationships" *(Brink 1977: 22)*. It is, in fact, his increasing narcissism which eventually leads Pink to madness, but it is clear that he attempts to employ ego defences long before his wall is completed.[2]

As Fairbairn suggests, "[t]he earliest form of defence resorted to by the developing ego in a desperate attempt to deal with internalized bad objects is necessarily the simplest and most readily available, viz. repression"; in other words the bad objects are simply banished to the unconscious. Fairbairn describes four "classic" methods of defence (the paranoid, phobic, hysterical and obsessional) and states that they are only called into operation "when repression fails to prove an adequate defence against the internalized bad objects and these begin to threaten the ego"*(Fairbairn 1962: 65)*. Brink writes:

> Freud thought defences to be techniques by which the ego is protected against intolerable anxiety. Rycroft puts it more positively saying that defences may be 'taken to include all techniques used by the ego to master, control, canalize, and use forces which may lead to a neurosis.' That is, they mediate conflicts, which in their raw state would be intolerable, perhaps leading to depression or schizoid withdrawal. Defences do turn conflict to constructive uses in everyday life, but they can also take exaggerated and troublesome forms. *(Brink 1977: 37)*

When these defences do take "exaggerated" forms they appear as personality disorders, and Brink adds that they most often do not occur singly. Rather, "in their combined forms they lose the sharpness of definition which is convenient for discussion". Their characteristics will be explored, however, as the character Pink is seen to employ them throughout the work—to which I shall now turn my attention.[3]

* * *

The film version of *The Wall* opens with a provocative shot that slowly moves along the floor of a long hotel corridor. However, due to its unusual stale whiteness, the scene suggests the corridor of a mental institution. The viewer later learns that it is the door to Pink's room at the end of the hallway which is being approached. Besides intimating the camera's intrusion into his womb-like space, the oddly-ridged ceiling of the corridor suggests that the viewer is burrowing deep into the labyrinth of Pink's self, beyond the bricks of the carpet which represent his wall. This idea is supported by the accompanying music—a song from the World War II era sung by Vera Lynn, a prominent figure in the second half of the work *(see below)*. Though we never hear the complete text of the song ("The Little Boy That Santa Claus Forgot" by Tommy Connor, Jimmy Leach and Michael Carr), it holds great significance for Pink:

> Christmas comes but once a year
> for every girl and boy.
> The laughter and the joy
> they find in each new toy.
> I'll tell you of a little boy
> who lives across the way.
> This little fella's Christmas
> is just another day.
>
> He's the little boy that Santa Claus forgot
> And goodness knows he didn't want a lot.

> He sent a note to Santa
> for some soldiers and a drum.
> It broke his little heart
> when he found Santa hadn't come.
> In the street he envies all those lucky boys
> then wanders home to last year's broken toys.
> I'm so sorry for that laddie...
> he hasn't got a daddy.

From this opening shot we cut to Pink's father who, like Waters' own, was a platoon commander in the Royal Fusiliers during the second world war. Sitting in a dug out, he is seen cleaning his revolver to the accompaniment of the first part of "When the Tigers Broke Free", a song which does not appear on the recording but was written specially by Waters for the film:

> It was just before dawn
> One miserable morning in black '44
> When the Forward Commander was
> told to sit tight, when he asked
> that his men be withdrawn.
> The generals gave thanks
> as the other ranks held back
> the enemy tanks for a while.
> And the Anzio bridgehead was held for
> the price of a few hundred ordinary lives.[4]

The music of the song, heard against a background of falling bombs, has a salutatory but sober quality which is partially achieved by its droning on a major chord, but also through the use of solo trumpet, male chorus and the funereal-type drum—all characteristics associated with military life. The music of the piece helps to convey how Pink's father has become an idealised internal object (all the more apparent later in the work), while the text alludes to "Us and Them" from *The Dark Side of the Moon (see p. 29)*, a song concerned with the divisions that human beings create between themselves, and the resultant apathy which tends to arise; in this case specifically, the generals' apathy towards the lower ranks. This, of course, foreshadows Pink's appearance as a hateful megalomaniac, the end result of having walled himself off from others.

The image of Pink's father fades into what is to become one of the major visual images of the film—a shot of Pink as a young boy running towards the camera across a rugby field. This scene, which director Alan Parker has referred to as "the recurring dream of Pink's childhood" *(Parker 1982: 1063)*, we shall see acts as a formal device; it appears at three key points in the film and helps to relate Pink's childhood to his present condition. As the work progresses, it becomes clear that this scene is intimately related to Pink's lost father, suggested initially here by the effective cinematographic fusion with the previous scene.

Next we see Pink, a successful rock musician in the midst of a long North American tour, sitting alone in his hotel room. The undisturbed ashes of a burned-out cigarette in his hand, and the crazed look on his face display Pink's highly active internal world. The sound of a maid attempting to open the chained door gives rise to Pink's imagined vision of emergency doors, held together by a thick steel chain which is under incredible tension from the crowds of fans behind it. As the chain snaps and the doors burst open, the viewer hears the opening strains of "In the Flesh?", the first piece that actually appears on the album. The startlingly loud entry denotes that we are at a Pink Floyd concert, and on the original recording this opening interrupts the peaceful music of "Outside the Wall"—the last piece of the work, and, as we shall see, one that could have been effectively titled "Outside the Concert Hall". The shock of this opening is significant when considered in the light of Waters' statements about the background of the work:

> ...[T]he idea for *The Wall* came from ten years of touring...rock shows. I think particularly the last few years in '75 and in '77 [when] we were playing to very large audiences, some of whom were our old audience who'd come to see us play, but most of whom were only there for the beer..., and consequently it became rather an alienating experience doing the shows. I became very conscious of a wall between us and our audience, and so this record started out as being an expression of those feelings.... The people who you're aware of at a rock show on stage are the front twenty or thirty rows of bodies. And in large situations where you're using what's euphemistically called 'festival seating', they tend to be packed together swaying madly, and it's very difficult to perform under those situations with screaming and shouting, throwing things, hitting each other, crashing about and letting off fireworks...it's a drag to try and play when all that's going on. *(Vance 1979)*

The aggressive feelings that arise from the situation that Waters describes take the form of Pink's hatred of his audience; towards the completion of his transformation into a kind of fascist demagogue, as Helen Sherrill observes from the film, "he imagines them brutalized by police" *(Sherrill 1991: 79)*. For Waters, these feelings culminated in an albeit less severe projection of hatred during the last concert of Pink Floyd's 1977 tour performed in front of 80,000 people at Montréal's Olympic Stadium:

> ...I personally became so upset during the show that I spat at some guy in the front row. He was shouting and screaming, and having a wonderful time, and they were pushing against the barrier. ...[W]hat he wanted was a good riot, and what I wanted was to do a good rock and roll show. I got so upset in the end that I spat at him, which is a very nasty thing to do to anybody. The idea is that these kinds of fascist feelings develop from isolation. *(Vance 1979)*

Although *The Wall*, according to Waters is "...an attack on parts of myself that I disapprove of..." *(Dallas 1987: 136-137)*, it also explores his impression of the behaviour of rock audiences. As the emergency doors break open at the concert venue, crowds of frantic people are seen running down an empty corridor. In his imagination Pink superimposes on this scene the trampling feet and screaming faces of battle, obviously related to the former thoughts of his father. Waters discusses this relationship:

> That kind of crazed rush into an empty auditorium is something that I used to watch from time to time in big, big places like the Cow Palace in San Francisco, that crazed rush to the front of the stage, to stand crushed against barriers for hour after hour. ...Clearly, the motivation behind people jumping off DUKWs and running up beaches in Anzio is that they've been bloody well ordered to do it, you know. And they thought, and they were probably right in thinking, they were fighting a

war that needed to be fought. Whereas the motivation for the kind of involvement in rock shows that I'm pointing at is a masochism. It's something I don't understand. I do not understand that thing of people going to rock shows and apparently the more painful it is the better they like it. There are lots of shows where the sound is just so awful and so loud that it's painful. And it becomes a kind of religious exercise almost, it seems to me. It's a bit like being a whirling dervish or something, you achieve ecstasy through continual repetition of some simple movement. Maybe that's what it is. Maybe it's a response to a lack of religious involvement. It's a bit like walking on hot coals or something. Certainly you see people sometimes at shows where they've gone to be in the presence of their Gods and whatever happens, really, they're going to bloody well make all the right responses in all the right places, come hell or high water. *(Dallas 1987: 137-138)*

Considering Waters' comments above, the shocking effect achieved at the beginning of "In the Flesh?" connotes a sadistic attack by the performer and the audience's masochistic response.

As Waters suggests, however, he is less inclined to blame the fans for the oddness of this relationship than the group itself:

[I]t was a situation we'd created ourselves through our own greed...the only real reason for playing large venues is to make money. ...[T]hey're only expressing their response to what it's like. In a way I'm saying they're right...that those shows are bad news....There is an idea, or there has been an idea for many years abroad that it's a very uplifting and wonderful experience and that there's a great contact between the audience and the performers on the stage and I think that that is not true. I think there've been very many cases where it's actually a rather alienating experience...for everybody. *(Vance 1979)*

This self-blame is reflected in the parodic title of the piece, taken from their 1977 tour which was dubbed *Pink Floyd—In the Flesh*, the question mark obviously challenging the validity of the title. Hence, during the stage performances of *The Wall*, it was not the group that took the stage during this opening piece, but a surrogate band composed of backup musicians; and in Waters' 1990 performance of the work in Berlin, the surrogate band (played by the German rock group The Scorpions) are ceremoniously driven directly on to the stage in a limousine—itself an act of self-parody. Similarly in the film when Pink Floyd takes the stage it is not as himself, but as a neo-nazi skinhead singer. Just as the soldiers at Anzio fall victim to the hatred of fascist Germany, Pink's fans become the victims of his hatred later in the work.

"In the Flesh?" also explores the issue of the power possessed by rock musicians,[5] obviously in the portrayal of Pink as a demagogue, but also through musical events. That there is something unsettling about this power is displayed at the outset of the recording where a quiet speaking voice comes in midway through a sentence and the music of "Outside the Wall" is heard softly played on acoustic instruments. The disturbance comes with the sudden volume of the band entry, in combination with the sudden change of mode from C major to E natural minor. The rock star's power is portrayed through the guitar's extreme distortion and the accompanying organ. As Robert Walser notes:

In Western musical history, the only other instrument capable of indefinite, unarticulated sustain is the organ (and its contemporary descendant, the synthesizer), which shares one other singular attribute with the electric guitar: the capacity to produce power chords...[which are] sometimes employed to similar effect: to display and enact overwhelming power—usually, in that context, for the greater glory of God. *(Walser 1993: 42-43)*

In this context, however, the overall effect is employed to represent the power of the fascist Pink.

Soon after the E minor modality has been firmly established, the piece uncomfortably shifts to a D minor modality with the use of a pedal tone (on D) in the bass guitar. At this point the listener hears the primary musical figure (A) which, in various guises, is used throughout the entire work (most easily identified as forming the basis for the three parts of "Another Brick in the Wall"):

Immediately preceding this figure is another harmonic figure (B) which also appears in those pieces, but at the end of each verse:

Figure (B) formed the basis for the odd verses of "Time" from *The Dark Side of the Moon (see page 20)*, where it evoked feelings of claustrophobia or constraint due to its circularity and narrow range. Figure (A), likewise, evokes a similar effect, and usually threatens to trap the ear into the narrow space of the interval of a minor third wherever it is used. As we shall see, numerous attempts to transcend these stifling melodic figures exist throughout the work.

The first such attempt appears here. The discomfort of these figures gives way during the second repetition of figure (A)—where the constrictive interval of a minor third is transcended and the piece rises to the main harmonic section in A major. As will become obvious, it is only after Pink's metamorphosis from the oppressed into the oppressor that a real sense of transcendence is possible. The film conveys Pink's sense of satisfaction when in the midst of the scenes of fans being brutalised by police, the camera focuses, during this harmonic shift, on a billboard which contains a soft drink advertisement. The ad pictures a smiling baseball player with the words *Feelin' 7up*.

The "fanfare-like" quality of this music, achieved primarily by the slow, and sequenced melodic riff prepares a regal entrance for Pink, whose power is further displayed by the entranced looks on the faces of the listening fans when he begins to sing:

> So ya'
> Thought ya'
> Might like to go to the show.
> To feel the warm thrill of confusion,
> That space cadet glow.

Tell me is something eluding you sunshine?
Is this not what you expected to see?
If you want to find out what's behind these cold eyes
You'll just have to claw your way through this
Disguise....

The contrast set up lyrically between "warm thrill" and "cold eyes" is also apparent between the music and the lyrics. While the music evokes both the typically "fun" music of The Beach Boys and Sha Na Na through use of the simple, "innocent" sounding organ, and 1950s quality background vocals, the lyrics convey the condescending and unfriendly tone of the singer. This contrast seems to communicate the sado-masochistic relationship of performer and audience to which Waters referred earlier.

At the same time, the music appears to satirize the power of the rock star facade—the background vocal style being one, which was normally reserved for providing support for popular solo singers, many of whom became big stars. The effect is one in which the lead voice always appears as the leader of the group. That Pink's power appears to be mocked here is illuminated by the comments of Bruce Johnston, one of The Beach Boys who actually sang on the album with Toni Tennille:

Musically, I've got to represent a vast amount of saccharine. Toni's got to represent a lot of fluff. There we are singing songs about worms on this album that certainly has to be about 180 degrees from what the Beach Boys do. *(Hogan 1980: 24)*

The effect here is that Pink, through the music, is apparently portrayed as a "teeny bop" star, the likes of which are normally idolised by children. That Waters' intends to ridicule the notion of the "rock star" seems apparent, especially in the light of his comments regarding *The Wall* performances:

...[I]n 'The Wall' we provided the audience with enough stuff so that it was almost impossible not to be involved in it, if you were in the audience, *I* think. And that was what the intention was, really, to do a rock show which didn't have to rely necessarily on the feeling of being in the presence of divine beings, or getting some contact-high from being close to power and wealth and fame... *(Dallas 1987: 140)*

Pink, on the other hand, is unwilling to allow his listener any contact with him, and the addressee must instead "claw" through his "disguise" or "wall". The use of the word "behind" here also suggests "origins", and the image intimates that the addressee must explore the mind which lies behind the "cold eyes" to explain his present personality. The work now proceeds to do exactly this.

In the film (immediately after Pink sings the last line of "In the Flesh?") the viewer returns to the previous images of the battle at Anzio to probe one of the roots of Pink's pathology. A Stuka bomber dives toward the battle and Pink's father is seen cranking a field telephone. The bomb explodes and the viewer sees what will become a leitmotif throughout the work—an incomplete telephone call displaying the inability to establish contact.

Back at the show (on the album) Pink can be heard angrily shouting the stage directions "Lights!...Roll the sound effects!...Action!" over the returning instrumental section. His hatred is communicated by the last directions which he shouts—"Drop it! Drop it on 'em! Drop it on them!!!!". As Schaffner notes, "[Waters'] original film script called for 'a rock and roll audience being bombed and, as they were being blown to pieces, applauding, loving every minute'" *(Schaffner 1991: 210)*. The remorse that Pink feels over the loss of his father to the evils of fascist Germany is transferred into his own fascist hatred and subsequently directed at his audience. His father's fate is about to become that of his fans, but in the place of the dropped bomb we hear the cry of a baby, and return to Pink's childhood.

At the same moment his father dies at Anzio, Pinks mother is seen sleeping in the garden at home while her new born son is seen crying in his pram. The pram is located at a bizarre distance from his sleeping mother. As Brody and Axelrad suggest:

> Possibly two extreme kinds of treatment of the young infant may increase narcissism: one in which there is too little reduction of narcissism by appropriate dosage of relief and of stimulation, the other in which stimulation is so high that the infant gets too little or too erratic experience in tension tolerance. In any case, narcissistic lability may be highest during the period of infancy when differentiation between the self and the external world is least perceived. *(Brody and Axelrad 1970: 361)*

Here can be seen the roots of Pink's infantile dependence—his inability to differentiate, in Holbrook's terms, "the *me* from the *not me*"; or, in other words, failure to establish an independent identity. It will be seen that Pink's mother is most often characterised as overprotective, but this scene reveals that she is not always so. Rather she is seen to fluctuate between both extremes of unsatisfactory, inconstant mothering.

As the camera cuts to the aftermath of the battle at Anzio and the medics are seen moving in, an extreme musical contrast is achieved. "The Thin Ice" begins as a reassuring lullaby from Pink's mother,[6] and its serenity contrasts the former onslaught that occurred during "In the Flesh?", just as the aftermath of the battle contrasts the battle itself. The familiarity of the "Stand by Me" chord changes (I—vi—IV—V) provide a comfort for the listener as does David Gilmour's gentle singing, until the repeated series of deceptive cadences which end the phrases beginning with "Oooh". The false hope she instills in Pink by referring to his father as if he were alive, as we shall see, will prove detrimental:

> Mamma loves her baby
> And Daddy loves you too
> And the sea may look warm to you babe
> and the sky may look blue
> but Oooh babe
> Oooh baby blue
> Oooh babe
> If you should go skating
> On the thin ice of modern life
> Dragging behind you the silent reproach
> Of a million tear stained eyes
> Don't be surprised when a crack in the ice
> Appears under your feet
> You slip out of your depth and out of your mind

With your fear, flowing out behind you
As you claw the thin ice.

Though the mother, at first, seems to provide reassurance, another side of her is displayed, which is signified by Waters' vocal entry at the beginning of the "skating waltz"—an ironic musical event at this juncture because it normally denotes a jovial, romantic situation. Because waltzing is normally an activity performed by lovers, and due to the fact that his mother is singing, its use here also seems to foreshadow Pink's psychosexual disorder.

Waters' sharp enunciation of consonants and his dry, harsh, vocal effectively establish the contrast in the mother's characterisation. Brink observes that "in sub-optimal instances of mother-infant interaction, conflicting internalized models of reality are generated in the ego" *(Brink 1982: 12)*. In cases such as this, the mother is commonly experienced as both loving and persecutory at the same time. The mother's persecutory aspect here is associated with her failure to help her young son mourn his father's death. That it is this aspect of her which warns him about the "thin ice" is an ironic signal that she herself is greatly responsible for his pathological grief, which is symbolically represented by the long row of soldiers walking into the mist and the subsequent "silent reproach of a million tear stained eyes" which he drags behind him. As suggested by the image of Pink floating in the swimming pool, like Christ he piles the world's grief upon his back, and consequently suffers for it. Waters' repetition of the word "claw" here (previously used at the end of "In the Flesh?"), in combination with Pink's actual clawing of himself during his outburst of grief, appears to suggest that his attempt to "claw" through to his bottled up or "walled in" emotions will be as fruitless as trying to "claw" the thin ice in order to regain his sanity.

This is also portrayed musically. What started out as a peaceful lullaby, changes to a fit of madness with a loud drum and electric guitar entry. This section reiterates the melody which accompanied the three lines that began "Oooh", but whereas before.

the figure was harmonised in C major, it is now performed only in octaves, giving the ear the impression that we are now in a sinister A minor modality. The figure is what Rudolph Reti calls an *interversion* of figure (A)—an arrangement of the same notes, only in a different order:[7]

After the first statement of the figure, the higher pitched guitar bursts into a short solo, seemingly attempting to escape the confines of the figure which the lower sounding guitar continues to repeat. It appears to succeed on the second repetition as it bursts into a solo once again, but its failure is suggested when in the last statement it joins the lower guitar in repeating the melody. Just before the piece concludes, the lead guitar breaks its melodic bonds again by jumping up to the leading tone of the key; instead of rising to the tonic however—(as it would normally do in a perfect cadence like this one), the lead guitar vanishes into the mix, leaving the lower guitar to play the final chord of the piece, and the listener's expectations consequently unfulfilled. The lead guitar fails to establish a feeling of transcendence, just as Pink will ultimately fail to regain the "ice"; and the staggering drum fill which ends the piece foreshadows his lapse into madness.

The removal of the original C major harmonisation, and the apparent lack of chordal roots anticipates Pink's "fading roots", or oncoming disintegration of mental stability. A similar effect of unrootedness and uneasiness is achieved during the last chord of the tune (C major), which is heard together with the first chord (D minor) of "Another Brick in the Wall (Part I)", creating a confusion to the ear as it is simultaneously presented with two different tonics.

This sense of confusion seems to become Pink's when, in the next scene, he is seen as a small boy about five years of age playing in a church while his bereaved mother mourns the loss of her husband. That he does not fully understand the situation is apparent:

> Daddy's flown across the ocean,
> Leaving just a memory.
> A snapshot in the family album,
> Daddy, what else did you leave for me?
> Daddy, what d'ya leave behind for me?
> All in all it was just a brick in the wall.
> All in all it was just bricks in the wall.

The continued separation which exists between Pink and his mother again illustrates that she is not adequately helping him deal with his own loss, but is seemingly trying to protect the small boy from grief. Brink writes:

> ...[A]ny disruption of early parental attachment calls for special adaptations which are more or less supported or thwarted by circumstances over which the child has a minimum of control....If the surviving parent is strong and supportive but does not impinge or arouse persistent conflict, chances of a successful adaptation are increased....But there are also less fortunate circumstances surrounding loss in which true mourning and adaptation are unlikely to occur; then denial and suppression of affect are apt to cover for effective reintegration. *(Brink 1982: 6)*

The preceding scene of the adult Pink barely afloat in the swimming pool displays that "denial and suppression of affect" have taken the place of proper grieving. Instead of moving toward the stage of accepting the loss, the young Pink's mourning process is arrested in the stage of anger (communicated by the shouted repetition of the fourth line and the forceful distorted power chords which precede it).[8] At this point in time, rather than acknowledging his father's death, the young Pink seems to feel that his father has merely deserted him. According to Levin, this has particular implications:

> ...desertion may be experienced not only as a loss but also as an attack...there may be subtle differences between reactions to loss and attack. Loss may lead to effort to retrieve the object, followed by redistribution of libido to other objects; but when an attack is experienced, a severe narcissistic injury may occur, and the ego may attempt to undo the injury by persistently seeking excessive narcissistic supplies or by developing excessive narcissistic aspirations. *(Levin 1966: 151)*

That this is the case is evident. His agony is conveyed by the scream heard towards the end of the track, and his increasing narcissism is communicated by the repetition of the last line: rather than providing merely a brick for Pink's wall (as the line originally states), this early experience contributes many bricks.[9] One of the primary reasons for the severe trauma caused by this event is best expressed by Erna Furman in *A Child's Parent Dies: Studies in Childhood Bereavement* (1974):

> An adult distributes his love among several meaningful relationships— his spouse, parents, children, friends, colleagues—as well as in his work and hobbies. The child, by contrast, invests almost all his feelings in his parents. *(in Brink 1977: 18)*

With the reprise of "When the Tigers Broke Free"[10] young Pink, now approximately ten years old, discovers his father's uniform along with a scroll and some bullets. As Brink states, "'[p]ermission' by the remaining parent or caretaker to mourn is a key factor in releasing the child from the chance of later disturbance over dependency" *(Brink 1977: 18)*, but these articles are, of course, "hidden away" in the bedroom of Pink's mother:

> And kind old King George
> Sent Mother a note
> When he heard that Father was gone
> It was I recall in the form of a scroll
> with gold leaf and all
> And I found it one day
> in a drawer of old photographs, hidden away.
> And my eyes still grow damp to remember
> His Majesty signed with his own rubber stamp...
>
> It was dark all around
> There was frost in the ground
> When the Tigers broke free.
> And no-one survived from
> The Royal Fusiliers Company C
> They were all left behind
> Most of them dead
> The rest of them dying
> And that's how the High Command
> Took my Daddy from me.

In this piece can be seen one of the roots of Pink's hatred and distrust of authority figures, a characteristic which later culminates in an obsessional ego defence, or, in other words, his own need for power. Perceiving his father as victimised, particularly in the light of his own victimisation later in school *(see below)*, increases his sense of identification with him. As Sherrill suggests, "Pink puts on his father's hat and, standing straight, looks at himself in the mirror, attaining some union and identity with his missing father" *(Sherrill 1991: 82)*. Sol Altschul observed with many of his patients however:

> The mechanisms of denial, hypercathexis in fantasy, or "acting out" often combined to avoid reality recognition of the loss and to preserve the object. Use of these mechanisms in adapting to the trauma resulted in failure to complete the necessary work of mourning. It also seemed to 'freeze' the ego at that level of object relations and developmental conflicts achieved at the time of loss. *(in Levin 1966: 144)*

Pink's inability to accept his father's death, and his increasing identification with him, becomes a primary factor in his failure to achieve mature dependence. As Elizabeth Zetzel emphasises:

> Before an object loss can be recognised and tolerated, self-object differentiation and some ego identification must have occurred...ego gains through identification depend upon the capacity to recognize and accept the possibility of object loss. *(in Levin 1966: 145)*

Pink's idealisation of his father is again made apparent in this scene, but, as Zetzel suggests, the potential ego benefits from this identification are ultimately unrealizable due to his inability to accept the reality of the loss.

That Pink is unable to "complete the necessary work of mourning" is also displayed in "Goodbye Blue Sky":

> Did you see the frightened ones?
> Did you hear the falling bombs?
> Did you ever wonder
> Why we had to run for shelter
> When the promise of a brave new world
> Unfurled beneath a clear blue sky?
> Did you see the frightened ones?
> Did you hear the falling bombs?
> The flames are all long gone
> But the pain lingers on.
> Goodbye Blue Sky
> Goodbye Blue Sky
> Goodbye.

At the beginning of this song the peaceful sound of a chirping bird is heard. However, this peace is soon broken by the sound of an aeroplane, which once again gives rise to the image of bombers and the painful memories associated with them. Gerald Scarfe, the artist of *The Wall* film's animation sequences, describes the footage that accompanies this piece:

> The dove of peace explodes and from its entrails a terrible eagle is born. This menacing creature tears great clods from the countryside with its gigantic talons, destroying whole cities. Swooping low it gives birth to the War Lord, a gargantuan figure who turns to metal, and sends forth bombers from its armpits. The bombers turn to crosses as the frightened ones run to their shelters. The ghosts of soldiers fall and rise again continuously and on a hill of bodies a Union Jack turns to a bloody cross. Blood runs through the corpses and pointlessly trickles down the drain. *(in Schaffner 1991: 224-5)*

Musically the entire song reflects a continued disturbance of peace. The introductory figure is performed on nylon-stringed guitar, which provides a gentler effect than that achievable on steel strings. Corresponding to the appearance of the "Germanic eagle of war" *(Parker 1982: 1062)* is the entry of the dark, ominous sounding synthesizer and a shift from the D major vamp to one on A minor. This section is characterised by its use of a B major chord over the droning A bass note, a combination which creates a great degree of tension due to the resulting tritone between A and D sharp. A similar process governs the passages sung to the syllable "Oooh"; the falling melody begins with a vamp on a D major chord, but always ends with one on B minor.

The thought of all the wasted lives evoked by the image of blood trickling down the drain is accompanied by a fade out of the opening musical figure, whose suspended fourth continually receives great emphasis due to its being a syncopated anticipation of beat three. The resulting effect is one of continual yearning, and this is enhanced by the fact that the piece fades out during this figure—the fade out being a common signification of continuing in perpetuity. A relevant and important aspect of early object loss that, therefore, should be mentioned here, and one which Zetzel illustrates, is "failure to relinquish the object investment, leading to a continued search for the object in adult life" (in Levin 1966: 145). The perpetual yearning, portrayed musically above, returns later in the work when Pink searches for his lost father internally.

Meanwhile, Zetzel's further observations are highly relevant for Pink:

> The absence...of either parent from a very early age on will have continued sequelae throughout growth and development. The progress from one-to-one to triangular relations may be impaired; the differentiation between identification and object investment may not be explicit. Furthermore, the loss of either parent before the resolution of the infantile neurosis may lead to regressive defenses and interference with the integration of a genuine sexualized identity. (in Levin 1966: 145)

Evidence of all these characteristics become apparent in Pink throughout the work. It should be noted, however, that this single traumatic experience is often enough to cause severe problems, but in Pink's case there exist many other contributing factors which compound the traumatic effects. The work at this point proceeds to explore these.

The film's next scene sees Pink distributing his father's bullets between two of his friends at the side of a railway track outside the entrance to a tunnel. Due to the approach of the oncoming train, Pink's friends are too frightened to accompany him into the tunnel in order to place one of the bullets on the steel rail. Instead they leave him to accomplish the task alone, and he flattens himself against the side as the train approaches the tunnel. As it roars past him Pink sees, through the slats, people packed into the goods train like cattle. This allusion to the inhumane acts of the Nazis in World War II sets up a comparison between the Nazis' inability to recognise Jews as individual human beings (portrayed by the pink masks which are worn in the place of faces), and a more recent example of a similar phenomenon: as Pink's face turns into a mask also, his teacher is seen at the opening of the tunnel brandishing his cane and shouting, "You—yes you—stand still laddie!".[11]

"The Happiest Days of Our Lives", a phrase usually reserved for describing the fond memories of school days, is the ironic title of the next piece which illustrates another of Pink's traumatic experiences:

> When we grew up and went to school
> There were certain teachers who would
> Hurt the children any way they could
> By pouring their derision
> Upon anything we did,
> And exposing every weakness,
> However carefully hidden by the kids.

At this point in the film the teacher, after finding a book of Pink's poems on his desk, humiliates him in front of the rest of the students by mocking his abilities. After reading aloud an excerpt from one of his poems (from "Money", a song on *The Dark Side of the Moon*), the teacher says, "absolute rubbish lad-die...get on with your work!" and strikes him. This discouraging experience, in light of Brink's hypothesis in *Creativity and Repair* (1982), is likely a major contributing factor in Pink's inability to accept his father's death:

> From the Romantic period of the eighteenth and early nineteenth centuries onward, the concept of imagination has increasingly been tied to the psychology of creativity. Developments in psychodynamic theory during the last few decades prompt a new attempt to be more precise about what imagination seeks to accomplish within the total psychological economy. I believe that its most important function is reconstructive in situations of loss of essential attachment figures, whether they be parents in early life or some combination of disruptions of the developmental process and later losses of sustaining personal relationships....Every reader of literature, and of the biographies of writers, has noticed the high incidence of parent loss and forced adaptation among those who later become creative.[12] *(Brink 1982: 3-4)*

By discouraging his writing of poetry, the teacher threatens to rob Pink of a potentially powerful restorative activity.

According to Waters, this part of the work is very much drawn from his own experience:

> My school life was very like that. It was awful...really terrible. When I hear people whining on now about bringing back grammar schools it really makes me quite ill to listen to it. I went to a boy's grammar school and although...I want to make it plain that some of the men who taught there were very nice guys...it's not meant to be a blanket condemnation of teachers everywhere...but the bad ones can really do people in, and there were some at my school who were just incredibly bad and treated the children so badly, just putting them down—putting them down all the time. Never encouraging them to do things, not really trying to interest them in anything, just trying to keep them quiet and still, and crush them into the right shape, so that they would go to university and 'do well' . *(Vance 1979)*

The image of "crushing" people into the right shape is symbolically represented throughout the work by hammers—tools used by blacksmiths to mould or shape metal. The first appearance of this symbol is a musical one, which occurs at the beginning of "The Happiest Days of Our Lives". The hammer blows first appear in the guise of sharply accented shots performed together by bass guitar, bass drum and high-hat, but appear once again after the first melodic phrase when the teacher is heard striking Pink.

The introduction of the piece features a D tonic but, preceding the vocal entry, the harmony shifts to an A tonic representing the teacher's imposed constraint. The rigid school environment is portrayed through the mechanical bass drum appearance on every beat. This section, a slower rendition of which reappears later forming the middle section of "Waiting For the Worms" (a song portraying Pink as the leader of a fascist rally), is for the duration of the first melodic phrase comprised of a transposed interversion of figure (B)—both melodically and harmonically:

During the second melodic phrase, however, the stifling limits of this figure are broken and, with the third melodic phrase, the piece escapes the imposed A minor tonality and returns to the original D tonic. This music, along with the revengeful tone in Waters' voice, accompanies the somehow slightly reassuring knowledge that the teacher too is victimised:

> But in the town, it was well known,
> When they got home at night, their fat and
> Psychopathic wives would thrash them
> Within inches of their lives.

This melodic phrase ends by modulating to the relative major (F), bringing with it also a great deal of satisfaction. This sense is also conveyed at this point as the drums escape their rigid beat, breaking into a rhythmically free section for the duration of the piece. During the transition is heard a high shriek, apparently a battle cry announcing the students' impending revolt in "Another Brick in the Wall (Part II):

> We don't need no education.
> We don't need no thought control.
> No dark sarcasm in the classroom,
> Teachers leave us kids alone.
> Hey! — teacher! leave us kids alone.

During this selection is a portrayal of what Waters describes in a draft of the film's screenplay as "the factory farm techniques employed in schools to produce a docile and unquestioning workforce" (G. R. Waters 1981). The children are marched mechanically through a maze and on to a conveyer belt where they disappear behind a brick wall. They reappear on the other side of the wall sitting at their desks, and now wearing the pink masks which rob them of their identity. Along with the cogs and wheels that run this huge mechanical apparatus are hammers, which ultimately force the children into a mincer from which they emerge in a ground down state.

Eventually the kids rip off their masks and demolish and set fire to the school. Taking the remnants of the desks and blackboards outside, they hurl them on an enormous fire and then drag the teacher towards it as well. This liberating act of revenge is accompanied by a musical one portrayed by the lengthy guitar solo, which is supported by powerfully sustained organ chords which rise higher and higher throughout.

Waters' observations from his own experience are, once again, illuminating:

...we had a fair number [of teachers] who were serving their time and who were extremely bitter about all sorts of different things and who, as I say, were so frustrated and bitter about their lives that they treated the kids at school abominably....they would often pick on the weak ones as well and make their lives a misery for them....[I]t was a real war with lots of them...and sometimes the battle was won by the kids, and I can remember teachers at my grammar school having nervous break-downs....Because of the way we felt and the fact that we felt it was a battle, in fact, we behaved in the same way. We followed their example. The nasty sarcastic ones that picked on the weak kids...that affected us to the extent that we picked on the weak teachers. *(Dallas 1987: 135-6)*

As the guitar solo abruptly ends and the organ support disappears, however, it is made clear that this revolt took place only in the young Pink's imagination. Back in the classroom sitting at his desk, he still feels the effects of his alienation at the hands of the teacher, an experience which contributes to his increasing narcissism:

All in all it's just another brick in the wall
All in all you're just another brick in the wall.

The experience, as we shall see, will also play a major role in forming Pink's obsessive personality. As Sherrill observes:

Miller speaks of the pattern of the abused child, masochistically trying to please the oppressor, futilely trying to gain acceptance. Finally, losing all hope, he polarizes in the manner of enantiodromia from the masochist into the sadist. The child's rage merges with the introjected cruelty of the adults who victimize him, and the vicious cycle is perpetuated. *(Sherrill 1991: 85)*

Though his experience with the teacher is crucial in Pink's personality development, it is the next song "Mother" which provides the ultimate origin of his obsessional disorder.

Before the song begins the adult Pink appears in his hotel room attempting to call the United Kingdom in order to talk to his wife. Finding her not at home he imagines himself sharing an intimate moment with her, which soon transfers into a memory of snuggling up to his mother in bed. Fairbairn's observations of the characteristics of individuals with a schizoid element in their personality are useful. He finds evidence of the following features:

(1) that in early life they gained the conviction, whether through apparent indifference or through apparent possessiveness on the part of their mother, that their mother did not really love and value them as persons in their own right; (2) that, influenced by a resultant sense of deprivation and inferiority, they remained profoundly fixated upon their mother; (3) that the libidinal attitude accompanying this fixation was one not only characterized by extreme dependence, but also rendered highly self-preservative and narcissistic by anxiety over a situation which presented itself as involving a threat to the ego; (4) that, through a regression to the attitude of the early oral phase, not only did the libidinal cathexis of an already internalized 'breast-mother' become intensified, but also the process of internalisation itself became unduly extended to relationships with other objects; and (5) that there resulted a general over-valuation of the internal at the expense of the external world. *(Fairbairn 1962: 23)*

That Pink's mother is primarily over-protective is made apparent by Waters:[13]

> If you can level one accusation at mothers it is that they tend to protect their children too much. Too much and for too long. That's all. This isn't a portrait of my mother, although...one or two of the things in there apply to her as well as to, I'm sure, lots of other people's mothers. *(Vance 1979)*

It is clear that Pink's incomplete telephone call presents itself as a threat to his ego, and this gives rise to a renewal of his fixation on his mother. At the end of the piece when Pink discovers that his wife has cheated on him, it is clear that she (following Fairbairn's fourth feature) becomes internalised also, and that the experience leads him further toward his "over-valuation of the internal at the expense of the external world".

The song begins with some of Pink's insecurities, including the fear of falling victim to his father's fate, and the fear of castration at the hands of the establishment:

> Mother do you think they'll drop the bomb?
> Mother do you think they'll like the song?
> Mother do you think they'll try to break my balls?
> Mother should I build a wall?

The fear of castration is an image which has often denoted a lack of control or loss of power in our predominantly patriarchal history. That the image denotes also a threat to one's masculinity has implications with regard to Pink's inability to establish a genuine sexualised identity. Rochlin's comments are pertinent:

> One of the most familiar problems to analysts is that created by the early loss of a parent, whether by death, divorce, or separation, which results in the remaining parent's (more often the mother) absorbing the whole of the young child's love and, thus, promoting early, persistent sexual conflicts. In the case of boys whose fathers are absent, emotional disturbances appear and are usually of a particular aggressive nature. These problems soon become associated with their developing masculinity. *(Rochlin 1980: 48-9)*

Evidence of the "aggressive nature" of Pink's emotional disturbances becomes apparent later both in "One of My Turns" and "Don't Leave Me Now". What appears to be a defence of his masculinity, or power, is seen during the film at the moment when Pink's wife comes home and, acting as the aggressor, tries to seduce him. Watching a soccer game on television (an activity which connotes competition), Pink ignores her advances only to try and initiate contact later after she has fallen asleep, but to no avail. Henry Biller's comments are pertinent considering the absence of Pink's father as a role model:

> Having observed his father's relationship with his mother, [the boy] has learned basic skills in interacting with females. He can communicate adequately with females. He does not feel intimidated by women, yet he does not have to constantly dominate them. He can accept their femininity because he is secure in his masculinity. *(Biller 1974: 84)*

That this is not true of Pink becomes evident in the third verse of the song.

The second verse, however, continues Pink's preoccupation with powerlessness at the hands of the establishment, the first line of which connotes his later lust for absolute power (a tactic which will eventually serve to counter these fears):

> Mother should I run for President?
> Mother should I trust the Government?
> Mother will they put me in the firing line?
> Mother am I really dying?[14]

The last two lines illustrate, once again, Pink's affinity with his father. The accompanying film footage reveals that, as a child, he experienced a disease that could have possibly proved terminal; his fears are augmented when the doctor calls his mother out of the room to talk privately.[15] According to Joseph Natterson, "fear of death and object loss are closely related; moreover, the ego may actually employ the fear of death in coping with object loss" (in Levin 1966: 148).

The Mother's response to Pink, sung by Gilmour, betrays her complex character. She appears to be driven partially by contempt for her son, but as Holbrook observes, "[o]ver-mothering was found by [D. M. Levy] to be a form of compensation in some cases for unconscious hostility" *(Holbrook 1971: 148)*. One suspects that if this is the case, her hostility may be due to her son representing, for her, a constant reminder of her deceased husband:

> Hush, now baby don't you cry.
> Mama's gonna' make all of your
> Nightmares come true.
> Mama's gonna' put all of her fears into you.
> Mama's gonna' keep you right here
> Under her wing.
> She won't let you fly, but she might let you sing.
> Mama will keep baby cosy and warm.
> Oooh babe, oooh babe, oooh babe
> Of course Mama's going to help build the wall.

It is clear from the last line that, in consonance with Brink's findings, "distortion of maternal care leads to increased narcissism" *(Brink 1977: 19)*. In addition to being helpful in analysing Pink's inhibitions in his relationship with his wife, Brink also offers an explanation of the mother's apparent ambivalence through his comments concerning the obsessional defensive technique:

> It's origin, to state it simply, is with an oppressive mothering, rather than with a deficit to which the hysteric reacts....Ambivalent attitudes toward mother, and consequently toward later attachments to women, will come in question....In the obsessional defensive technique, it has been said, both good and persecutory aspects of the mother are internalized in the ego, the good being identified with while the persecutory are controlled; the mother is thus powerfully internalized in what might be called object surplus, rather than object loss. Nevertheless a sort of developmental deprivation results, with the individual feeling himself unfree to make spontaneous moves toward other and more appropriate attachment objects. At its most severe, he is monopolized by a one-parent identification standing in the way of the diverse experiences among which an optimal maturational course may be chosen. *(Brink 1977: 40-41)*

Evidence of Pink's ambivalent attitude toward his mother appears in the film when, after we first see him as a sick child going downstairs to his mother's bedroom to seek consolation by crawling into bed with her, the shot is later repeated showing his father's corpse beside her. This seems to display an unconscious fear that it was, perhaps, his mother who killed his father through her suffocating tendencies. That this corpse lies in her bed also seems to act as the foundation for his later view of his wife as a sexual predator in "Empty Spaces/What Shall We Do Now?".

This ambivalence forms the basis of his "developmental deprivation", which is apparent through his fears of his wife expressed in the third verse. The first line also displays Pink exhibiting the common schizoid characteristic of "'sense of superiority' to others" *(Holbrook 1971: 148)*:

> Mother do you think she's good enough for me?
> Mother do you think she's dangerous to me?
> Mother will she tear your little boy apart?
> Mother will she break my heart?

Brink's comments, again, are helpful:

> It thus appears that the obsessional comes by his interest in substitute objects..., not so much by wanting their love as by clinging to them in a testing, managing way. He cannot tell whether they are friend or foe and forever tries to discriminate between what are two sides of the same predicament....The male obsessional's deepest preoccupation is with the overly strong mother, and predatory approaches to versions of her are to be expected....Thus to show the obsessional defence at its most lethal is only to indicate what is found in literature and art in many modified forms recalling this primal 'myth' of the feared danger of woman assuming mastery over man. *(Brink 1977: 41-42)*

Pink's sexual conflict also appears to have been enhanced by his mother's apparent involvement with his romantic life, especially with her preoccupation with "dirty" women:

> Mama's gonna' check out all your girlfriends for you
> Mama won't let anyone dirty get through.
> Mama's gonna' wait up till you get in.
> Mama will always find out where
> You've been.
> Mama's gonna' keep baby healthy and clean.
> Oooh babe, oooh babe, oooh babe,
> You'll always be a baby to me.

That Pink has been unable to establish his own identity, or differentiate himself from his "primary object", due to her overprotective nature, is shown in the film by the reappearance of the pink masks subtly emblazoned on the drapes behind the girl who young Pink asks to dance at the ballroom-type affair he attends with his mother. His infantile dependence is symbolically portrayed when he assumes the foetal position on his bed, still attempting to reach his wife on the phone. As Fairbairn suggests:

> Dependence is exhibited in its most extreme form in the intra-uterine state; and we may legitimately infer that, on its psychological side, this state is characterized by an absolute degree of identification and absence of differentiation. Identification may thus be regarded as representing the persistence into extra-uterine life of a relationship existing

before birth. In so far as identification persists after birth, the individual's object constitutes not only his world, but also himself; and it is to this fact...that we must attribute the compulsive attitude of many schizoid and depressive individuals towards their objects. *(Fairbairn 1962: 47)*

As Fairbairn observes "[the infant] has no alternative but to accept or to reject his object—an alternative which is liable to present itself to him as a choice between life and death"; thus Pink's infantile state arouses sympathy. His innocence is portrayed musically in "Mother" through the abundance of acoustic instruments in the piece, particularly through the choice of acoustic guitars and, in the last verse, piano.

Pink's mother's domineering influence and his attempt to assert himself against her is also portrayed musically. The sections of the piece which are sung by the mother are exclusively in six-eight time (again denoting a lullaby), whereas Pink's sections are predominantly in four-four. The comfort of this straight four feel is interrupted however: first of all, during the first two lines of each of his verses (where a bar of five-eight is inserted), and secondly where a bar of three-four appears preceding the end of each verse. Both of these interruptions appear to represent the mother's continued crippling effect on Pink's character. Pink appears to assert himself, however, transcending the wall of his overprotective mother's influence during the guitar solo whose harmonic changes match those of the verses that he sings.[16] This entire section is in an uninterrupted straight four feel, but the sense of escape achieved is lost with the return of the third verse. The prominent organ part throughout the piece and the continuously repeated plagal chord movement of the mother's section (F - C) conjures the verbal image of "Amen", which translated from the Greek means "So be it". This affirmation of Pink's mother's undying influence on him he recognises in the last line of the song; expressing dismay at his increasing narcissism he asks of the wall, "Mother did it need to be so high?". His feelings of incompleteness are communicated by the last chord of the piece which, rather than ending on the tonic, ends on the sub-dominant. This line, in the film, immediately precedes the answering of his phone call home, which, rather than being answered by his wife, is picked up by another man—the result of the barrier he has erected between his wife and himself.

The image of Pink sliding down the wall with the phone still in hand again reminds the viewer of the similar scene when Pink's father dies at Anzio. His thoughts are portrayed in the following animation sequence where a red rose and a lily grow and blossom. After they caress, the rose takes the guise of a penis and the lily that of a vagina. They make love but the peace is broken (symbolically portrayed by the two doves that fly away past the flowers) when they begin to fight. The female flower, a predatorial version of Pink's devouring mother (transferred now into a fear of women), eventually consumes the male flower, then metamorphoses into a pterodactyl and flies away.[17] That he portrays himself as a red rose, a common symbol for love, suggests that Pink truly loves his wife but is unable to express his love due to his insecurities. That Pink's wife is portrayed as a lily, a flower associated with death, displays that the experience with his wife has become the beginning of the end. Considering the initial connection made between Pink and his father noted above, and the portrayal of his wife as death, Guntrip's observation is relevant:

The ultimate unconscious infantile weak ego is very clearly experienced con-

sciously as *a fear of dying*, when its threat to the stability of the personality is being felt.
(Guntrip 1969: 215)

The scene of the flowers is accompanied by the music to "What Shall We Do Now", a track which does not appear on the album, but whose introduction is musically the same as "Empty Spaces" only transposed from E minor to D minor. Figure (A) is heard in augmentation; its location far back in the mix adds to its ominousness, as does the presence of backward recorded speech which gives the impression of an arcane language.[18] The constriction of this figure is broken when the melody, escaping the interval of a minor third, jumps up to A (the fifth), and this is accompanied by the penetration of the vagina and subsequent love making. The sense of freedom achieved is immediately questioned when the A falls back within the minor third interval to E (the second), and this serves to foreshadow the fighting which begins as, after the above process is repeated, the E falls back to the tonic to repeat the original figure. The rose tries to reunite with the glowing lily as the figure ascends by step to A again, but the descending bass line signals the devouring of Pink by his wife, and his subsequent increase in narcissism as he once again becomes trapped in figure (A) during the vocal entry:

> What shall we use to fill the empty spaces
> Where waves of hunger roar.

Accompanying these lines is the mechanical pulse of a synthesizer and the image of a wall of buildings and consumer goods which Waters refers to as "[t]he wall of post war reindustrialisation" (G. R. Waters 1981). Both Brink's and Rochlin's observations help to explain this portion of the animated sequence:

> That loss of attachment objects increases narcissism is explained by Gregory Rochlin, who notes that resupply of objects may be of an altered or pathological sort. 'When an important object is lost, there is an unconscious wish to give up object [attachment] and to react further with an increase of narcissism; despite this tendency, however, even in the most narcissistic states, objects are still sought, although in greatly modified or pathological forms. A valued relationship, therefore, never seems to be entirely relinquished.' A variety of means, including acquisition of inanimate objects, may be used to make good a felt deficit so as not to lose self-esteem. *(Brink 1977: 21)*

Mingled with images of consumer goods throughout the song are other things which Pink imagines might allow him to assert an identity, or establish some feeling of significance. While a lot of these, as Waters suggests, display the idea of "adopting somebody else's criteria for yourself...without considering them from a position of really being yourself" (Vance 1979), the majority of the images betray Pink's desire for power, whether it be economic, physical, or through the adulation of his fans:

> Shall we set out across this sea of faces
> In search of more and more applause?
> Shall we buy a new guitar?
> Shall we buy a more powerful car?
> Shall we work straight through the night?
> Shall we get into fights?

Leave the lights on?
Drop bombs?
Do tours of the East?
Contract diseases?
Bury bones?
Break up homes?
Send flowers by 'phone?
Take to drink?
Go to shrinks?
Give up meat?
Rarely sleep?
Keep people as pets?
Train dogs?
Race rats?
Fill the attic with cash?
Bury treasure?
Store up leisure?
But never relax at all
With our backs to the wall.

The last two lines recall *Animals* (1977) and the unease created by the competitive "back stabbing" of the dogs in order to achieve "pig" status. Whereas the narrating dog on that record was content to bury a single bone,[19] Pink first contemplates burying "bones", and then towards the end of the piece "training dogs" *(see p. 67)*. This progression seems to point to Pink's ambition to become a powerful pig, which is made apparent later after his transformation during *The Wall* performances: a large, evil-looking pig emerges from behind the wall during the piece "Run Like Hell", representing Pink's megalomania.

Following the slow introduction of this piece figure (A) is once again performed, but this time with a forceful rhythm and power chords in the electric guitar, suggesting an extremely anxious attempt on Pink's behalf to escape the continuous inward movement toward schizoid withdrawal. The visual images that accompany this figure, however, suggest that the wall of "reindustrialisation", which "overshadows human feelings and crushes them beneath the weight of its inexorable cycle of production and consumption" (G. R. Waters 1981), will prove to be only a further impediment. This is illustrated by the screaming face that emerges from it; the shift of attention from organic to inorganic portrayed by a flower's transformation into barbed wire as the wall goes by it; the baby that grows up to be an unfeeling nazi, clubbing another over the head; and the overall shattering of spiritual values as the wall bursts through a cathedral, whose bricks reform and are transformed into a neon temple housing bricks of gold—indicating now a reliance only on material wealth. The music, at first, seems to offer a faint opportunity for escape through its harmonic movement (D minor to A minor) but the initial melodic figure, which begins with an escape of the minor third interval, returns to its midst each time:

Shall we   buy   a   new   gui - tar

This sets the stage for the mechanical delivery of the rest of the text (beginning "Shall we get into fights?"), which becomes trapped in the continuous vamp on

D minor. Compounding frustration is communicated by the entry of the background vocal at "bury bones", and this continues until the end of the piece when, seemingly unable to withstand the pressure, the "guard is dropped" (the D minor vamp is broken as the harmony returns to A minor), and the forceful image of a hammer blow is seen. The hammer's blow is also *felt* due to the abrupt ending of the piece.

Appearing on the album in the place of "What Shall We Do Now?", "Empty Spaces" takes a different approach to replacing the gap where Pink's wife formerly was:

> What shall we use to fill the empty spaces
> Where we used to talk?
> How shall I fill the final places?
> How shall I complete the wall?

The last line of the piece signifies that Pink's next tactic will eventually increase his narcissism further. "Empty Spaces" segues directly into "Young Lust", which serves to answer the question stated at the end of the former song:

> I am just a new boy,
> Stranger in this town.
> Where are all the good times?
> Who's gonna show this stranger around?
> Oooh I need a dirty woman.
> Oooh I need a dirty girl.

The film shows Pink sitting in a trailer in the backstage area of a concert venue after one of his performances. He eyes a groupie whom he eventually decides to take back to his hotel room. As Brink suggests, the obsessional defence "is not in practice to be fully dissociated from the hysterical....It's quest in the hyper-dependent mode, however, is less for beautiful inanimate objects and sublime scenes than for persons" *(Brink 1977: 40)*.

That Pink is not merely filling the "empty space" where his wife was is suggested by his desire for a "dirty" woman. Remembering his mother's abhorrence of such women (in "Mother"), it appears that Pink is attempting to escape her influence and assert his selfhood by going against her overbearing principles. Once again it is also clear that he is attempting to assert his masculinity:

> Will some cold woman in this desert land
> Make me feel like a real man?
> Take this rock and roll refugee.
> Oooh babe, set me free.

Musically the song exudes a renewed confidence in Pink. This is conveyed through Gilmour's strong, raspy singing (made even more powerful by the excessive reverb applied to it); the numerous guitar fills in conjunction with Gilmour's use of artificial harmonics; the long sustained organ chords, highly rhythmic bass playing, and the song's overall "swaggering" rhythm. The piece also boasts the first extended guitar solo in the work since "Another Brick in the Wall (Part II)". The various blues elements that are present within the song serve to connote a sense of confidence sexually as well—the blues being a popular platform from which to express sexual prowess.

This sense of confidence is not sustained in the next piece however.

Immediately after Pink and the groupie enter his hotel room, he slumps into his chair and switches on the television. Schizoid-like he is completely unreceptive to her attempts to converse. As she waves her hand in front of his face to see if he is indeed conscious, he raises his hands to his temples. Sympathetically she asks "Are you feeling okay?", and begins to tenderly and sensuously suck on his fingers. We hear Pink's thoughts during "One of My Turns", and realise that he is thinking about his wife. His movement from the general, in the first two lines, to the personal in the third suggests that the image of a dying man is related to his own disintegrating ego, and his diminishing capacity to feel love:

> Day after day love turns grey,
> Like the skin of a dying man.
> Night after night, we pretend it's all right
> But I have grown older and
> You have grown colder and
> Nothin' is very much fun anymore.
> And I can feel one of my turns coming on.
> I feel cold as a razor blade,
> Tight as a tourniquet,
> Dry as a funeral drum.

The connotations of the series of similes that describe his decaying feelings in the last three lines suggest thoughts of a suicide attempt. The adjectives ("cold", "tight", and "dry") also suggest the image of an unaroused vagina. Rochlin's comments about one of his patients are interesting when applied to Pink:

> The key to the underlying persistent problem was in the unconsciously held feminine identification that was incompatible with his masculine development. He had not been able sufficiently to relinquish it or find expression for it in a way that was relatively free of conflict. He illustrated that when masculinity remained exaggeratedly bound to its infantile aspirations for power, performance, and prowess, they become associated with the erotic aims of the same period. The moderating effects of intimacy is precluded by the ruling masculine narcissism. As a result, a fusion of infantile masculine and erotic aims occur. The feminine identification, normally a necessary, unconscious defense against extravagant boyhood masculine yearnings that are associated with brutal relations, remains ineffective. When he felt 'feminine,' he pictured himself a hapless victim. *(Rochlin 1980: 270)*

At this point Pink begins to experience one of his turns. Leaping out of his chair, he once again metamorphoses from the role of victim to that of the sadistic persecutor. Fairbairn's observations about schizophrenics are useful:

> When feelings do assert themselves..., they are usually out of keeping with ideational content and quite inappropriate to the occasion; or alternatively, as in catatonic cases, emotional expression assumes the form of sudden and violent outbursts. *(Fairbairn 1962: 20)*

Pink chases the girl around the hotel room, demolishing it on his way:

> Run to the bedroom, in the suitcase on the left
> You'll find my favourite axe.[20]
> Don't look so frightened
> This is just a passing phase,

Just one of my bad days.
Would you like to watch T.V.?
Or get between the sheets?
Or contemplate the silent freeway?
Would you like something to eat?
Would you like to learn to fly?
Would you like to see me try?
Would you like to call the cops?
Do you think it's time I stopped?
Why are you running away?

That his outburst is unconsciously directed at his mother's overbearing influence on defining his sexual identity is communicated by the ironic questions "Would you like to learn to fly?" and "Would you like to see me try?" (the image of flying evokes the idea of freedom, and recalls the earlier use of the flying image "I wont let you fly" in the song "Mother"). That Pink feels the effects of his wall as a prison is portrayed in the film when the majority of objects that he destroys are either framed or box-like.

Pink's outburst is also portrayed musically. The first half of the piece is sung to the accompaniment of a gentle sounding synthesizer. Its long sustained chords provide a type of comfort, but this sense of comfort is continuously broken when, after being reaffirmed each time by a plagal cadence, the tonic chord (C major) is disturbingly played detached. Because the tonic chord is commonly understood as the ultimate "resting place" of any particular key, this musical device is all the more effective.

The contrast between Pink's outburst and his calm state of dissatisfaction is achieved through an incredibly abrupt modulation of all musical characteristics: the sudden shift in dynamics from very soft to very loud; the full band entry (including piano whose percussive qualities contrast the predominantly smooth timbre of the synthesizer); the shift in time from a light six-eight to a driving and deliberate four-four; the octave-and-a-half leap in Waters' vocal range which gives the effect of screaming; and the unprepared harmonic modulation.

Rather than satisfying the ear by returning to the tonic following the decorated dominant seventh chord (a progression which the ear most expects), the piece abruptly modulates to D phrygian. This unsuspected shift in mode, along with the other abrupt modulations in musical characteristics, is comparable to the shift which suddenly takes place in Pink's character as his outburst begins. Walser's comments about the phrygian mode are pertinent:

> Affectively, the Phrygian mode is distinctive: only this mode has a second degree only a half step away from the tonic instead of a whole step.[21] Phenomenologically, this closeness means that the second degree hangs precariously over the tonic, making the mode seem claustrophobic and unstable. Hedged in by its upper neighbor, even the tonic, normally the point of rest, acquires an uncomfortable inflection in this mode. *(Walser 1993: 47)*

The unstable nature of this mode reflects Pink's own instability, and the claustrophobic feelings caused by his increasing narcissism have been observed above. It is interesting that the "closeness" that Walser mentions most strongly appears during the line "Would you like to see me fly?", where an E flat major chord descends to D minor. After he says "Would you like to see me try?", the D minor changes to a D major chord and the piece modulates momentarily to G major giving the impression of a sense of escape. During the guitar solo which immediately follows, however, we are thrust back into the phrygian mode again.

The guitar solo also fails to achieve a sense of transcendence, partially because its identical first and third phrases rhythmically follow the chord changes (E flat major / B flat to B flat major). Furthermore, while the second phrase is comprised of a sequence which seems to ascend with great difficulty (it stops abruptly on single notes before again continuing its ascension), the last phrase begins over a D minor chord and ends when the piece rises back up to an E flat chord—making both the listener and Pink experience this "closeness" once again.

Both the film scene and the music have very unsettling endings. Pink, after throwing the television out the window, drives a piece of the broken glass into his hand as he grabs the pane and teeters on the high window ledge half inside and half outside the bedroom window. The song, instead of finishing on the tonic, ends on a G minor chord with Waters holding for a long time a minor ninth above the root—a dissonance foreign to the rest of the song which makes the absurdity of Pink's final question even more disturbing. Also relevant is Brink's observation that "among people with obsessional complaints, 'there is an unusually high celibacy rate of 40 per cent to 50 per cent...'" *(Brink 1977: 40)*.

The next scene first has Pink lying Christ-like in the pool again, and the visions of his wife making love with another man conveys that the biblical comparison is now one of feelings of betrayal and forsakenness. Next he is seen indoors once again in front of the television which, along with the standard lamp and chair, has become the only object he has retained during his continued withdrawal.

The unsettling mood created in the previous song continues at the beginning of "Don't Leave Me Now"; the opening bass note (E) appears just after the final chord of "One of My Turns" (G minor), and the tritone relation between the third of the chord (B flat) and this E is strongly felt.[22] Uneasiness is also created by the sound effects of heavy breathing, the unnaturally slow echo that is used on the guitar, and Waters' continued use of the high range that he utilised vocally during Pink's "turn" in the previous scene.

The harmonic and melodic dissonances of the piece are also disturbing. The root movement of the repeated progression of four chords (F flat augmented seventh, D flat major seventh [add 9], B flat eleventh, G to G augmented) outlines a diminished seventh chord—a chord comprised of two overlapping tritones. That the piece is entirely non-functional harmonically seems to reflect Pink's diminishing stability. The vocal enters, after the first iteration of the chord progression, during the G augmented chord. Waters' first note (A) is a tritone above the sharpened fifth of the chord, and he descends melodically down to this note on the first chord of the progression. Much discomfort is created throughout the melody of the piece due to the fact that most of the time when a phrase ends, Waters is either singing one of the most dissonant notes in the accompanying chord or a non-chord tone.

As Brink suggests, "[a]nger against the mother may cause attraction to forms of the breast to be thrown in reverse, and instead of selecting good secondary attachment objects, substitutes are treated with irony, hatred or contempt" *(Brink 1977: 26)*. The lyrics of the piece convey that in Pink's past relationship with his wife, he has displayed further characteristics of an obsessional personality disorder:

> Oooh babe
> Don't leave me now
> Don't say it's the end of the road.
> Remember the flowers I sent?
> I need you babe,
> To put through the shredder
> In front of my friends.
> Oooh babe,
> Don't leave me now,
> How could you go?
> When you know how I need you
> To beat to a pulp on a Saturday night.
> Oooh babe
> Don't leave me now.
> How can you treat me this way?
> Running away.
> I need you babe.
> Why are you running away?
> Oooh babe.

Brink, in referring to the "dominant controlling ways" obsessional persons have, explains Pink's behaviour:

> When the object is associated with the avoided mother, it may be honorifically idealized, covering fear with impossible desire. The obsessional's aim is to master and control the split, ambivalently held internalized object; he may well do so by fantasies of dominance, forced submission and punitive control, while at the same time idealizing the object so as to placate it. *(Brink 1977: 41)*

That Pink idealises his wife appears apparent from the section of music that closes the piece *(see below)*.

The film makes it clear that Pink also attempts to employ the paranoid ego defence. While he is watching television, the camera shows the shadow of his wife sneaking up behind him. She then momentarily metamorphoses into a king cobra, and then into a praying mantis—an insect the female species of which is commonly known to devour her mate after copulation. She next metamorphoses into the fanged flower/vagina that was seen previously in "Empty Spaces", and chases Pink around the room terrorizing him. According to Guntrip, "[t]he paranoid individual faces physical persecution (as in dreams of being attacked by murderous figures)":

> When an individual is inwardly menaced by an involuntary schizoid flight from reality and depersonalisation (as when too deep fear is too intensely aroused) he will fight to preserve his ego by taking refuge in internal bad-object fantasies of a persecutory...kind. Then, unwittingly projecting these on to outer reality, he maintains touch with the world by feeling that

people are...plotting his ruin. *(Guntrip 1969: 57-58)*

At this point in the work, it is also worthwhile to note Guntrip's comment that people "do undoubtedly maintain persecutory anxiety as a defence against the development of a feeling of 'fading out into nothingness'. *(Guntrip 1969: 75)*

Fairbairn describes the paranoid position by contrasting it to the hysterical:

Whereas the hysteric overvalues objects in the outer world, the paranoid individual regards them as persecutors; and, whereas the hysterical dissociation is a form of self-deprecation, the attitude of the paranoid individual is one of extravagant grandiosity. *(Fairbairn 1962: 45)*

Fairbairn's comments inadvertently show an important similarity between the paranoid and obsessional attitudes, namely that of "extravagant grandiosity". The combination of these defences contribute to Pink's later imagined transformation into a nazi-type leader.

That he has failed to control the ambivalently held internal object through the obsessional defence is illustrated by Pink's attempt to externalise his bad internal object in the form of an hallucination. Guntrip helps to explain further the need that some individuals have of internal objects:

The entire world of internal bad objects is a colossal defence against loss of the ego by depersonalization. The one issue that is much worse than the choice between good and bad objects is the choice between any sort of objects and no objects at all. Persecution is preferred to depersonalization. The phenomenon of internalization of bad objects has hitherto been regarded as arising out of the need to master the object. We have now to see it as arising even more fundamentally out of the need to preserve an ego. *(in Holbrook 1971: 170)*

The absurd size of the room in this scene helps to convey effectively the reality of Pink's diminishing sense of self.

His desire for his wife and his last expression of regret over his ever increasing narcissism is portrayed through the music that accompanies his hallucination, which is launched by the full band entry. Pink's transformation back from the persecutor to the persecuted is conveyed by the return to a functional tonality (A minor), and his yearning is conveyed through the repetition of "oooh babe" (his shift in character is signified by Gilmour singing now), and by the repeated suspended seconds in the following chordal figures which "beg" for resolution:

When the piece cadences on the tonic, Pink's immediate conflict has been solved in that he has stopped hallucinating. He finds himself alone, however, cowering in the corner.

Pink's renunciation of intimacy is expressed through his smashing of the television set when a romantic scene appears there. This violent outburst immediately precedes his "mass-withdrawal of libido" in the next song. Fairbairn's comments are, again, notable:

> Whether such a mass-withdrawal of libido can properly be ascribed to repression is a debatable question, although where the process is restricted to a withdrawal from object-relationships it gives that impression....There can be no doubt, however, that withdrawal of libido from the conscious part of the ego was the effect of relieving emotional tension and mitigating the danger of violent outbursts of precipitate action....There can be equally little doubt that much of the schizoid individual's anxiety really represents fear of such outbursts occurring. This fear commonly manifests itself as a fear of going insane or as a fear of imminent disaster. It is possible, therefore, that massive withdrawal of libido has the significance of a desperate effort on the part of an ego threatened with disaster to avoid all emotional relationships with external objects by a repression of the basic libidinal tendencies which urge the individual on to make emotional contacts. *(Fairbairn 1962: 52)*

In "Another Brick in the Wall (Part III)", it is clear that Pink has formerly used drugs to mitigate his violent outbursts, but he renounces them just as he does everything and everyone else:

> I don't need no arms around me.
> I don't need no drugs to calm me.
> I have seen the writing on the wall.
> Don't think I need anything at all.
> No don't think I need anything at all.
> All in all it was all just bricks in the wall.
> All in all you were all just bricks in the wall.

Accompanying this song in the film is a montage of all the experiences that have led to Pink's state. That his wife is not the persecutor that he makes her out to be is evident by the image seen of her screaming in agony.

As is the case in all of the parts of "Another Brick in the Wall", there is an attempt here to escape the stifling feeling of the minor third that constitutes figure (A). The first attempts occur during the second and third lines, in an upper direction initially, but then in a downward one:

I don't need no drugs to calm me I have seen the wri- ting on the wa - ll

Due to the continuing harmonic vamp on D minor, however, a true sense of transcendence is not achieved until the G chord where the melody leaps from D to a G also. This is only temporary, however, as the tune ends harmonically with a double statement of figure (B). In combination with the steady bass drum and the violent guitar power chords that occur after each line of the verse, the background harmony vocal in the last lines seems to display a sense of confidence, but this is countered by the termination of rhythmic intensity as the drums suddenly drop out. According to Fairbairn:

> Reference has already been made to the narcissism which results from an excessive libidinization of internalized objects; and such narcissism is specially characteristic of the schizoid individual. Accompanying it we invariably find an attitude of superiority which may manifest itself in con-

sciousness to a varying degree as an actual sense of superiority. It should be noticed, however, that this attitude of superiority is based upon an orientation towards internalized objects, and that in relation to objects in the world of outer reality the basic attitude of the schizoid individual is essentially one of inferiority. It is true that the externally oriented inferiority may be masked by a facade of superiority based upon an identification of external with internalized objects. *(Fairbairn 1962: 50-51)*

Pink's withdrawal into himself is portrayed in "Goodbye Cruel World" through the massive reduction in texture to only bass guitar and vocal. That we are now back to the beginning of the work is conveyed in the film by the image of Pink sitting in his hotel room with a long, undisturbed ash on his burned-out cigarette. A sense of separation is achieved in this piece through the aural partition which is created by mixing the bass guitar in one speaker and the vocal in the other. His contentedness is conveyed by Waters' use of a major key, and the satisfying perfect cadences (V—I) which characterise the piece; but this sense is disturbed with the uncomfortably abrupt ending of the song as Pink says "goodbye" for the last time:

> Goodbye cruel world
> I'm leaving you today.
> Goodbye.
> Goodbye.
> Goodbye.
> Goodbye all you people,
> There's nothing you can say
> To make me change
> My mind.
> Goodbye.

Because the lyrics of this song remind one of a suicide note, Pink's withdrawal appears figuratively to be compared to death. Remembering Guntrip's comments that "the ultimate unconscious infantile weak ego is very clearly experienced consciously as a fear of dying", his further remarks are pertinent:

> This can be associated with 'fear of breaking down into a regressed illness, or more mildly still feeling unable to cope....On the other hand, when exhaustion begins to develop as it periodically does, out of the struggle to master this internal breakdown threat, then it may be experienced as *a wish to die*'. *(in Holbrook 1971: 170)*

As the camera burrows through Pink's eye into his mind, the scene of him as a boy running across the rugby field reappears. The initial connection made with his deceased father in its first appearance *(see page 63)* suggests that Pink's overwhelming identification with his father is portrayed again here through his own metaphorical death. At the same time it becomes clear later in "Comfortably Numb", noting Guntrip's comment above, that this scene is related to Pink's nearly terminal childhood illness.

Guntrip's further comments are relevant in understanding Pink's "wish to die":

> This is felt 'in less uncompromising terms', says Guntrip, as 'a longing to regress, to escape from life...'. The most poignant aspect of the Regressed Ego as manifest 'most undisguisedly' in schizoid suicide is that the 'life-tiredness' expressed in the withdrawal...is an attempt at rebirth. *(in Holbrook 1971: 170)*

That this is true of Pink is apparent during his internal search for his father. His hope to begin life anew is illustrated by his returning to his earliest major trauma in order to "make right" the experience which first led him to begin building his wall.

At this juncture in the live performance, the last brick is placed in the wall which has been gradually built throughout the performance. It entirely separates Pink Floyd the group from their audience, just as it does Pink the character from the external world. Regarding the schizoid individual Fairbairn writes:

> ...he erects barriers between his objects and himself. He tends both to keep his objects at a distance and to make himself remote from them. He rejects his objects; and at the same time he withdraws libido from them. This withdrawal of libido may be carried to all lengths. It may be carried to a point at which all emotional and physical contacts with other persons are renounced; and it may even go so far that all libidinal links with outer reality are surrendered, all interest in the world around fades and everything becomes meaningless. *(Fairbairn 1962: 50)*

That everything becomes "meaningless" for Pink is apparent in the next song "Hey You", which is not included in the film.

Following the intermission in the live performance, the musicians continue the concert by performing behind the wall, which obscures the performers and the audience from one another. Just as "Hey You" marks Pink's attempt to reestablish contact with the outside world it also marks an attempt on behalf of the performers to reestablish contact with the audience. Pink begins to reach the same conclusion of which Rochlin speaks:

> Many studies...verify the conclusion that isolation or separation from those whom we value and the things that represent them is usually tolerated only temporarily....Deprived of social experience, we are not self-sustaining. *(Rochlin 1973: 3)*

Just as Pink's withdrawal was communicated by a reduction of texture, his attempt to reemerge is portrayed through the gradually increasing instrumental texture, marked initially by the entry of acoustic guitar, fretless bass and then electric piano. His fragility is communicated through the brittle timbre of the acoustic guitar. According to Andy Aledort:

> The haunting opening acoustic guitar part was played on the album with a very unusual tuning, created by a very unusual *stringing*. Like "Nashville" tuning, which simulates a 12-string but with the normal strings removed (leaving only the high octave strings for the low E, A, D and G strings), this tuning is the same but the low E is replaced by another *high* E string, two octaves higher than normal. This creates a beautiful, crystalline sound enhanced by the sustained arpeggiating of the chords....This guitar is also treated with flanging, giving it an even more ethereal sound. *(Aledort 1993)*

The timbre of this guitar serves to help create the impression of a cold atmosphere devoid of any human warmth. This is enhanced by the dissonances played by the electric piano and its cold timbre (the result of its lack of overtones).

Although the song is basically in E natural minor, the chordal movement in the introduction from an E minor (add 2) to D minor (add 2) threatens to cast the piece into the claustrophobic phrygian. That the chords are both in second inversion rather than root position also helps to bestow them with an unstable quality, and this is not alleviated by the bass guitar entry; although almost all of its phrases ascend to the root, the phrases inevitably end by sliding back down the string. This movement, in combination with the stifling threat of the phrygian mode, anticipates Pink's failure to transcend his claustrophobic wall. Pink's efforts to break out of his prison are also portrayed through the forceful rhythm played together by the bass and drums after the latter's entry in the second verse.

Although to a great extent it is clear that Pink is trying to establish contact with the audience beyond the wall, his efforts will ultimately prove fruitless because as Waters says "he's only singing it to himself" (Vance 1979). This is clear from the fact that the characteristics of his addressee basically describe himself:

> Hey you! out there in the cold
> Getting lonely, getting old, can you feel me?
> Hey you! standing in the aisles
> With itchy feet and fading smiles, can you feel me?
> Hey you! don't help them to bury the light,
> Don't give in without a fight.
> Hey you! Out there on your own sitting
> naked by the 'phone would you touch me?
> Hey you! with your ear against the wall
> Waiting for someone to call out would you touch me?
>
> Hey you! would you help me to carry the stone?[23]
> Open your heart, I'm coming home.

At this point Pink confidently believes he is going to transcend the wall, and this is conveyed through the guitar solo which appears over a background of guitars playing figure (A). The sheer height of the wall is portrayed by the expanded range of the figure, both through its harmonisation at the interval of a tenth, and through its repetition on the sub-dominant as well as the tonic. Consequently his attempt to escape his confinement is once again thwarted. Rochlin's observations help to explain Pink's sudden change of heart, in relation both to his audience and the outside world in general:

> Alone, we seem unable to fully perceive our own worth—or to have an enduring conviction in it. The intelligent work, the creative act, the kind overture, in and of themselves, do not accomplish the endless task of self-confirmation. We require social approval and support for our very being....when the grim realities are unrewarding, whether we have had a part in fashioning them or not, we turn to fantasies and dreams in which we ourselves can furnish, or so it seems for awhile, the all-important missing element—the company and concern of others from whom we draw support for our self esteem. *(Rochlin 1973: 128)*

That Pink has "furnished the all-important missing element" through fantasy is also communicated to the listener by the intervening narrator (whose part is sung by Waters rather than Gilmour who sang the first two verses) in the bridge of the song:

> But it was only fantasy.
> The wall was too high, as you can see.

No matter how he tried he could not break free,
And the worms ate into his brain.

Pink's repeated efforts to break out are conveyed during the musical accompaniment to this section. The piece modulates to G major where a IV—V—I progression accompanies each line. The satisfaction that would normally be achieved by this cadential figure is thwarted when the meter momentarily shifts from four-four to two-four for one bar each time. During this bar, which begins with the tonic chord (I), the progression is quickly reversed. The tonic chord falls back to the dominant (V) and then, once again, to the sub-dominant (IV)—where the progression initially began. During the last line of the bridge, a deceptive cadence (V - vi) effects the return to the less fulfilling E minor.

The bridge features the first reference to "the worms". According to Waters:

> ...the worms have a lot less to do with the piece than they did a year ago;
> a year ago they were *very* much a part of it. If you like they were my sym-
> bolic representation of decay...the basic idea of the whole thing really is
> that if you isolate yourself you decay. *(Vance 1979)*

That Pink is beginning to decay is also displayed by the sound of flies, which are portrayed by the "buzzing" timbre of the synthesizer which enters during the recapitulation of the introduction. Guntrip's description of a common schizoid tendency, as we shall see, applies to Pink:

> Fear of loss of contact with the external world constantly motivates effort
> to regain contact with it, but this cannot be done by loving relationships,
> and therefore can only be done in terms of the other two basic emotion-
> al reactions, fear and aggression. *(Guntrip 1969: 101)*

Pink's process of decaying eventually takes the form of his loss of all human feelings, at which point he reacts only aggressively. He adopts the forceful image of the hammers and becomes the evil fascist figure who was seen at the beginning of the work during "In the Flesh?".

Pink's increasing desperation is conveyed in the third verse, when Waters takes over the lead part singing an octave higher than Gilmour did:

Hey you? out there on the road
Always doing what you're told, can you help me?
Hey you? out there beyond the wall
Breaking bottles in the hall, can you help me?
Hey you! don't tell me there's no hope at all,
Together we stand, divided we fall.

Again while the first pair of lines are addressed to himself (on the road being a common expression for touring), the next two lines display Pink's desperate pleas to his audience.

Pink's constant efforts to escape his stifling prison are also evident musically in the body of the verses. The first two lines of every verse, like the instrumental interlude in "The Thin Ice", is an interversion of figure (A):

The claustrophobic confines of figure (A) are broken in each verse during the fifth line and this occurs in conjunction with the transition from the group of minor chords in the first two pairs of lines (E minor and B minor) to the following group of major chords:

The last line of each verse, however, once again returns to the confines of this figure, and a descending series of minor chords representing his fall:

At the end of the song the lines "we fall" continue to echo after the song's conclusion, gradually receding away from the listener into the back of the mix. Pink's sense of separation becomes the listener's also when it is clear that Pink "falls" back into himself.

That Pink is still in his hotel room is conveyed by the sound of the television being turned on again, and the sound of cars driving by outside his broken window. The film surrealistically illustrates his extreme sense of alienation when he is seen first clawing, and then throwing himself against a massive brick wall. The wall's immensity is portrayed through the sense of great space created by the vast range between the low, ominous pedal point and the high strings which comprise the opening of "Is There Anybody Out There?". The high keyboard sounds which occur after the first vocal phrase, connote the sound of water drops, and their reverberations give the impression of dropping in a large cave. With the return of the sound of the buzzing flies (conveying Pink's continued decaying), a sound effect that was formerly used in "Echoes" from *Meddle* (1971) is heard. In that piece the sound effect was associated with an albatross, and therefore connotes the bird's image here. The albatross was made famous in Samuel Taylor Coleridge's "The Rime of the Ancient Mariner" (1798), and its use normally symbolises frustration or guilt; in this instance it would appear to be the former.

Pink begins to comprehend the reality of his isolation. Holbrook, quoting an American writer, Hora, describes a state which is now Pink's:

> Existential anxiety stems from the need to have our existence confirmed by our fellow man. We are driven to reach out with our voices, and experience a connection through being heard by another power. *(in Holbrook 1971: 164)*

With his ear against the wall, Pink does just this singing "Is there anybody out there?" in an attempt to confirm his existence. His increased feelings of isolation are portrayed in the second half of the piece, and throughout the next two songs also where, in each case, a solo instrument (either classical guitar or piano) is pitted against orchestra.

The next scene shows Pink in a desperate attempt to preserve his ever-decaying ego. Waters describes the scene in the screenplay:

> PINK now dressed in jeans and a T-shirt, obsessively sorts all his possessions and lays them out symmetrically down the centre of his living room, like a demented soldier preparing for kit inspection. He lays out everything, paying attention to the minutest details. Having dealt with his own possessions, he then incorporates the remains of several room service meals into the symmetry of his obsession. Stale bread. Chicken bones. Pieces of bacon. Throughout this gentle madness we hear the acoustic guitar bridge. *(G. R. Waters 1981)*

It is interesting to note Brink's comments:

> The obsessional defence against depressive or schizoid withdrawals, with its expected range of normal to pathological effects, is said by one observer to comprise 'excessive cleanliness, orderliness...perhaps also a fondness for collecting things....'Fondness for collecting things' signifies [the dominant controlling ways obsessional persons have], suggesting that in addition to a need to control persons for fear of being controlled by them, there is a deficit of undemanding attachment being served by substitute objects. *(Brink 1977: 40-41)*

Similar behaviour, as we shall see, continues in the next piece "Nobody's Home".

Waters' above comparison of Pink to a soldier suggests that Pink has now begun to take refuge in his overwhelming identification with his father. That his regression has begun is apparent by the use of both classical guitar and orchestra. The latter is employed throughout his entire return to childhood and search for his father, until Pink is revived to be taken to his next show in "The Show Must Go On"—a piece which exclusively returns to the more typical rock instrumentation. The use of orchestral instruments connotes a return to an earlier time musically, making their presence appropriate for Pink's regression.

The melody of the acoustic guitar bridge features a transposed variation of figure (A):

The figure, which has now been reduced to two semi-tones, appears to illustrate an increase in Pink's claustrophobic feelings, while the descending scale-like passages which follow its occurrences always fall back to the stifling pedal on A minor with which the piece began.

The next scene shows Pink shaving, and during this process he decides to shave his chest, hair and eyebrows. Sherrill, citing Kernberg, "suggests that such masochistic acts discharge aggression toward the self or release anxiety" *(Sherrill 1991: 93)*. He returns to the television, seemingly the only external object which can penetrate his wall, but it becomes clear that it too does not provide any satisfaction. As "Nobody Home" begins it is clear that Pink's thoughts are predominantly elsewhere:

> I've got a little black book with my poems in,
> I've got a bag with a toothbrush and a comb in,
> When I'm a good dog they sometimes throw me a bone in.[24]
> I got elastic bands keeping my shoes on,
> Got those swollen hand blues,
> Got thirteen channels of shit on the T.V. to choose from.
> I've got electric light,
> I've got second sight,
> I've got amazing powers of observation.
> And that is how I know,
> When I try to get through
> On the telephone to you
> There'll be nobody home.

Pink begins compulsively to enumerate his attributes and possessions in a vain attempt to affirm his identity. The "scanning" of objects is a tendency which is characteristic of the hysterical defence, which commonly collaborates with the obsessional. As Brink writes:

> Scanning refers to taking visual inventory of good objects, whose dis-covery in the environment gives pleasure and reassurance. Object selection is the scanner's method of preferential treatment of some objects over others—those most congenial in association and meaning to the ego, more readily activating imagination when taken in as stimuli. Hyper-dependence is the habitual way of depending for reassurance, for maintenance of ego strength, on the visual stimuli of selected objects...
> *(Brink 1977: 38)*

That these substitute objects are not successful in bringing Pink reassurance is made clear when an intimate scene appears on the television. As his hand caresses the television remote control, he is reminded about his inability to connect with his wife. He continues however:

> I've got the obligatory Hendrix perm,
> And the inevitable pinhole burns
> All down the front of my favourite satin shirt.
> I've got nicotine stains on my fingers,
> I've got a silver spoon on a chain,
> I've got a grand piano to prop up my mortal remains,
> I've got wild staring eyes,
> I've got a strong urge to fly,
> But I've got nowhere to fly to.

> Oooh babe, when I pick up the 'phone
> There's still nobody home.[25]

It is clear that Pink's deterioration is again compared to dying. In the first verse he speaks of having the sensation of "swollen hands", a symptom of his almost terminal childhood fever, while in the second he speaks of propping up his "mortal remains" at the piano.

Pink lists all of the possessions and features which he has, but they are all countered at the end by what he doesn't have. He has a strong urge to escape the stifling environment of his prison, but is unable to do so because he has cut himself off from others. His efforts are portrayed musically. During the line "I've got a strong urge to fly", the melody of the verse hits its highest point thus far but proceeds to fall back down during the next line, which is followed by a rapidly descending synthesizer effect. That he is now completely alone is most strongly conveyed to him through the loss of his wife, and his desperation is conveyed when Waters leaps momentarily into his high register to sing the penultimate line of the verse.

As an alternative, Pink takes flight further inwards. He is now pictured with his television and standard lamp in what Waters refers to as "[a] desolate lunatic wasteland of mouldy decay" (G. R. Waters 1981), which is characterized by dead trees, barbed wire and the charred hammers which foreshadow the end result of his decaying later in the work. His desire for rebirth is figuratively effected in his metamorphosis back into a small boy. As he sets off to look for his father the song ends:

> I've got a pair of Gohills boots,[26]
> And I've got fading roots.

While at the same time suggesting his decreasing stability, the last line also seems to anticipate Pink's inability ultimately to locate his father. This sense of instability and incompleteness is also communicated musically through the song's abrupt ending and the unresolved E seventh chord at its conclusion.

Young Pink wanders into a bunker and stumbles upon a section reserved as a sickbay. Finding no signs of any other people he continues to explore, and eventually finds a room with barred windows; in this room he discovers his adult self completely mad and flees. According to Fairbairn, this would confirm that Pink's ego is split:[27]

> Amongst other schizoid phenomena which may be mentioned here are a sense of being wasted, a sense of unreality, intense self-consciousness and a sense of looking on at oneself. Taken together, these various phenomena clearly indicate that an actual splitting of the ego has occurred. This splitting of the ego must be regarded as more fundamental than the impotence and impoverishment of the ego already noted. It would seem, however, that withdrawal of libido from external objects has the result of intensifying not only the effects of the splitting process, but the actual extent of the splitting process itself. *(Fairbairn 1962: 51)*

Young Pink continues his search walking through muddy trenches where he discovers a large number of dead soldiers, but he does not find his father among them. He is seen looking on again, dream-like, at his present adult self who still sits watching television. He walks off into the mist where a steam train appears, which brings returning men in uniform who are greeted by their families. As he approaches the scene, we hear the beginning of "Vera":

> Does anybody here remember Vera Lynn?
> Remember how she said that
> We would meet again,
> Some sunny day.
> Vera! Vera!
> What has become of you?
> Does anybody else in here
> Feel the way I do?

Vera Lynn became a symbol of hope for Britain during the second world war through her optimistic songs such as the one Waters refers to here—"We'll Meet Again", a song written by Ross Parker and Hughie Charles with which she closed her radio series "Sincerely Yours". Waters makes reference to the following excerpt of the song:

> We'll meet again,
> Don't know where,
> Don't know when.
> But I know we'll meet again some sunny day....

Pink seems to suggest that Vera Lynn has vanished from the limelight for having disappointed so many people after filling them with a sense of false hope. In an attempt to allay his feelings of isolation, he asks whether anyone else on the receiving platform feels the same sense of futility that he does.

This sense of false hope is conveyed musically. The piece opens with a statement of figure (B) in the bass:

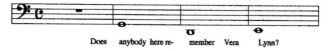

The listener is given the impression from this figure that the piece is in G major, but as the song progresses it becomes clear that it leans more toward E minor. This tonal ambiguity characterises the piece throughout, but when it ends on an E minor chord the sad truth is felt. This occurs in the film during the moment when Pink, after wandering through the crowds, tugs on the coat of a man who resembles his father. No sooner has the man turned around when he is greeted by his own family, and Pink sadly walks away. The false hope that Pink harbours as he searches for his father is also portrayed through the sense of escape from the bounds of figure (B) throughout the piece, but his impending anguish is felt through the desperation in Waters' vocal performance and in the tritone bass movement, which appears every time the chord progression G, D / F sharp, C is heard. That Pink is unable to find his father is unsurprising when considering Fairbairn's statement that "[i]n our inner unconscious world where we repress and lock away very early in life our original bad objects, they remain always rejecting, indifferent, or hostile to us according to our actual outer experience". *(in Holbrook 1971: 116)*

The idea of alienation which was conveyed through the relation between solo instrument and orchestra, is prolonged when the entire crowd of arriving soldiers and families turn toward young Pink and sing the jubilant "Bring the Boys Back Home":

> Bring the boys back home.
> Bring the boys back home.
> Don't leave the children on their own...No No
> Bring the boys back home.

The choral arrangement of this piece, along with its fluttering piccolo and flourishing runs in the strings, establishes the piece as both a celebratory and optimistic expression of the singing people. The repeated IV—V—I progression strongly conveys their sense of satisfaction, but this sense is entirely lost at the end when the progression changes to IV - V - vi which illustrates Pink's unfulfilled expectations. As this last chord is reached in the film, Young Pink is seen at the platform now suddenly alone once again, resignedly walking towards his chair and television which mysteriously appear there. In the recorded version of the song, this same sense is strongly conveyed as the choir suddenly drops out leaving Waters' anguished voice (now at the front of the mix) holding the last note alone, before it too drops out seemingly exhilarated.

That the song has a double meaning is conveyed by Waters:

> ...it's partly about not letting people go off and be killed in wars, but it's also partly about not allowing rock and roll, or making cars, or selling soap, or getting involved in biological research or anything that anybody might do...not letting *that* become such an important and 'jolly boy's game' that it becomes more important than friends, wives, children, or other people. *(Vance 1979)*

Waters' statements display that Pink's career ambitions have partially contributed to his isolated condition, and this idea is reinforced as he is brought back to a state of semi-consciousness by a knock on the door of his hotel room telling him that it's "time to go" to the show which he has to perform this night. That he is not fully conscious is illustrated by the rest of the sound effects in the tape loop montage, which illustrate the various things from earlier that move through his mind; these include the teacher shouting "Wrong...do it again!", the unconnected telephone calls to his wife, the groupie asking "Are you feeling O.K.?", and the operator saying "There's a man answering...but he keeps hanging up". The knock on the door prompts Pink to ask, once again, "Is there anybody out there?".

The next scene shows the adult Pink slumped in his chair, seemingly the victim of a drug overdose, and therefore unable to respond to the door which is now being broken down by his manager and entourage. Paramedics push his irate manager out of the way and a doctor is seen attempting to revive him:

> Hello?
> Is there anybody in there?
> Just nod if you can hear me,
> Is there anyone at home?
> Come on now,
> I hear you're feeling down.
> I can ease your pain,
> And get you on your feet again.
> Relax,

I'll need some information first,
Just the basic facts.
Can you show me where it hurts?

The return of rock instruments in this song connotes Pink's state before his withdrawal; the combination of rock and orchestral instruments, however, suggests a state of semi-consciousness. He is conscious of the doctor but, as the film shows, he is still partly in his state of regression *(see below)*. That the doctor is "only coming through in waves" for Pink is evident by the echo effect used both in the guitar part and on Waters' vocal during the first line of each section of the verse. The doctor mistakes his pain for physical pain, but Pink, whose part is sung by Gilmour here, attempts to explain his situation:

> There is no pain, you are receding,
> A distant ship smoke on the horizon,
> You are only coming through in waves,
> Your lips move but I can't hear what you're saying.
> When I was a child I had a fever,
> My hands felt just like two balloons.
> Now, I've got that feeling once again,
> I can't explain, you would not understand,
> This is not how I am,
> I have become
> Comfortably numb.

As Pink's response to the doctor begins, the orchestral strings suddenly come to the foreground, illustrating that he is still very much in a state of regression. In the film, as this section of the piece begins, the scene of Young Pink running across the rugby field reappears. This time, however, we see that he has discovered something; he bends down to pick up a dying rat. Holding it carefully in his arms and petting it, he takes it home to show his mother who tells him to take it back outside. He runs with the rat to the garage, where he lays it in a box containing straw, and takes off his sweater which he uses to cover the dying creature. Following this we see the scene, which first appeared in "Mother", of Young Pink sick in bed, visited by the doctor. In his above response, Pink directly compares his present condition to that of his childhood sickness, which at this point would appear to be an ailment known as "rat-bite fever".[28] Whereas he feared as a child that he was physically dying, now Pink feels as if he is dying emotionally. His feelings seem to have completely decayed as illustrated by the visual imagery of worms; he is, as a consequence, numb to all pain.

The comfortable quality of Pink's state is communicated through the shift from B aeolian (a "minor" mode) to D major, and through the shift from Waters' sharp enunciation of consonants to Gilmour's much smoother articulation. Preceding the guitar solo, chimes are heard (a common signification, particularly in films, for a state of altered consciousness) illustrating Pink's dream-like state, and his sense of escape is portrayed through Gilmour's pleasantly melodic solo which occurs over the D major chord changes. This sense of transcendence or escape was also portrayed visually during the live performances of the work when Gilmour performed the guitar solo from atop the wall.

The return of the B minor modality signifies the doctor's intrusion into his comfortable state. The doctor gives him an injection of some sort in order to revive him:

> O.K.
> Just a little pin prick,
> There'll be no more aaaaaaah!
> But you may feel a little sick.
> Can you stand up?
> I do believe it's working, good,
> That'll keep you going through the show,
> Come on it's time to go.

After Pink lets out an agonised scream, his manager is seen stuffing money in the pocket of what appears to be a very worried promoter. The doctor is clearly only concerned that Pink is in good enough shape to perform. Waters describes the situation and shares his own experience:

> ...they're not interested in any of these problems. All they're interested in is how many people there are and tickets have been sold and the show must go on, at any cost, to anybody. I mean I, personally, have done gigs when I've been very depressed, but I've also done gigs when I've been *extremely* ill, where you wouldn't do any ordinary work...[because] they've paid the money and if you cancel a show at short notice, it's expensive. *(Vance 1979)*

Again Pink attempts to express himself:

> There is no pain you are receding,
> A distant ship smoke on the horizon.
> You are only coming through in waves,
> Your lips move but I can't hear what you're saying.
> When I was a child
> I caught a fleeting glimpse
> Out of the corner of my eye.
> I turned to look but it was gone.
> I cannot put my finger on it now,
> The child is grown,
> The dream is gone,
> And I have become
> Comfortably numb.

In the film, immediately before the singing of this verse, Pink briefly sees the image of his father holding the dead rat. Next Young Pink, now cured from his illness, runs back to the garage where he finds the rat now dead. Dejectedly he picks it up by its tail and drops it into the neighbouring canal. That the rat is, for Pink, symbolically related to his father is evident. Sol Altschul's comments are useful:

> To adapt by mourning to...loss requires a redistribution of internal cathexis to an object that is still needed for current as well as future developmental tasks. The cases presented suggest that development was hampered not only by denial and incomplete mourning but also by the absence of a suitable object for interaction. *(in Levin 1966: 144-145)*

It would appear that the rat became a substitute object for Pink in order to help him cope with his father's death. Having invested much hope in being able to nurse it back to health, its death served to impede any future hopeful "glimpses" that Pink might have.

The closing guitar solo occurs over the B minor changes, representing the loss of Pink's freedom to the interests of the music industry people. The entourage of the barely conscious Pink dress him in his stage clothes and begin to carry him out of the building. This loss of freedom is also portrayed in the song "The Show Must Go On"—a piece which is not included in the film nor the stage performance. The piece is based on the chord changes from Pink's verses in "Mother", and the lyrics seemingly represent a continuation of his previous concerns about his primary objects, or mother and father. That this is no longer his immediate worry, however, is conveyed by the fact that all of his lines (sung by Gilmour) express either his lack of desire to perform or his concern about his apparent loss of feelings. Meanwhile the background vocalists (representing the music industry people) *pretend* that they are interested in his personal crises:

> Oooh Ma, Oooh Pa
> Must the show go on?
> Oooh Pa take me home.
> Oooh Ma let me go.
> There must be some mistake,
> I didn't mean to let them
> Take away my soul.
> Am I too old? Is it too late?
> Oooh Ma, Oooh Pa
> Where has the feeling gone?
> Oooh Ma, Oooh Pa
> Will I remember the songs?
> The show must go on.

The insincerity of the background vocalists is initially portrayed through the confident, undisturbed four-four meter with which the song begins. They attempt to appear genuine when, during the third and fourth lines, the harmony shifts back and forth from a D major to a D diminished seventh chord (a movement which creates much tension due to the latter's being comprised of two overlapping tritones), but their unauthenticity is displayed by the uninterrupted reassuring meter. The meter switches to three-four in the fifth line during Pink's entry, and this change, in combination with the complex rhythmic figures executed by the bass and drums, displays both his lack of confidence and his weak attempt to assert himself. His failure is displayed when the piece moves back to a straight four feel, but this is anticipated by the "bittersweet" quality of the major seventh chord (a chord comprised of a major and minor triad) over which Pink sings these lines. The major seventh chord evokes a positive impression because of Pink's expression of regret over the loss of his soul or human feelings, but it also evokes the sad realisation that for him it *is* "too late". This is illustrated at the end of the piece when it becomes apparent that the music industry people are not genuinely interested in his troubles with his mother and father, but are actually concerned with the show going on as planned. During the last line, their voices overpower his to assert that "the show must go on".

As Pink is being dragged out of the hotel, his skin gradually decays to the point where he metamorphoses into what Waters calls "the PINK Scarfian dummy"—a portrayal of Pink as a flimsy rag-doll non-entity which appears later in the film during "Waiting for the Worms" and "The Trial". Pink is thrown into the waiting limousine whose "door slams closed like a prison door". Waters describes the following scene in the draft of the screenplay thus:

> He starts to fight back for the first time....He twists and turns from one window to another. His nails dig deep into his own 'flesh'. He begins to rip off the pink skin from his body. Passive no more. Piece by piece the dead layers of decaying skin are torn away revealing first a Nazi-like arm band, and then eventually the whole uniform. *(G. R. Waters 1981)*

Having failed in his first attempt at rebirth, Pink is now reborn as the fascist demagogue who wears the symbols of crossed hammers on his sleeve—the figure that was seen at the beginning of the work during "In the Flesh?".

When he arrives at the concert hall, Pink is escorted to the stage by similarly uniformed, jackbooted guards. The hall is filled with banners bearing the crossed hammer insignia, and the atmosphere of the place is, as Waters suggests, like "an unholy marriage between Nuremburg 1936, Red Square on May Day, and a Klu Klux Klan meeting" (G. R. Waters 1981). As the curtains are opened, Pink is welcomed exultantly by the crowds. He gives them the hammer salute (symbolised by crossed wrists), and they enthusiastically respond likewise. Now Pink has completely relinquished the position of victim for that of the sadistic persecutor. He approaches the podium to sing the reprise of "In the Flesh", and the punctuated shots in the drums provide the necessary hammer blows:

> So ya'
> Thought ya'
> Might like to
> Go to the show.
> To feel the warm thrill of confusion,
> That space cadet glow.
> I've got some bad news for you sunshine,
> Pink isn't well, he stayed back at the hotel,
> And they sent us along as a surrogate band,
> And we're going to find out where you fans
> Really stand.

At this point Pink begins to isolate victims in the audience, who are then brutally dragged away by members of the hammer guard:[29]

> Are there any queers in the theatre tonight?
> Get 'em up against the wall.
> There's one in the spotlight,
> He don't look right to me,
> Get him up against the wall.
> That one looks Jewish,
> And that one's a coon.
> Who let all this riff raff into the room?
> There's one smoking a joint and
> Another with spots,
> If I had my way
> I'd have all of you shot.

As Pink concludes, the audience sadistically cheers in support of his mass condemnation. Fairbairn's remarks are interesting in the light of this projection of hatred:

> When, accordingly, an individual with a schizoid tendency makes a renunciation of social contacts, it is above all because he feels that he must neither love nor be loved. He does not always rest content with a mere passive aloofness, however. On the contrary, he often takes active measures to drive his libidinal objects away from him. For this purpose he has an instrument ready to hand inside himself in the form of his own differentiated aggression. He mobilises the resources of his hate, and directs his aggression against others—and more particularly against his libidinal objects....In so doing, he not only substitutes hate for love in his relationships with his objects, but also induces them to hate, instead of loving, him; and he does all this in order to keep his libidinal objects at a distance. *(Fairbairn 1962: 26)*

That the audience has been induced to hate is evident by the many T-shirts worn by people in the audience which actually say "hate". Their enthusiastic chanting (on the album) of "Pink Floyd" after the conclusion of "In the Flesh", however, displays their sado-masochistic tendencies. Eventually they begin to chant "hammer" as their support of his hatred grows.

Pink's oppressive display of power over his unthinking audience is displayed during the opening of "Run Like Hell" when they all begin to move as one mechanical mass. Their faces suddenly turn into identical pink masks, as did those of the students in response to the teacher's oppression earlier in the work. Like the teacher before him, Pink now wants to create an expressionless society, where everyone is the same. People will now be made to feel guilty for their former actions, and any deviations from the norm will be punishable by the hammers:

> You better make your face up in
> Your favourite disguise
> With your button down lips and your
> roller blind eyes,
> With your empty smile
> And your hungry heart
> Feel the bile rising from your guilty past.
> With your nerves in tatters
> As the cockleshell shatters
> And the hammers batter
> Down the door,
> You better run.

The oppressive force of the hammers is expressed here through Waters' use of rhyme (tatters, shatters, batter) and the resultant consonance achieved using the harsh "t" sound. The image of the "protective shield" is now compared to the frailty of a cockleshell, which defends unsuccessfully against the forceful hammer blows which easily shatter them.

As the violence breaks out of the concert hall, the "blackshirts" are seen terrorizing the streets. They go into a restaurant and demolish it while beating up some black men, and then a family of Pakistanis are seen being driven from their house. They come upon a car, where a black boy is seen kissing a white girl, and smash the windshield with a bat. The boy is dragged away and beaten, while the girl is raped. The song continues, and the hammers of oppression now also become the hammers of repression:

> You better run all day
> And run all night
> And keep your dirty feelings
> Deep inside. And if you're
> Taking your girlfriend
> Out tonight,
> You better park the car
> Well out of sight,
> 'Cos if they catch you in the back seat
> Trying to pick her locks
> They're gonna' send you back to Mother
> In a cardboard box.
> You better run.

It is clear that this element of repression, again due to the use of the word "dirty", is rooted in Pink's mother. Now he is instilling his fears in others, as evidenced by the last frightening image.

The imagery of being hammered "into the right shape" is portrayed through the musical processes of this song. An ominous air is established at the beginning of the song with the guitar due to its odd "scratchy" timbre, the brevity of its initial entry, and its unnaturally fast echo. As the rhythm section enters, the bass guitar begins to "hammer" the tonic on every beat. Suspense is created by the long cymbal rush, which introduces the attack of the electric guitar, whose chords do not stray outside the D major tonality set up by the pedal point in the bass. With the disappearance of the pedal point, and the sudden occurrence of an F chord (a chord very much unrelated to D major), we suddenly receive the repeated warning to "run". As this warning is reiterated, we immediately conform and return to a D major tonality; an A major chord (V) follows the F, and then we return to D. The D vamp becomes unsettling with the return of the fast echoing guitar which performs a minor pentatonic fill against the D major chord.

The verse suddenly shifts to a progression, the root movement of which outlines the claustrophobic phrygian mode (E major, F major, E major, C major, B major, E major). These feelings of claustrophobia represent the result of the addressee's withdrawal from the oppressive forces represented by Waters' intimidating singing style (which with every line approaches the listener from alternating speaker channels giving the impression that this relentless attack is coming from all directions). As Waters' screams "you better run" at the end of each verse, the piece returns once again to the oppressive D pedal point.

Following the second verse is a synthesizer solo, which seemingly takes over Waters' vocal. This solo, the only one played on synthesizer throughout the whole album, appears over a repetition of the phrygian progression. Remembering Walser's comments (page 65) about the synthesizer's potential for sustain and its implications for power, the solo represents the threat of Pink's power.

The fear to conform is conveyed to the listener by the sound effects which appear over the D pedal in the outcourse of the piece. These include the sounds of the "blackshirts" running, their insane laughter, and the sounds of car tires squealing. Before the final entry of the D major guitar riff, the "battle cry" originally heard at the beginning of the students' revolt in "Another Brick in the Wall (Part II)" is heard; its appearance this time is more frightening because of the evil intentions of the attacking force.

The next song "Waiting for the Worms", which even features a German count-in, illustrates the spread of Pink's decay as it increasingly takes on Nazi-like proportions. The oppressive force of the hammers, shown marching unopposed down the deserted street, has now caused the building of walls on a mass scale; as they march by houses, their inhabitants close their curtains and, in Waters' words, "retreat into themselves" (G. R. Waters 1981). The opening of the piece, a reprisal of the beginning of "The Show Must Go On", recalls Pink's state just before his transformation—suggesting that all the other citizens will now undergo similar metamorphoses. This is conveyed by the chorus of singers who sing the initial lines. Their false sense of "comfort" or safety being portrayed by the initial upward octave leap:

> Oooh you cannot reach me now,
> Oooh no matter how you try.
> Goodbye cruel world it's over,
> Walk on by.

The oncoming transformations of the background singers are depicted by their singing behind Pink during the next lines—behind both Gilmour's and Waters' voices. Because Gilmour sings the lead (in the same style as "The Show Must Go On"), this also suggests a flashback to Pink's state before his transformation. Waters explains:

> 'Waiting for the Worms', in theatrical terms, is an expression of what happens in the show, when the drugs start wearing off and what real feelings he's got left start taking over again...he keeps flipping backwards and forwards from his real, or his original persona if you like, which is a reasonably humane person into this 'waiting for the worms to come' persona, which is cracked...flipped, and is ready to crush anybody or anything that gets in the way... *(Vance 1979)*

This continual reversion between both personaes is indicated by the return of Waters' voice which interjects, each time, with the line "Waiting for the worms to come":

> Sitting in a bunker here behind my wall,
> Waiting for the worms to come.
> In perfect isolation here behind my wall,
> Waiting for the worms to come.

That Pink still attempts to take refuge through his identification with his father is illustrated by his imagined increase in protective sheltering; he is not only behind his wall now, but also in a bunker.

The film shows the hammers setting up a street rally, and Pink is seen shouting through a megaphone. Waters, again, explains the situation:

> ...you hear a voice through a loud-hailer...it goes 'testing one-two' or something, and then it says 'we will convene at one o'clock outside Brixton Town Hall', and it's describing the situation of marching towards some kind of National Front rally in Hyde Park....So all that shouting and

screaming, because you can't hear it...if you listen very carefully you might hear 'Lambeth Road'..., 'Vauxhall Bridge'...,'we might encounter some Jewboys'. It's just me ranting on. *(Vance 1979)*

During Pink's speech the piece returns to the A minor vamp, which first appeared during "The Happiest Days of Our Lives" and represented the Teacher's "imposed constraint". The force of the marching hammers is now represented through the detached rhythmic playing of the guitar and bass, and through the deep male voices which support Pink at the beginning of each phrase singing "waiting". Waters' melody is almost exclusively constructed from the claustrophobic figure (B):

> Waiting to cut out the dead wood,
> Waiting to clean up the city,
> Waiting to follow the worms,
> Waiting to put on a blackshirt,
> Waiting to weed out the weaklings,
> Waiting to smash in their windows
> And kick in their doors,
> Waiting for the final solution[30]
> To strengthen the strain,
> Waiting to follow the worms,
> Waiting to turn on the showers
> And fire the ovens,
> Waiting for the queens and the coons
> And the reds and the Jews,
> Waiting to follow the worms.

Although Pink's drugs are wearing off, it is clear that his real personality, as well as the personalities of the town's inhabitants, have begun to be affected by the worms. This is displayed by the reappearance of the original background singers, and the return of Gilmour's voice when the following lines are sung:

> Would you like to see Britannia
> Rule again my friend?
> All you have to do is follow the worms.
> Would you like to send our coloured cousins
> Home again my friend?
> All you need to do is follow the worms.

Pink imagines the idea of Britain, once again, becoming a colossal colonial or imperial power. Like Hitler, he envisages raising the Anglo-Saxon race back to its former strength and purity.

These lines are separated by a return of figure (A) in the electric guitar, which reappears during the outro in combination with the latter half of figure (B):

The combination of these figures is repeated over and over, while Pink contin-

ues to shout instructions over the megaphone. The film shows the forceful animated hammers marching ever onward, and the crowds' shouting of "hammer"
becomes increasingly loud as Pink's evil and hatred assume control; everyone
is forced first to withdraw, and then become part of this evil after their own
feelings decay.

At the height of this crescendo Pink realises the frightening aspect of his
hatred. There is a sudden reduction of musical forces to piano and solo voice
as he ends his nightmarish hallucination screaming "Stop". His impending
madness is portrayed in the piano's chromatic dissonances, and in the surreal-
istic echoing of his words. The film shows Pink pathetically sitting in one of
the arena's washroom stalls beside a toilet bowl. With bottle in hand, he sings
to himself from his "little black book" of poems, and then sings:

> Stop.
> I wanna' go home,
> Take off this uniform
> And leave the show.
> And I'm waiting in this cell
> Because I have to know,
> Have I been guilty all this time?

Pink's sudden feelings of guilt are, in part, related to the fantasy of his projected hatred. Fairbairn discusses two of the common motives for the schizoid's
substitution of hate for love:

> There are two further motives...by which an individual with a schizoid
> tendency may be actuated in substituting hating for loving—curiously
> one an immoral, and the other a moral motive....The immoral motive is
> determined by the consideration that, since the joy of loving seems
> hopelessly barred to him, he may as well deliver himself over to the joy
> of hating and obtain what satisfaction he can out of that....The moral
> motive is determined by the consideration that, if loving involves destroy-
> ing, it is better to destroy by hate, which is overtly destructive and bad,
> than to destroy by love, which is by rights creative and good. *(Fairbairn
> 1962: 26-27)*

It would appear that Pink's motive has been the "immoral", and his feelings of
guilt initially stem from this realiation.

A security officer, who has entered the bathroom, discovers Pink in the stall. As
he opens the door the animated scene of "The Trial" begins. It is immediately
clear that Pink, once again, becomes the victim—he is again portrayed as "the
pink Scarfian dummy", and is guarded by two hammers at either side of the
door. Like his former victims from the reprise of "In the Flesh", he is literally
"up against the wall". Waters describes the scene:

> A double door opens, which gives on to an enormous stadium. Inside the
> stadium, strange music business figures jabber at one another. A stage,
> made of writhing worms produces itself, an actor-cum-lawyer preens
> himself in front of a dressing room mirror. This is the prosecutor, invent-
> ed by PINK in his subconscious, as a tool with which to pick the locks of
> his own guilty feelings. A large worm rears up. Upon its faceless head it
> wears a judge's wig. It sways menacingly in the air, like a cobra ready to
> strike. *(G. R. Waters 1981)*

That this piece satirizes both the judicial system and stadium rock is evident. It compares trials to spotlighted performances, whose lead actors are clearly the lawyers, and whose function has become, in part, entertainment. At the same time, it mocks the immensity of packed stadiums; this is displayed by the huge wall which runs down the center, dividing one half of the people from the other (also portrayed on the inner sleeve of the original vinyl recording). The satirical nature of the work is not only conveyed by the visual images, but also by the music. The piece, through its orchestration, chromatic colourings and characteristic repeated bass figure, recalls the music of Kurt Weill—particularly that for the stage works written in collaboration with the satirical poet and dramatist Bertolt Brecht.

The piece creates an aura of doom immediately when the foreboding bells chime thrice three times. The chimes also set the stage for the three hammer blows portrayed through the judge's pounding of his gavel. Pink's alienation is reflected both in the excessive use in the melody of the interval of a tritone above the bass, and in the return of the claustrophobic phrygian root movement of the opening chord progression (E minor, F major / E, E minor, C, B seventh); the same root movement which appeared previously in the verses of "Run Like Hell".

The prosecutor begins his address, and then calls his first witness the teacher, who appears as a marionette dropped over the wall by his wife:

> Good morning Worm your honour
> The crown will plainly show
> The prisoner who now stands before you
> Was caught red handed showing feelings,
> Showing feelings of an almost human nature.
> This will not do.
> Call the Schoolmaster.
> I always said he'd come to no good
> In the end your honour
> If they'd let me have my way I could
> Have flayed him into shape
> But my hands were tied.
> The bleeding hearts and artists
> Let him get away with murder.
> Let me hammer him today.

According to the prosecutor, Pink is guilty for having displayed feelings by halting his sadistic spread of decay. The teacher metamorphoses into a hammer and offers to crush him into the right shape; his threatening aspect is conveyed by the ascending chromatic run in the low basses.

Pink's instability is communicated during his entry, where the rising tritone figure reappears in his melody (forming an E diminished chord). Its affect is heightened, however, due to its being held for two beats before resolving upward. When this figure is repeated two bars later, it forms a B major seventh chord, and the "bittersweet" quality evokes the listener's sympathy. Pink's fears of disintegration are conveyed in his response, and confirmed both by the appearance of the diminished chord at the end of his lines, and by the line sung by the chorus which follows:

> Crazy, toys in the attic, I am crazy.
> Truly gone fishing.
> They must have taken my marbles away.
> Crazy, toys in the attic, he is crazy.

Pink's "unrootedness" is illustrated, in the film, through his portrayal as an ever-falling leaf.

Next the prosecutor calls Pink's wife—his second witness. In the form of a snake she slithers beneath the wall, and then stings him after she metamorphoses into a scorpion. Her testimony differs from that of the teacher, and conflicts with the prosecutor's charge:

> You little shit, you're in it now,
> I hope they throw away the key.
> You should have talked to me more often
> than you did, but no, you had to
> Go your own way. Have you broken any
> Homes up lately?
> "Just five minutes Worm your honour
> Him and me alone."

As Pink's wife asks the judge to give him to her to punish, his mother bursts forth from out of the wall and flies to protect him. Her descent in the form of a bomber coincides with her rapidly descending pitch (also the string slides in the violins), and her voice flies from the right speaker channel to the left where the wife was located:

> Babe,
> Come to Mother baby, let me hold you
> In my arms
> M'Lud I never wanted him to
> Get in any trouble
> Why'd he ever have to leave me
> Worm your honour, let me take him home.

In the form of a pair of giant lips, Pink's mother sucks him up and, turning into herself, snuggles him in her arms. She then turns into a gigantic wall. Pink, again, expresses his torment. That he is crazy is supported again by the chorus:

> Crazy, over the rainbow, I am crazy,
> Bars in the window,
> There must have been a door there in the wall
> When I came in.
> Crazy, over the rainbow, he is crazy.

During this internal self-examination, it is evident that Pink's bad objects have escaped from his unconscious. This, according to Fairbairn, would explain his sudden sense of guilt which was expressed in "Stop". Fairbairn suggests that guilt is a defence against the release of bad objects from the unconscious—a defence he terms 'the moral defence':

> The essential feature, and indeed the essential aim, of this defence is the conversion of an original situation in which the [individual] is surrounded by bad objects into a new situation in which his objects are good and he himself is bad. The moral situation which results belongs, of course, to a higher level of mental development than the original situ-

ation; and this level is characteristically a 'civilized' level. It is the level at which the super-ego operates, and to which the interplay between the ego and the super-ego belongs...most analytically minded psychotherapists may be expected to make it their aim to mitigate the harshness of the patient's super-ego and thus to reduce guilt and anxiety. Such an endeavour is frequently rewarded with excellent therapeutic results.[31]
(Fairbairn 1962: 68-69)

The super-ego is continuously characterised by Guntrip as sadistic in *Schizoid Phenomena, Object Relations and the Self* (1969), due to the intensity of the guilt to which it gives rise in people. The judge in "The Trial" is clearly Waters' portrayal of Pink's super-ego, and it is therefore appropriate that he appears first in the form of a worm (a symbolic representation of decayed feelings), and later as an asshole. It is clear that Pink's employment of "the moral defence" fails, due to the fact that his objects are still portrayed as bad, and that they *are* released from his unconscious. Fairbairn explains this phenomenon:

> There is now little doubt in my mind that...the deepest source of resistance [to psychotherapy] is fear of the release of bad objects from the unconscious; for, when such bad objects are released, the world around the patient becomes peopled with devils which are too terrifying for him to face....At the same time there is now little doubt in my mind that the release of bad objects from the unconscious is one of the chief aims which the psychotherapist should set himself out to achieve...for it is only when the internalized bad objects are released from the unconscious that there is any hope of their cathexis being dissolved. The bad objects can only be safely released, however, if the analyst has become established as a sufficiently good object for the patient. Otherwise the resulting insecurity may prove insupportable....The release of such objects obtained in analytical treatment differs...from a spontaneous release of such objects in that it has a therapeutic aim—and ultimately a therapeutic effect in virtue of the fact that it is a release controlled by the analyst....Here it should be noted that the release of repressed objects of which I speak is by no means identical with that active externalization of internalized objects, which is the characteristic of the paranoid technique. The phenomenon to which I specially refer is the escape of bad objects from the bonds imposed by repression. When such an escape of bad objects occurs, the patient finds himself confronted with terrifying situations which have hitherto been unconscious. *(Fairbairn 1962: 69 and 75-76)*

It must be remembered that the cathexis of internal bad objects must be dissolved in order to free an individual's libido from being narcissistically directed within, so that it can be directed externally toward appropriate objects.

When the judge approaches Pink in order to deliver his verdict he is literally in the form of an asshole on legs. As he approaches Pink, the wall forms a cylinder which surrounds the defendant, walling him in ever tighter. His frightening power is conveyed through the sudden electric guitar entry, which plays figure (A) at the tonic and the sub-dominant—reflecting Pink's increasing feeling of constriction. The judge hovers above the cylinder which envelops Pink, as if over a toilet bowl and delivers his judgement:

> The evidence before the court is
> Incontrovertible, there's no need for

the jury to retire,
In all my years of judging
I have never heard before of
Someone more deserving
The full penalty of law.
The way you made them suffer,
Your exquisite wife and mother
Fills me with the urge to defecate.
Since my friend, you have revealed your
Deepest fear.
I sentence you to be exposed before
Your peers
Tear down the wall.

At this point we must recall Fairbairn's characterisation (from page 79) of the gradual transition from infantile dependence to mature dependence which features "a gradual change in libidinal aim, whereby an original oral, sucking, incorporating and predominantly 'taking' aim comes to be replaced by a mature, non-incorporating and predominantly 'giving' aim". His further comments are informative:

> In conformity with the predominance of taking over giving in the early oral attitude, individuals with a schizoid tendency experience considerable difficulty over giving in the emotional sense. In this connection it is interesting to recall that, if the oral incorporative tendency is the most fundamental of all tendencies, those next in importance for the organism are the excretory activities (defaecation and urination). The biological aim of the excretory activities is, of course, the elimination of useless and noxious substances from the body; but, although, in conformity with their biological aim, the child soon learns to regard them as the classic means of dealing with bad libidinal objects, their earliest psychological significance for him would appear to be that of creative activities. They represent the first creative activities of the individual; and their products are his first creations—the first internal contents that he externalizes, the first things belonging to himself that he gives. In this respect the excretory activities stand in contrast to oral activity, which essentially involves an attitude of taking. This particular contrast between the two groups of libidinal activity must not be taken to preclude the coexistence of another contrast between them in an opposite sense; for there is, of course, also a respect in which the oral incorporative attitude towards an object implies valuation of the object, whereas the excretory attitude towards an object implies its devaluation and rejection. What is relevant for the immediate purpose, however, is the fact that, at a deep mental level, taking is emotionally equivalent to amassing bodily contents, and giving is emotionally equivalent to parting with bodily contents. *(Fairbairn 1962: 14)*

As the judge shits images of his past life at him, Pink displays his knowledge that he is, in fact, guilty. The crime he was initially charged with was "showing feelings of an almost human nature", which he did throughout the work by withdrawing further into himself in order to protect them. This is not the crime with which he is charged however. The crime he is ultimately charged with and punished for is not having *expressed* his feelings—an inaction which resulted in his making others suffer. It is this observance of suffering which gives the judge (or Pink) an urge to defecate or "give".

Pink's deepest fear was to expose his weaknesses, a fear which prevented him from making any true human contact.[32] By tearing down the wall, Pink displays his realisation about the detrimental effects of his narcissism or "self love" on others. When considering Fairbairn's belief that we are all fundamentally schizoid to varying degrees, it is appropriate that the listener is addressed in the work's final piece—"Outside the Wall":

> All alone, or in twos,
> The ones who really love you
> Walk up and down outside the wall.
> Some hand in hand.
> Some gathering together in bands.
> The bleeding hearts and the artists
> Make their stand.
> And when they've given you their all,
> Some stagger and fall, after all it's not easy
> Banging your heart against some mad bugger's
> Wall.

This piece accompanies the final scene of the film, which shows a group of children helping to clean up the debris where rioting has taken place. That the cycle of building walls has already begun again is suggested by the young boy who is seen collecting bricks. This idea is also illustrated on the album through the incomplete statement at its conclusion which is completed as the record begins, making the album endlessly cyclical; it says, "Isn't this where we came in?". The film ends with an image of hope however. Another small boy, who closely resembles the young Pink, finds a Molotov cocktail from which he removes the rag and, after retching at its smell, empties the liquid from the bottle displaying his innocent distaste at bringing harm to others.

That Pink's realisation comes too late makes him a tragic figure, but through his symbolic gesture he emancipates himself from guilt. Pink Floyd the group, under Waters' supervision, did likewise by choosing to perform the work in smaller venues—shows which proved to be the last that Waters would perform with the group. Following the performances the barrier between the group and its audience came tumbling down, after which they strolled amongst the rubble and performed "Outside the Wall" using acoustic instruments—a signification of authenticity and innocence, which was portrayed also by the children's voices on the studio version of the piece. The work's ultimate meaning is allegorically powerful, and is best expressed by its author who says "the show is about redemption, and we are redeemed when we tear our walls down and expose our weaknesses to our fellow man and sit around the fire and talk. That's the acoustic song at the end".[33]

Chapter 5 — The Final Cut:
A Requiem For the Post War Dream

'The pain of war cannot exceed the woe of aftermath...'.

Robert Plant[1]

Perhaps the greatest faculty a human being can demonstrate is empathy toward fellow human beings. Unsurprisingly empathy is often difficult to express, due both to the day-to-day concerns which individuals are forced to face, and to the increased removal they feel as the world moves closer and closer to becoming a global society. It is, however, a striving for empathy which plagues *The Final Cut* (1983)—in particular the struggle both to empathise with what Waters calls "the post war dream", and with those who fought for that aspiration in the Second World War (1939-1945).

Arising from Waters' fears that this dream had been betrayed (largely his reaction to the conflict which occurred between April and June 1982 between Great Britain and Argentina over the Falkland Islands),[2] the work is an admission of possible guilt for having also betrayed those like his father who were involved in defending it. He said of the album to Karl Dallas:

> It says something about a sense, I suppose for me personally, a sense that *I* may have betrayed him. He died in the last war and I kind of feel that I personally may have betrayed him, because we haven't managed to improve things very much. That the economic cycles still over-ride everything, with the best intentions, the cycle of economic recession followed by resurgence still governs our actions. *(Dallas 1987: 148)*

The feelings of conflict that Waters expresses are apparent in the two contrasting portraits which adorned the original vinyl album's inner sleeves—the first of which showed a hand holding out poppies to a uniformed soldier standing far in the distance, and the second displaying the same soldier standing in the foreground with a knife in his back. The work invites listeners to enter into this conflict; its message becomes increasingly more important as time distances us further from what was possibly our century's greatest tragedy, and as the number of people directly affected by this tragedy diminishes.

As the album begins, the listener hears a radio being tuned to various stations reporting the news. Among the snippets of information heard are talk of the plans to build a nuclear fallout shelter at Peterborough and Cambridge, the occurrence of rising violence in Third World countries like Bolivia, and an announcement that Japan will build the replacement for *The Atlantic Conveyor*, a British container ship lost in the Falklands conflict. The hearing of these then current events prompts the commencement of the requiem—a genre which, in the Roman Catholic Church, is a mass for the repose of the souls of the dead. Inasmuch as it is also a celebration of the Eucharist by the living, its primary concern traditionally appears to be that of "the after-life" rather than the present one. The work begins by introducing this supposition:[3]

> Tell me true, tell me why was Jesus crucified,
> Was it for this that Daddy died?
> Was it you? Was it me?
> Did I watch too much T.V.?
> Is that a hint of accusation in your eyes?

Though suspicious of whether or not Christ's sacrifice was truly intended to improve conditions in this life, Waters is certain that his father's was. As the aforementioned newscasts reveal, however, it appears not to have, threatening him with the idea that his father's sacrifice was a waste. This threat prompts him solemnly to ask who is to blame, and his sobriety is communicated through the deliberateness of his soft slow articulation of the words. The song acquires an air of religious seriousness both through its use of the organ-like harmonium, and through the appearance of the plagal embellishments which occur at the end of each iteration of the harmonic ostinato.

The next verse returns directly to one of the news bulletins heard previously. It documents an issue which was very much in the forefront of the world's attention and concern throughout 1982, as displayed by this excerpt from the editorial of the Canadian weekly news magazine *Maclean's*:

> The Japanese economic miracle is best described by one startling statistic. During the past three decades, the country's productivity has increased more than elevenfold, an annual growth of a least 8.5 per cent. The recent Canadian equivalent is almost too small to be meaningful. According to the Economic Council of Canada, productivity in this country between 1975 and 1980 grew by precisely one-quarter of one per cent per year. *(Newman 1982: 3)*

As the verse begins, the entry of French horns conjures the image of hunting (the horn has long been associated with hunting), once an activity required for one's survival, but one which has generally been replaced in the modern world by the need to acquire money.[4]

Heard against the background of the sound effects of someone counting change, the lyrics of the verse effectively illustrate the distraction of economics observed in the earlier quotation from Waters:

> If it wasn't for the Nips[5]
> Being so good at building ships
> The yards would still be open on the Clyde.[6]
> And it can't be much fun for them
> Beneath the rising sun
> With all their kids committing suicide.

The end of the verse, however, pinpoints the detrimental effects of Japan's economic success. According to Maurice Pinguet:

> Between 1965 and 1975, the number of under-fourteen suicides in Japan doubled from forty-six a year to ninety-five. In the same period there was a tenfold increase in the number of stomach ulcers among schoolchildren in the same age bracket. For a long time the suicide figure for minors (under twenty) stayed around the 700-a-year mark: then in 1977 it went to 784, and suddenly, in 1978, to 866....In a competitive society where conditions are no longer immutable, families want their children to 'succeed'. Japanese society has many tensions, springing firstly from competition among firms, but also from the get-ahead ambition within families. The adolescent is expected to be both child and adult, taking charge of his own future....One thing follows another: to get into a good firm you need a degree from a good university; to take the entrance examination for a good university you have to be from a good

school; to get into a good school you have to come from a good primary school. In short, competition starts in kindergarten... *(Pinguet 1993: 36-
37)*

This survey of the bleak conditions of his time prompts Waters to address the
then British Tory Prime Minister, Margaret Thatcher. The assignment of blame
to the general population is signalled by the entry of full orchestra—a musical
representation of the masses:

> What have we done? Maggie what have we done?
> What have we done to England?

The solemn tone of the introduction is angrily shattered as the piece breaks into
rock. The heavy drum entry, in combination with the harsh timbre which results
from sliding the pick down the top string of the distorted electric guitar, effectively contrasts the predominantly smooth texture which preceded. The sudden
increase in dynamics, and Waters' abrupt leap into his high vocal register also
help to communicate his anger as he sings:

> Should we shout, should we scream,
> "What happened to the post war dream?"
> Oh Maggie, Maggie what did we do?

The discomfort caused by the abrupt modulation of musical characteristics is
also accomplished melodically and harmonically. Dissonance arises through
the use of a chromatic passing tone (appearing on the first and last occurrences
of the word "we"), and due to the substitution of the major for the minor chord
which would normally appear on the mediant [III] (occurring on the word
scream). In the midst of this angry outburst, a hint of pathos arises when, during the singing of "What happened to the post war dream?", the sub-dominant
[IV] is altered to the minor sub-dominant.

As this outburst ends, the impression of resignation is conferred as all the musical characteristics modulate back to their original state. A solo trumpet takes
over the melody as the piece ends, providing a "taps-like" gesture (a bugle call
commonly used at a military funeral—in this case that of the post war dream).
The piece does not finish with a sense of finality, however, as a result of the rising major sixth interval which ends the trumpet's melody; every preceding
occurrence of this interval appeared during the midst of a melodic phrase. This
refusal of closure marks the beginning of Waters' inquiry which takes place
throughout the rest of the work.

During the segue into "Your Possible Pasts" a railcar is heard being backed into
a siding, a sound effect which anticipates the last line of the song's first verse.
A feeling of coldness arises as a result of the wind sound effects, but also
through the use of electric guitar for the typically acoustic guitar-style figure
which introduces the piece.[7] The lyrics remind listeners of the possible pasts
which delicately "flutter" behind them, the threat of which was dispelled by the
soldiers of the Second World War who defeated Nazi Germany:

> They flutter behind you your possible pasts
> Some brighteyed and crazy some frightened and lost
> A warning to anyone still in command
> Of their possible future to take care.

The threat of our possible pasts, as Waters observes, acts as a warning to those who are still capable of controlling future safety. By the long pause which follows the word "command", however, Waters seems to be suggesting that future safety depends very much on those in positions of authority.[8] The unsettling knowledge of possible threats to future safety is conveyed both through the continued insertion of a measure of two beats which disrupts the comfortable triple metre every other line, and by the simulated sound of a gunshot provided by the snare drum crack at the end of the third line. The abrupt shock of this event (an effect achieved also by the sudden volume of the power chords in the electric guitar and organ) immediately dissipates, illustrating that this is merely a false alarm. The last lines of the verse forebodingly warn of the poppies which now "entwine" because of insufficient care and cultivation. This refusal to remember threatens the possibility of a recurrence of organised genocide suggested by the "cattle trucks" or railcars which lie in wait:

> In derelict sidings the poppies entwine
> With cattle trucks lying in wait for the next time.

Though the present sense of safety is conveyed through the perfect authentic cadence (V—I) which ends the verse, the sudden modulation to the relative natural minor for the chorus disturbs this sense of satisfaction as does the increase in dynamics and Waters' screaming of the lyrics:

> Do you remember me? How we used to be?
> Do you think we should be closer?

Recalling the character Pink (from *The Wall*) who developed fascistic traits due to his isolation, the chorus suggests that being closer to one another may increase our power of empathy and help us to avoid future catastrophes. Waters' voice, however, displays the frustration of his own sense of isolation. This is communicated both through the melody of the chorus (a repeated occurrence of what was known in *The Wall* as Figure A—a figure which, due to its narrow interval, connotes feelings of claustrophobia or isolation), and through the echo effect on the word "closer", which ironically recedes away from the listener with each repetition.[9] Frustration gives way to a sense of quiet poignancy as a result of the dissonant major seventh contained in the chorus' final chord.

The next verse, anticipating "Sexual Revolution" from *The Pros and Cons of Hitchhiking* (1984), explores the sense of division between the sexes. Waters sustains the sense of coldness through the prostitute's fraudulent smile and "cold" eyes:

> She stood in the doorway the ghost of a smile
> Haunting her face like a cheap hotel sign
> Her cold eyes imploring the men in their macs
> For the gold in their bags or the knives in their backs
> Stepping up boldly one put out his hand
> He said, "I was just a child then now I'm only a man".

Although she feigns warmth as illustrated by the use of acoustic guitar during this verse, its electronic treatment betrays her insincerity. Not being interested in making genuine contact, the prostitute instead wants only money, or to be recognised (because of her femininity) as hard-done-by like the ex-servicemen she propositions. As the one who approaches her suggests, however, his unfair treatment had nothing to do with his gender; the background sound effects of children playing connotes innocence (a period when there is considerably less concern about the distinction between males and females), and anticipates the character's attitude that the fact that he is masculine is insignificant.[10] The intimidation that the man feels as he approaches the woman (which portends the traumatic difficulties of the hero in "The Hero's Return") is communicated through the recurrence of the "gunshot" sound effect. The man's warm gesture coincides with the sense of satisfaction that results from the perfect authentic cadence which ends the verse, but this is quickly dispelled again by the chorus.

The piece remains in the key of the relative minor for the guitar solo which follows. During the first half of the solo the harmony travels back and forth between the chords of E minor and C major, and the F sharp which appears above each chord sustains the chorus' dissonance harmonically. The solo appears to be a reaction by the narrator to his apparent inability to "connect" (expressed in the chorus). Ushered in by the flailing organ chords, the greater portion of the solo consists of a repeated figure which is played each time at the same pitch level and articulated by playing a note on the first string while bending the second up to the same note.[11] The repetition of this figure creates an effect of compounding frustration, while Gilmour's apparently indeterminant slides on the low E string add a sense of uncontrollable anger. The solo ends on a B (the major seventh interval above the C root), and this dissonance does little to ease the exasperation generated during the solo.

The lyrics of the third verse once again criticise Christianity's concept of the after life. Waters comments on the idea of being comforted by the thought that lost loved ones have not truly died, while at the same time being fearfully discomforted by the idea that one needs to be redeemed in order personally to achieve this state due to unconditional guilt (original sin). The lyrics sustain the motif of coldness:

> By the cold and religious we were taken in hand
> Shown how to feel good and told to feel bad
> Tongue tied and terrified we learned how to pray
> Now our feelings run deep and cold as the clay
> And strung out behind us the banners and flags
> Of our possible pasts lie in tatters and rags.[12]

The verse seems to suggest that continuous concentration on "other worldliness" makes one less empathetic toward events in this world, particularly those of the past, as a result of one's attention being primarily directed toward the "future". The last two lines propose that such perception contributes to our inability properly to commemorate events like the war, and consequently its "banners and flags", the memorials of our freedom, are destroyed.

Unwilling to express satisfaction with such a conclusion, Waters postpones the perfect cadence which ends the verse in an attempt to deny the listener a sense of gratification. This fulfilment inevitably comes, nevertheless, inducing a violent bash of frustration as the tonic is repeated before the chorus returns for the last time. Ultimately the listener is left ungratified, however, as the piece fails to end on the tonic, and as Waters' voice fades into the distance leaving him and the listener isolated.

"One of the Few" continues this sense of isolation, which is created initially by the ominous ticking of an alarm clock and the sounds of someone sleeping. This state of desolation, however, belongs to the returning Hero of the following piece—an ex-airman (Royal Air Force-RAF) referred to by Waters as the Bomber *(Dallas 1987: 150)*. That he is an airman is also made apparent by the piece's title, derived from Winston Churchill's epochal speech before the House of Commons on 20 August 1940 which included the statement, "Never was so much owed by so many to so few". Shortly afterward the British government published a poster showing five airmen with this quotation printed above as an expression of the nation's gratitude to the RAF.[13]

The music of the piece creates an eerie sense of unease for the listener, who is permitted to observe the thoughts of the sleeping airman. In combination with the unusually low dynamic level, the dark broad tone of the low droning pedal point creates an air of foreboding. The contrast achieved between the keyboard's tone and the comparatively high thin tone of the guitar gives the latter a quality of brittleness, providing the listener with the impression that something or, more appropriately, somebody is going to "break". Because the melody of the piece avoids the second scale degree, its mode is ambiguous; because of the guitar's slide from the minor third scale degree to the tonic at the end of both phrases of the instrumental introduction, however, the ear is initially inclined to hear the mode as phrygian.[14] The phrygian mode, as the reader may recall from the discussion of "One of My Turns" from *The Wall*, was characterised by Robert Walser as "claustrophobic and unstable", and the brief hints given of this affective quality encourage the listener to suspect that these may be attributes of the sleeping airman.

The modal ambiguity, nevertheless, reflects the ambiguity of the airman's situation, and his frustration is communicated both through Waters' sharp enunciation of the "k" and "t" sounds which occur throughout the piece, and through the nature of the melodic phrases—both gradually descend to the tonic after the large initial upward leaps which signify a sense of striving:

> When you're one of the few to land on your feet
> What do you do to make ends meet?
> (Teach)

The lyric's initial image (and one that variedly is repeated throughout the album) is that of an airman who survived air battle and, unlike those who didn't return, landed on his feet. The second line has a double meaning: besides asking what type of profession he can adopt in order to secure his sustenance (foreshadowing his appearance as a classroom teacher in the next song), through the archaic meaning of the word "meet" (meaning suitable or proper), the airman also expresses his concern that the resolution which he and others fought for not be compromised. His instincts, as communicated through the subliminal pronouncement of "teach" (an effect achieved through the use of echo and the word's background position in the soundscape), tell him that he should attempt to educate others in order that they too will have a sense of the horrors that he experienced first hand. Aware of the general difficulty in identifying with a situation that one is removed from, however, the airman's next question is how to teach others of his experience:

> Make them mad, make them sad, make them add two and two,
> Or make them me, or make them you,

make them do what you want them to,
Make them laugh, make them cry, make them lay down and die?

Among the alternatives which the airman considers is that of appealing to people's emotions; making them "put two and two together"; changing them into those who are already sympathetic; or through amusing them. The sense of ambiguity established by the uncertainty of mode dissipates as the subtle background instrument finally provides the major second before the last line of the verse (confirming that the mode is actually aeolian). This sudden clarity anticipates that which the airman seems to arrive at by the end of the song: he suspects that, in general, people will be so removed from his situation that they will be unable to empathise with his knowledge of death and pain unless they personally are harmed. The frightening laugh, which precedes the verse's last line, demonstrates the maddening effect that the frustration of this suspicion creates in the mind of the Hero.

The transition to "The Hero's Return", a song documenting the character's difficulty in readjusting after his return from the war, recalls that between "Another Brick in the Wall (Part I)" and "The Happiest Days of Our Lives" from *The Wall*. The listener hears the sound of children playing, and the teacher's approaching footsteps are heard before the door opens on the classroom havoc which is portrayed by the sudden dynamic increase with which the piece begins.

The Hero's frustration is conveyed during the instrumental introduction of the song (a section forming the basis of the music for its first and third verses). This material is characterised by its strong quadruple rhythm which is articulated by the rhythm electric guitar, but a great deal of tension is created by the drums and the melody of the lead guitars (one a twelve-string acoustic and the other a distorted electric) because of their creation of eight beat phrases against the rhythm guitar's consistent four feel. The effect is further enhanced by the electric guitar's articulation of the melody occuring on off-beats, while the acoustic guitar plays on the beat. The cymbal rolls also portray the Hero's frustration; normally the tension created by such a gesture is released with a crash, but the cymbals are muted here at the height of their crescendo, consistently frustrating the listener's expectations.

The piece is predominantly in D mixolydian—a mode which, as a result of its flattened seventh note, contains the interval of a tritone between its third and seventh tones; the first two phrases of the melody, by outlining this interval, accent its harshness.[15] During the last phrase of each appearance of this introductory section, however, there is a shift to the ionian or major mode where the seventh is sharpened, thus creating a temporary sense of relief. This brief abatement, however, only succeeds in intensifying the dissonance which immediately returns at the beginning of each verse as the piece reverts to mixolydian.

The lyrics express the hero's inability to relate to his students. His frustration is again conveyed through Waters' use of consonance ("t"), rhyme ("about", "clout", "out"), and the electric guitar power chords which punctuate each line:

Jesus Jesus what's it all about?
Trying to clout these little ingrates into shape
When I was their age all the lights went out
There was no time to whine and mope about.

The narrator's estrangement is caused by the children's vast removal from his experience. Unlike them he was forced to grow up quickly due to the threat of air raids, and to him the things about which they complain seem trivial by comparison.

During the next verse the teacher's frustration gives way to desperation. The continually repeated descent from the tonic to the flattened seventh chord portrays his falling spirits, and the poignancy created by this process is intensified by the latter's major seventh dissonance. The rhythmic tension disappears, and the harshness of Waters' voice is reduced by the addition of a lower voice, the entry of which signals an internal visit to the hero's traumatizing past. His sad sense of alienation is communicated by the verse's melody which, like the chorus of "Your Possible Pasts", is formed from the claustrophobic Figure (A) from *The Wall*. Waters sustains the allusion to his previous album, further illustrating the reasons for this teacher's "dark sarcasm":

> And even now part of me flies over
> Dresden at angels one five
> Though they'll never fathom it behind my
> Sarcasm desperate memories lie.

The Bomber confesses to the listener of the horrors created by his participation in the 13-14 February 1945 Allied raids on the defenceless city of Dresden which, according to the "conservative" casualty estimations, resulted in the deaths of at least 135,000 civilians, a large percentage of which were refugees *(Bidinian 1976: 51)*. With part of him still flying at 1500 feet over the burning city, the Hero reveals his anxiety about what historians commonly refer to as "an unnecessary tragedy" *(Morrison 1982: 291)*. One imagines the Bomber's feelings to be similar to those expressed by the American Captain Laurence Critchell, quoted in Alexander McKee's *Dresden: The Devil's Tinderbox (1982)*:

This strange state of mind which fell upon us for a little while after the guns had been silenced was a vague obscenity. It was the faint, lingering aftertaste of having achieved something monstrous. We had unleashed powers beyond our comprehension. Entire countries lay in waste beneath our hands—and, in the doing of it, our hands were forever stained. It was of no avail to tell ourselves that what we had done was what we had to do, the only thing we could have done. It was enough to know that we had done it. We had turned the evil of our enemies back upon them a hundredfold, and, in so doing, something of our own integrity had been shattered, had been irrevocably lost....We who had fought this war could feel no pride. Victors and vanquished, all were one *(McKee 1982: 308)*.

In combination with the extreme reduction of texture and dynamic level, the return of the ticking alarm clock signifies that the teacher is back at home in bed once again. The lyrics of the verse make it clear that his difficulties are not just limited to his relationship with the students however:

> Sweetheart sweetheart are you fast asleep, good
> 'Cos that's the only time that I can really speak to you
> And there is something that I've locked away
> A memory that is too painful

To withstand the light of day.

The Hero's trauma also affects his ability to relate to his wife or lover. His internal torture is contrasted by the image of outer celebration as the return of the lower voice marks a return to his past once again:

> When we came back from the war the banners and
> Flags hung on everyone's door
> We danced and we sang in the street and
> The church bells rang.

Although the memory of the war has all but disappeared from the minds of the general public, the sense of desperation communicated during these lines demonstrate that, for the narrator, the anguish caused by the experience continues.

Through the acoustic guitar texture so typical of "the confessional", the Hero discloses through Waters' half whispered vocal the agonizing memory which he has been unable to share. Its halting effect is communicated as the sixteenth-note motion of the rhythm electric guitar gives way to the quarter note motion of the acoustic guitar—an effect which is magnified by the shift to triple time. The piece seems to modulate at this point to G major, giving the listener a false sense that resolution will occur. This impression is soon dispelled, however, with the sudden pang caused by each repetition of the tritone bass movement (G, G / F sharp, C). Even more strongly this time, his concealed inner woe profoundly contrasts the former images of celebration, and the sharpness of his pain is conveyed by Waters' piercing enunciation of the "t" in the last word of the first line:

> But burning in my heart
> The memory smoulders on
> Of the Gunner's dying words on the intercom.

By finishing on an E minor chord the piece ends in E aeolian, and the haunting affect this creates is enhanced by the discord created in the melody as it ends on the second scale degree (F sharp). This immediately precedes the chilling sound effects of the Gunner's dying words before he, seemingly unable to evacuate, is forced to go down with the plane.

The next song, "The Gunner's Dream", displays the power of the Hero's empathy. Waters surrealistically portrays the character imagining that he is the Gunner (one of the Few who was not fortunate enough to land on his feet), falling to his death and thinking of the dream for which he has offered his life. This effect is achieved firstly as the sound of the falling plane is transformed into the sound of cold winds, and secondly by the use of a pedal point (a device connoting stasis) in the piano throughout the first five bars of the piece. The sensation of stasis anticipates the slow motion image as the Bomber contemplates himself "floating" rather than falling to the ground:

> Floating down through the clouds
> Memories come rushing up to meet now
> But in the space between the heavens
> And the corner of some foreign field
> I had a dream
> I had a dream.

As he imagines himself descending, the Gunner's memories ascend towards him from his unknown grave located somewhere in "the corner of some foreign field"—an image that Waters has borrowed from the poem "The Soldier" by Rupert Brooke (1887-1915). For the Hero, the most important memory, however, is that which he imagines was the Gunner's last as he fell to the ground—the vision of a post war dream.

During this first verse, the combined timbres of the acoustic and electric pianos create a mixed sense of warmth and cold. The impression of warmth increases dramatically in the second verse with the addition of orchestral strings, but the imagery present in Waters' lyrics ("silver", "cold November air", "tolling bell") helps to sustain the initial mixture after the third line. The sudden warmth created by the string entry seems to reflect the imagined spirit of the Gunner looking down after a Remembrance Day ceremony attended by his mother and a character called Max, who together honour the Gunner's dream. The Gunner's spirit addresses Max—a character who would appear to be the Hero himself:

> Goodbye Max
> Goodbye Ma
> After the service when you're walking slowly to the car
> And the silver in her hair shines in the cold November air
> You hear the tolling bell
> And touch the silk in your lapel
>
> And as the tear drops rise to meet the comfort of the band[16]
> You take her frail hand
> And hold on to the dream.

The image of the Hero raising his hand to touch the poppy in his lapel recalls the album's front cover,which features a view of the front of his uniform where a portion of the poppy and his war medals are pictured.[17] As Max takes the hand of the Gunner's mother the earlier scene from "Your Possible Pasts" is evoked, where the ex-serviceman offers his hand to the prostitute; with the existing doubt of whether or not the prostitute ever took his hand, the listener is allowed to savour this image of warm human contact due to the delayed cadence which ends the verse. The beauty of this image is momentary though as a result of the disturbing aspect of the Hero's sudden outburst (portrayed by Waters' screaming vocal). This outburst would appear to be the result of his uncertainty as to the objective feasibility of the dream, and the consequent threat that the Gunner's sacrifice was a meaningless waste *(see below)*—an idea sparked by the sound effect of the tolling bell, which in his mind signifies the death of the post war dream.

The saxophone's solo becomes a personification of the Hero's conception of the "dream", as Waters' singing of the word is transformed into the sound of the instrument. The saxophone struggles to exert itself against the oppressive forces represented by the background instruments which appear simultaneous to its own entry.[18] The appearance of three fast ascending runs (at least an octave each time) throughout the solo help to communicate a sense of striving, and the last appearance of this gesture coincides with a reduction of these oppressive forces (achieved primarily through the departure of drums). The solo at this point gives the semblance of slowly dying, however, as a result of its short last phrases, its continually descending pitch, and owing to the listener's impression that the saxophonist has run out of breath. This idea is also supported by the cadencing of this section in the aeolian mode (natural minor), rather than the ionian (major)—a process which has been continually threatened throughout the piece.

In the next verse the Hero defines the Gunner's post war dream through Waters' calm sounding voice. His inner strife is revealed, nonetheless, by the disturbed shouting heard in the background of the recording mix. This intense frustration is also communicated to the listener by the incredible tension achieved through the verse's highly irregular poetic meter—the result of Waters' abundant use of alliteration, assonance, consonance and rhyme:

> A place to stay
> Enough to eat
> Somewhere old heroes shuffle safely down the street
> Where you can speak out loud
> About your doubts and fears
> And what's more no-one ever disappears
> You never hear their standard issue kicking in your door
> You can relax on both sides of the tracks
> And maniacs don't blow holes in bandsmen by remote control
> And everyone has recourse to the law
> And no-one kills the children anymore
> And no-one kills the children anymore.

The snare drum's depiction of the sound of someone kicking in the listener's door increases the sense of apprehension already apparent in the verse. It is also enhanced by the rhythmic acceleration of the lyric, beginning midway through the sixth line and ending with "standard issue" (the standard boots worn by police or soldiers). The reason for this uneasiness is the same as before: the Hero is inclined to believe that the dream is dead. This conclusion is reached through his allusion in the ninth line of the verse to the incident which took place 20 July 1982 in London; during a concert by the Royal Greenjackets Band under a Regent's Park bandstand, six army musicians were blown apart and twenty-eight people were injured when a bomb planted by the Irish Republican Party (IRA) exploded.

The Bomber's attempt to empathise with the Gunner proves to be too overwhelming. Suffering another outburst he reverts back to his tormented self again, and the substance of his lines recalls the former sound effects of ticking clocks earlier in the work:

> Night after night
> Going round and round my brain
> His dream is driving me insane.

With the Hero's long agonised scream fading into the background, Waters himself seems to narrate the rest of the piece (an interpretation partially made by the lyrics of the next song).[19] He encourages the listener to honour the Gunner's dream, in order that his sacrifice not be considered insignificant:

> In the corner of some foreign field
> The Gunner sleeps tonight
> What's done is done
> We cannot just write off his final scene
> Take heed of the dream

Take heed.

As the piece disappointedly ends in aeolian, the listener feels the Hero's alienation—the result of feelings of madness brought on by his attempt to honour the
dream in the face of everything which surrounds him. His unfulfillment is
expressed in the song's unresolved last chord, and in the sound effect of his
slow sad shuffle which was anticipated in the song's third verse.

"Paranoid Eyes", a song addressed to the saddened Hero, appears to feature
Waters in the role of narrator again. The song documents the Hero's reservations about facing the external world and attempts to comfort him. This sense
of consolation is portrayed through the snappy rhythm of the repeated piano
figure and the shift back to the ionian mode (major); the warmth provided by
the use of brass instruments and strings; and through Waters' voice, which is
treated with less reverb than usual, and appears slightly further in the front of
the mix giving the impression of closeness.

Waters' understanding of the Hero's plight is also expressed musically, however, suggesting that Waters can relate to his condition (foreshadowing his own
expression of similar feelings later in "The Final Cut"). A variety of musical
elements express a sense of discomfort or dissatisfaction. Among these are the
interruptions of the comfortable twelve-eight metre with a bar of six-eight
before the last line of each verse, and the insertion of a bar of nine-eight during the second line of the first verse. Another musical characteristic which
helps to achieve this effect is the delayed cadence which ends each verse (basically a highly embellished plagal cadence)—an effect which is augmented after
the last verse where the cadence is delayed even further than previously. In
addition to these elements is the piano's characteristic withholding of the thirds
of chords throughout the first half of every verse; it alternates between the
chords of G sus 4 and C sus 2, and these suspensions create tension and a desire
for resolution. Waters reacts against the frustrating external forces (represented
by this characteristic of the piano) by providing the thirds in the melody of the
vocal, attempting thereby to lessen the feelings of tension. Waters' tone is supportive and reassuring, but his own sense of frustration with the situation portrayed appears to be betrayed by the short, harsh quality of his internal rhyme
("lip", "slip", "grip") at the beginning of the first verse:

> Button your lip and don't let the shield slip
> Take a fresh grip on your bullet proof mask
> And if they try to break down your disguise with their questions
> You can hide hide hide
> Behind paranoid eyes.

Waters attempts to instill confidence in the traumatised Hero suggesting that he
can successfully conceal his anguish from others. Through the reappearance of
the tritone bass figure (G, D/F sharp, C—used initially by the Hero at the end
of "The Hero's Return" to express the pain of his haunting memory) after the
third line of the verse, Waters again displays his understanding.

The insincere prostitute from "Your Possible Pasts" can be heard proposition-
ing the Hero as he passes her by on his way "over the road":

> You put on your brave face and slip over the road for a jar
> Fixing your grin as you casually lean on the bar

> Laughing too loud at the rest of the world
> With the boys in the crowd
> You can hide hide hide
> Behind petrified eyes.

With the threat of exposing his true disenchantment with others by "laughing too loud", Waters reassures the Hero that he is able to avoid further alienation by concealing his torment. The instrumental interlude, which divides the second from the third verse, seems to convey that the Hero has successfully integrated himself into the bar room atmosphere. This is suggested by the confident strumming of the acoustic guitar, the section's undisturbed meter and the piano's free provision of the thirds of chords.

The third verse, however, imparts the Hero's general feeling of unfulfillment again. The verse expresses his frustrated expectations—the result of his society's misleading "success" stories, which are represented by the sound of the trumpet-calls that beckon members of the society to action. Sounding immediately after the first line of the verse, the trumpets (like the piano) sustain the G sus 4 chord and deny its desire for resolution:

> You believed in their stories of fame fortune and glory
> Now you're lost in a haze of alcohol soft middle age
> The pie in the sky turned out to be miles too high
> And you hide hide hide
> Behind brown and mild eyes.[20]

Similar to the symbol of the elevated pig from *Animals*, the "pie in the sky" or the capitalistic definition of "success" proves to be unattainable for the Hero, who is driven to alcohol by his disappointment. The mocking laugh that is heard preceding the last line of the song is complemented by the apparently ridiculing piano which light-heartedly provides the tonic chord's third at the end. This resolution only comes as the Hero is finally forced to withdraw; it is heard as he leaves the noisy bar. It is clear that this moment of resolve is still not his, though, as he is heard back in the street disturbingly shouting "Oi!".

The opening of the second half of the work also features this expletive, but this time it is followed by the sound of somebody angrily yelling "Get Your Filthy Hands Off My Desert". Following this the listener hears the sound of an exploding missile, which signals Waters' reference to some of his time's primary betrayers of the post war dream. He first refers to the former Soviet Union's invasion of Afghanistan in December 1979 under the direction of President Leonid Brezhnev, and to the Israeli invasion of Lebanon and subsequent encirclement of Beirut in June 1982 under the administration of President Menachem Begin.[21] Waters then refers to the 2 April 1982 Argentinean capture of the British ruled Falkland Islands (located in the South Atlantic 12,800 km / 8,000 miles away from the U.K.) through the leadership of the head of the ruling Junta, Lt. General Leopoldo Galtieri.

The invasion of the Islands was supposed by many to be an attempt by Galtieri to distract the Argentinean public from concerns about their worsening economy (which may in part be true), but the seizure of the Islands must also be considered a reaction to the U.K.'s failure to resolve the 17 year dispute over the sovereignty of what U.S. President Ronald Reagan called "that little ice cold bunch of land down there" *(Facts on File 1982: 317)*. Margaret Thatcher's response to the invasion was to dispatch a naval task force to the South Atlantic (a two week trip from the United Kingdom), where Britain announced that as of 30 April it would impose a total air and sea blockade around the Islands—it would intercept all ships and planes, civil and military, of all nations, within the previously announced 200-mile war zone:

> Brezhnev took Afghanistan
> And Begin took Beirut
> Galtieri took the Union Jack
> And Maggie over lunch one day
> Took a cruiser with all hands
> Apparently to make him give it back.

The latter half of the song refers to the 2 May sinking of the Argentine Cruiser *General Belgrano* by the submarine *HMS Conqueror*. With a loss of 368 Argentinean lives, this action began the conflict's heavy fighting.[22] The decision to sink the cruiser was purportedly made by Thatcher and members of her inner war cabinet while lunching at Chequers *(Dalyell 1983:20)*. It is seemingly the latter fact which prompts Waters to utilise a string quartet as the main performance force of the piece. Due to its being a genre largely developed and popularised by Franz Joseph Haydn (who for most of his life was a court composer), the string quartet retains its continued association with elitism. Its use intensifies the image of a monarch who sits being entertained while she carelessly controls the lives of others (an image immediately reinforced in "The Fletcher Memorial Home" through the condemnation of "incurable tyrants and kings").

The sinking of the Argentine cruiser carried further implications however:

> The *Belgrano*...was torpedoed when it was about 35 miles (56 kilometers) outside the 200-mile (320 kilometer) war zone Britain had declared around the Falklands. British officials claimed that the cruiser, which was accompanied by two destroyers, was sunk because it posed a serious threat to British ships. Nevertheless, the sinking quickly aroused controversy because of the heavy loss of life and the fact that the ship had been outside the 200-mile war zone. *(Facts on File 1982: 317)*

Waters' use of the word "apparently" in the last line of the song, reflects the growing suspicion among many that the decision to sink the Argentine Cruiser was made for political rather than military reasons. This was suspected by Tam Dalyell, a Labour Party shadow minister who was dismissed from his position on the front bench after opposing his party's support of the Conservatives' decision of sending the task force in the first place. After the conflict was over (mid June), Dalyell called for an investigation into the *Belgrano* sinking after he was able to reveal that the original Government account of the circumstances surrounding the sinking of the cruiser was almost entirely false *(see Dalyell 1983)*. It was Dalyell's belief that Thatcher should possibly be charged with a war crime, because of his suspicion that she had had full knowledge of a Peruvian diplomatic settlement (supposedly acceptable to Galtieri, and one which the world would have expected her to accept) when she ordered that the cruiser be sunk:

> The fusing of personal vanity and political calculation can lead to dreadful results. A tribunal might well take the view that electoral considera-

tions in Britain were not the paramount reason why the Prime Minister ordered the sinking of the *Belgrano*. It might perceive that it had even more to do with the leadership of the Conservative Party, because who doubts that in the absence of a scrap...and military victory *per se*, the return of the fleet would have raised all sorts of doubt about the wisdom of dispatching the task force in the first place. *(Dalyell 1983: 23-24)*

Dalyell's efforts prompted an investigation by the House of Commons Select Committee on Foreign Affairs which consisted of seven Conservative Party members and four members of the Labour Party.[23] Due to what were undoubtedly partisan biases, the committee split with the Conservatives producing one report and the Labour Party members another—the former becoming the Majority Report and the latter the Minority Report, which was rejected by the committee by six votes to four (the committee chairman, Sir Anthony Kershaw did not vote). As quoted in the 25 July 1985 edition of *The Times*, the Minority Report (unlike that of the Majority) did not exonerate Thatcher's government:

'The view of the Labour minority is that the possibility of a link between the Peruvian initiative and the sinking of the Belgrano is still an open question.'

It is one of the many matters which, they insist, a fresh parliamentary inquiry should consider ([1]).

Because the Minority Report was rejected by the committee, there has never been any further inquiry. As the additional evidence available to the Committee has never been made public (supposedly for the protection of military intelligence), the truth of the matter is unknown.[24]

Nevertheless the Falklands conflict instilled an intense patriotism in England and the U.K.'s military victory, as Lawrence Freedman notes, appeared to ensure the future of Thatcher's government:

In the aftermath of the 1983 general election it was widely believed that the 'Falklands factor' had been the key to the Conservative Party's re-election. Prior to the war dissatisfaction with Mrs. Thatcher's administration had been running high. By the end of the conflict it enjoyed substantial popular support and it never again trailed in the polls. *(Freedman 1988: 100)*

It is clear, however, that the resort to arms did absolutely nothing to solve the dispute between the two nations, which, of course, poses the threat of future armed conflicts over the Islands—a fact which was made apparent in the 1989 Argentine Presidential elections through the statements of the subsequent President Carlos Saul Menem. As Facts on File records:

In one of the most controversial statements of the campaign, Menem had implied that he would attempt to conquer the British-ruled Falkland Islands (Malvinas) militarily. 'I don't know how much blood we will have to shed, but our territory will return to the Argentine people', he had said. *(Facts on File 1989)*

The danger of a recurrence of hostilities is sure to increase with time, especially as the U.K. continues to refuse to discuss the issue (talks between the two countries in 1993 excluded any discussion of sovereignty).

By 1992 the total expenditure on the War, on Fortress Falklands and on the economic aid extended to the Islands since 1982 would cost British taxpayers in excess of £5 billion *(Dillon 1989: 237)*. This figure becomes even more staggering when it is considered that the Islands are inhabited by approximately 1,800 people. More disturbing, however, was the cost in human life—on both sides, approximately 1,000 men were killed and 2,000 injured or maimed. But, as Michael Bilton suggests, the effects of the war do not stop there:

> Rather than decreasing, the casualties from the Falklands War are actually increasing. Psychiatrists who travelled with the Task Force began treating soldiers and sailors even before the landings at San Carlos. Battle stress was a significant feature among the casualties in the South Atlantic: forty out of the 770 were judged to have psychiatric problems of one kind or another. As is shown in this book, the symptoms of stress due to acute battle reaction can vary from the sailor who, in his own words, put his wife and kids through hell for eighteen months after returning home, to the Royal Marine who twice tried to kill himself after surviving the bombing of *Sir Galahad* at Fitzroy in which forty-eight soldiers and crewmen were killed....Now military and civilian psychiatrists are dealing with increasing numbers of men from the Falklands campaign suffering from the effects of delayed-stress syndrome....Their patients are both officers and other ranks. The Royal Naval Hospital in Portsmouth has so far treated 500 of these cases, and they expect to receive, on average, one a week for the next ten to fifteen years. Many of their patients have not been able to talk about their experiences, believing that their loved ones—families, parents and friends—just wouldn't understand what they had been through. *(Bilton and Kosminsky 1989: 4)*

Bilton's last statement recalls the agony of the returned Hero. Waters' reaction to the conflict, which appears to have achieved nothing except Margaret Thatcher's political success, is expressed in the next piece.[25]

Waters attempts to sustain the element of mockery in the lyrics of "The Fletcher Memorial Home", but the seriousness of his dismay is soon revealed. The piece, taking its departure from the sense of childishness conveyed in the previous song's title, suggests building a type of communal playpen for those political leaders who act like "overgrown infants":

> Take all your overgrown infants away somewhere
> And build them a home, a little place of their own
> The Fletcher Memorial
> Home for incurable tyrants and kings.

The desperation which is inherent in Waters' derision is made apparent through a number of musical elements, the most obvious of which is the employment of his high vocal register. In addition to the minor 9th dissonance (performed as a harmonic in the violins) which appears above the chord at the end of the first line, tension is also achieved through Waters' borrowing of the augmented chord (III) from the parallel minor (occurring on the word "place"). These musical depictions of anxiety prepare the listener for the solemn notion that this "playpen" is to be a memorial to the composer's lost father ("Fletcher" having been his middle name). They are reinforced both through the unison doubling of Waters' voice during the last two lines, and through his refusal to cadence on the tonic at the end of the verse (instead he does so on the sub-dominant).

The next verse conveys Waters' impression of the self-absorption of these politicians—a sentiment shared by Tam Dalyell who suggests that, during the Falklands conflict, Margaret Thatcher "gave the clear impression of being highly elated by her presence on the centre of the world stage, involved in a cause which she had almost instantly come to see in stark black and white terms" *(Dalyell 1982: 73)*. Waters suggests that in "The Fletcher Memorial Home", this vanity can be fuelled by the presence of "closed circuit T.V." so that the rest of the population need not watch:

> And they can appear to themselves every day
> On closed circuit T.V.
> To make sure they're still real
> It's the only connection they feel.

The last line of the verse conveys a sense of anger and frustration which is communicated by its cadencing in the natural minor (aeolian), and also through Waters' leap up to the highest tone of the song's melody—an effect which is combined with his short, accented articulation of the word "feel". The line asserts that these "incurable tyrants" are unable to empathise with anybody but themselves. Again Waters' suspicion is supported by Dalyell who, when referring to his initial hesitation about dispatching the Falklands task force, states:

> During my National Service, I had been tank crew with the Scots Greys in the British Army of the Rhine. Though never involved in actual fighting, 1950-52 was the time of the Korean War, and the possibility of combat was less than a far-fetched nightmare. Indeed, many of those with whom I did my basic training at Catterick and Aldershot, were sent to Korea. Some of them, among those who joined the Eighth King's Royal Irish Hussars, were badly shot up and never returned. Firing live ammunition and inhaling all the fumes in the turret of a Centurion tank was at least an experience which has made me feel that politicians should think twice before committing the members of their armed forces to military operations. It has seemed to me that, among leading politicians, those who were least enthusiastic in endorsing military action were precisely those who had 'a good war' in 1939-45—for example, Carrington, Healey, Heath, Pym and Whitelaw. With some exceptions, such as John Silkin, who had been a naval officer in dangerous waters in World War II, those who most vehemently endorsed the task force were those who had never put on uniform, for whatever reason. I could barely control a smouldering anger at Mrs Thatcher's hawkish stance when I reflected that she had not only not been in the services but that Grantham, where she was brought up, had never been bombed. In particular, it stuck in my gullet every time she caringly referred to 'our boys' in the South Atlantic. *(Dalyell 1982: 29)*

During the next section of the song, Waters calmly conducts a mock procession of some of the Home's inhabitants; the combined affect of musical events is an unsettling one however. Among the characteristics that contribute to this effect are the initial ambiguity of the E sus 2 chord which begins the section, combined with the quick sharp embellishment from the minor third down to the dissonant second by the flutes; the piano's accented and detached right hand chords in combination with its low dark left hand octaves; the repeated figure in the strings which emphasises the major seventh dissonance above the pedal point on C; and the prolonged pedal point itself whose connotation of stasis foreshadows the disturbing thought that these people will never leave the Home. Waters plays the master of ceremonies:

> "Ladies and Gentlemen, please welcome Reagan and Haig,
> Mr. Begin and friend, Mrs. Thatcher and Paisley,
> Mr. Brezhnev and party,
> The ghost of McCarthy
> And the memories of Nixon,
> And now adding colour a group of anonymous Latin
> American meat packing glitterati".[26]

The element of jest made in the last two lines is underlined by a hint of pathos as the section ends with the tritone bass figure (G, D / F sharp, C), which was used to communicate the grief caused by the Hero's traumatic memory. This pathos signals the return of Waters' sense of desperation as he returns to his high register to sing, "Did they expect us to treat them with any respect?". As the tritone figure returns to form the basis of the next three lines, both the memory of the Gunner's death and that of Eric Fletcher Waters is invoked. In combination with the reduction of musical forces, the decrease in dynamic level and Waters' employment of his lower vocal register, the lines take on a sombre quality:

> They can polish their medals and sharpen their smiles,
> And amuse themselves playing games for awhile
> Boom boom, bang bang, lie down you're dead.

Waters envisions a scenario where the political leaders will kill one another off rather than innocent people. A sense of mournful longing still lingers (throughout the first two utterances of the tritone figure), nonetheless, as a result of the sustained D in the violins—the note begs for resolution each time during the last chord (C major) of the figure. The last line continues this dissatisfaction by cadencing in the natural minor, and this effect becomes even more pronounced through the piano's E sus 2 chord (the vocal melody also disturbingly ends on the second of the chord).

The guitar solo which follows seems to be a passionate display of lament, as suggested by its slow short phrases and David Gilmour's expressive use of vibrato. This sense is also conveyed by the seemingly resigning, indeterminant string slides which seem to threaten collapse with each appearance, and strongly suggested by the dissonance caused by Gilmour's sustaining the major seventh (B) over the C MA 7 chord. Most of the solo is played by bending the strings upward, and the resultant impression of longing would appear to reflect a desire to alter the past. This is communicated even more strongly in the latter part of the solo where the tritone bass figure reappears, again conjuring the memory of the dead. With each appearance of the figure a harmony guitar part is added, compounding the sense of longing. An element of disturbance takes place at the end of the solo; once again this is partly because it cadences in the natural minor, but even more so the result of the guitar's upper embellishment which forms the interval of a tritone (C—F sharp). This quality of unease anticipates the song's disturbing conclusion *(see below)*.

The song returns to the major mode for the last verse, but Waters' vocal expresses the desperation which was initially apparent. He illustrates his recognition that the inmates of "The Fletcher Memorial Home" must be supervised by a "cold glass eye"—one that can neither see nor shed tears:

> Safe in the permanent gaze of a cold glass eye
> With their favourite toys
> They'll be good girls and boys
> In the Fletcher Memorial Home for colonial
> Wasters of life and limb.[27]

Through the stress applied to the word "wasters", Waters momentarily communicates a sense of intense anger. But this immediately subsides with the return of the tritone bass figure and the song's last lines:

> Is everyone in?
> Are you having a nice time?
> Now the final solution can be applied.

Heard immediately after the second line is the sound of a pained voice in the background yelling "Did they?" (implying the question "Did they have a nice time wasting the lives of others?"). The line ends with the chord C add 9—the ninth on top again begs for resolution—and, with the appearance of the last line, it is clear that this resolution can only come through retribution. With the phrase "final solution", Waters again alludes to the mass extermination of Jews in the Second World War. The song ends with the suggestion that this is the treatment that these "wasters of life and limb" should suffer in exchange for their wrongdoings. The haunting nature of this solution is conveyed by the reappearance of the aeolian cadence, and by the melody's dissonant second over the song's last chord.

This disturbance is quickly dispelled in "Southampton Dock" by the sounds of seagulls, the bright sound of the solo acoustic guitar (with capo), and by Waters' calm narrative which is located closer to the front of the mix and not treated with reverb—qualities which give it an air of intimacy. The lyrics of the song document the general feeling of sobriety (also conveyed by the drone of the deep nasal voices heard during the fourth and fifth lines) that was felt at the end of the war in 1945 because of the vast numbers of people who did not return:

> They disembarked in '45
> And no one spoke and no one smiled
> There were too many spaces in the line
> And gathered at the cenotaph
> All agreed with hand on heart
> To sheath the sacrificial knives.

With the knowledge of the heavy cost of war in terms of human life fresh in their minds, the English honoured its lost heroes by solemnly vowing to put an end to any further human sacrifices. The truth of this statement is immediately challenged, however, by the return of the background voice which again yells "Did they?". This exclamation precedes the contrast that is achieved between the past and present (in the first and second verses consecutively) with the words "but now", which create a jolting effect as a result of their treatment with reverb.

The second verse recounts the 8 April 1982 departure of a cruise ship from

Southampton dock, which contained 3,000 troops destined for the conflict in the South Atlantic. The sound of the cruiser is heard as a woman, apparently Margaret Thatcher, stands on the dock waving goodbye to the troops:

> She stands upon Southampton Dock
> With her handkerchief
> And her summer frock clings
> To her wet body in the rain
> In quiet desperation knuckles
> White upon the slippery reins
> She bravely waves the boys goodbye again.

Desperately attempting to hold on to the "slippery reins of power or state",[28] Thatcher cleverly suppresses her intense concern for the saving of her political skin. Her bravery, quite appropriate for one so safely "out of range", suspiciously coincides with the encouragement which she gave to the nationally televised, ignorantly patriotic display which accompanied the cruiser's departure. Her "quiet desperation" is matched by that of Waters, whose agitated high voice sings behind the one that calmly narrates in the last three lines. This concealment of his genuine feelings of intense anger, along with bringing a slight sense of irony to the initial impression of intimacy, anticipates "The Final Cut" *(see below)*. The cadence that ends the first section of the song repeats a process which occurred at the beginning of the album during the line "What happened to the post war dream?" (the sub-dominant is altered to the minor sub-dominant before it ends on the tonic). As a consequence, this question again arises in conjunction with the sense of poignancy which accompanies it.

Waters' voice regains its usual passionate quality with the piano's reappearance, and the religious connotations of its gospel-style playing signals a return of focus back to the death of the post war dream. The men who fought for this dream are seemingly stabbed in the back with the same knife with which they were sacrificed:

> And still the dark stain spreads between
> Their shoulder blades
> A mute reminder of the poppy fields and graves
> And when the fight was over
> We spent what they had made
> But in the bottom of our hearts
> We felt the final cut.

Besides acknowledging our guilt for killing the post war dream, the fifth line cleverly alludes to Waters' observation quoted at the beginning of the chapter: that our actions always seem to be determined by economics. The line implies that we cashed in or benefited from the peace and freedom which was earned for us by them. This realisation brings with it a sharp pang of guilt and, consequently, *we* feel "the final cut" of the "sacrificial knife"—the harshness of which is conveyed through Waters' articulation of the "t" in the word "cut". The feeling of disappointment that the song creates is reinforced by the ii - I cadence with which it ends (a V - I cadence would have ensured a feeling of contentedness).

"The Final Cut" documents the composer's own reaction to the pain caused by this guilt, and by that of the various other frustrations formerly presented in the work. That he is hesitant to share the seriousness of these feelings is communicated first as the listener hears him shudder, and then by the piano's slight hesitation before the vocal entry—an effect which conveys a sense of not wanting the song to begin. This inhibition is also apparent throughout the piano's initial chord progression. Reluctant to leave the comfort of the tonic chord (F major), the piano's right hand chord does not follow the left hand's movement to the dominant until the third beat of the second bar. The third measure's movement to the sub-dominant also demonstrates this unwillingness; the piano retains the pedal tone (C) in the top voice (present throughout the entire first half of the verse) forming the chord B flat add 9. This device provides the impression of an attempt to hang on to the haven represented by the tonic.

The lyrics attest to the composer's unhappiness:

> Through the fish eyed lens of tear stained eyes
> I can barely define the shape of this moment in time
> And far from flying high in clear blue skies
> I'm spiralling down to the hole in the ground where I hide.

Besides effectively describing the kaleidoscopic quality of vision that anyone experiences looking through tears, the image of the "fish eyed lens" (a very wide-angle lens) functions as a testament to the expansive depth of Waters' own perception, or power of empathy. It is exactly this intense ability to empathise, though, which causes both his unhappiness and his inability to demarcate his own position in the present. The image of "spiralling down" in the last line reveals that his thoughts are still in part with the traumatised Hero who, imagining that he was the betrayed Gunner, "floated down" to his location in "the corner of some foreign field". Sharing the Hero's desire to honour the dream, Waters also shares his sense of alienation, because of the world's apparent refusal to attempt to do likewise. Like the Hero, Waters acknowledges that he is also inclined to "hide".

The second section of the verse illustrates his desire to dissolve the barricades which he has found it necessary to erect. A sense of increased confidence is conveyed with the full band's entry on the push-beat, as he invites an outsider to penetrate his defences:

> If you negotiate the mine field in the drive
> And beat the dogs and cheat the cold electronic eyes
> And if you make it past the shotguns in the hall
> Dial the combination, open the priesthole
> And if I'm in I'll tell you what's behind the wall.

As listeners make it "past the shotgun", the disappearance of the full drum kit's confident pulse, in combination with the deceptive cadence (V—vi), leads them to suspect that the outsider's mission may not be accomplished. As the chord progression rests on G min 7 (ii) throughout the fourth line and the first half of the fifth (recalling the dissatisfying conclusion to "Southampton Dock"), this sense of suspense is sustained. Unable to finish the fifth line of the lyric, Waters displays his fear that admission of the outsider will prove to be devastating, as illustrated by the sound of a shotgun blast and the celebratory outburst of the shooter.

Before the tonic returns, at any rate, the dominant is heard in the bass, signifying that the outsider has been successful in penetrating the sophisticated defence system. Waters proceeds to confess his insecurities, but their painful nature is communicated both by his passionate singing and by the figure which is performed by the accompanying strings. The figure is characterised by its treatment of seconds throughout the entire chord progression which ensues:

The dissonance that characterises the appearance of the seconds in each chord continually promises to be appeased as the non-chord tones resolve to chord tones.[29] This process is repeated throughout the entire section, however, demonstrating his ongoing disquietude. The lyrics disclose a lack of confidence with women which is extended to his mate, and he suffers doubts about whether or not she actually expresses her true feelings to him:

> There's a kid who had a big hallucination
> Making love to girls in magazines
> He wonders if you're sleeping with your new found faith
> Could anybody love him
> Or is it just a crazy dream.

The music returns to that which began the piece and the melody is sung to the syllable "Ah", a syllable which often in poetry (particularly that of the Romantics) is an expression of intense pining as it is here.

The same effect is conveyed musically by the use of appogiaturas during the beginning of the next verse. Through the return of the sound of the alarm clock and the reduction of texture, Waters' struggle is linked to that of the Hero who was also fearful of fully exposing himself to his mate:

> And if I show you my dark side
> Will you still hold me tonight?
> And if I open my heart to you
> And show you my weak side
> What would you do?

Wondering how the addressee will react if he allows her to know him fully, Waters' anxiety is again expressed by singing in his high register. Among other things, he wonders if she would betray him to one of the leading American rock music magazines for monetary benefit:

> Would you sell your story to Rolling Stone?
> Would you take the children away
> And leave me alone?

And smile in reassurance
As you whisper down the phone?
Would you send me packing
Or would you take me home?

The last line of the lyric contrasts with all the previous lines in its expression of hope, and this is reflected in the satisfaction achieved through the reappearance of the perfect (V—I) cadence. This sense of contentment is fleeting, nonetheless, as a result of the chromatic dissonance which appears in Waters' vocal (on the word "me"), and because of the return of the unfulfilling figure performed by the strings. It is these feelings of unfulfillment which seemingly are reacted against in the following guitar solo.

In the last section of the song the composer fully exposes the extent of his vulnerability and pain:

> Thought I oughta bare my naked feelings
> Thought I oughta tear the curtain down
> I held the blade in trembling hands
> Prepared to make it but just then the phone rang
> I never had the nerve to make the final cut.

Waters shares the knowledge about an attempt permanently to end the feelings of disquietude. For the first time in the song, this section of music does not articulate the dominant before it returns to the tonic; instead the bass guitar slides up to the mediant (III) before the verse ends. This effect, in combination with the return of both the dissonant figure (performed this time by strings and harp) and the chord progression which began the piece, signifies the continuation of his feelings of distress. The voice that is heard on the other end of the phone is oblivious to his plight. Its eruption into laughter parallels the contrast between the gentle timbre of the harp and the mechanical timbre of the organ swell into which it is altered at the beginning of the next piece.

Unlike any other track on the album, "Not Now John" is a boisterous heavy rocker which satirizes not only the British, but all Western societies.[30] The song dismisses the quest for empathy which characterised the rest of the work saying "Fuck all that!", and suggests that there is no time to think about such things. Instead, it returns to the economic concerns alluded to at the beginning of the album. David Gilmour sings the lead in an unsympathetic rough voice and for the first time on the album, the lead voice has the support of the masses as conveyed by the chorus of background singers:

> Fuck all that we've got to get on with these
> Got to compete with the wily Japanese
> There's too many home fires burning
> And not enough trees
> So fuck all that
> We've got to get on with these.

The singer, only concerned about competing with the Japanese, complains about the vast quantity of unemployed people (there are not enough trees to fuel all of their fireplaces).

In combination with the sound effects of machinery and the incessant delivery of the text from all directions of the speaker spectrum, the lyrics of the next section portray the strain of the technological and mechanistic capitalist society. The static quality of this lifestyle is conveyed by the vamp on one chord:

> Can't stop lose job mind gone silicon
> What bomb? get away pay day make hay
> Breakdown need fix big six
> Clickity click hold on oh no brrrrrring bingo!

Too busy to worry about the "bomb", the singers of this song are more concerned with the rewards reaped through their labours—vacations ("get away") and "pay day"—regardless of the "breakdowns" they inevitably will suffer. Appropriately, everyone yells "bingo" at the end of the stressful delivery of words.[31]

In the next portion of the song, Waters acknowledges that he too has been susceptible to becoming a slave of the capitalist economic machine. The piece hearkens back to "One of the Few", where he and the Hero formerly expressed a concern with educating people. By the end of the first line, however, art has been transformed into money-making entertainment:

> Make 'em laugh, make 'em cry, make 'em dance in the aisles,
> Make 'em pay, make 'em stay, make 'em feel ok.

In order to ensure that consumers will attend future concerts, they must be provided with a good time. This sentiment also provides the focus of the next verse, where Hollywood is the "pot of gold" which lies "at the end of the rainbow":

> Not nah John
> We've got to get on with the film show
> Hollywood waits at the end of the rainbow
> Who cares what it's about
> As long as the kids go
> So not now John we've got to get on with the show.

Although "John" probably has something meaningful to say, the narrator merely brushes him off.

Gilmour effectively portrays the narrator through his guitar solo, which is characterised by its flashiness instead of the usual melodic quality with which he plays. Launched by a power chord, the solo seems to convey that the narrator is more interested in asserting rather than expressing himself. Again he has the support of the background singers who, in the second half of the solo, urge him on as he begins to play an ascending passage. When the display commences, they again endorse him saying "got to get on".

The next two sections of lyric also show the narrator abruptly dismissing "John". The first illustrates him being distracted by his work, but the second seemingly illustrates the same behaviour extended at home:

> Hang on John
> We've got to get on with this
> I don't know what it is
> But it fits on here like.....
> Come at the end of the shift
> We'll go and get pissed
> But not now John

I've got to get on with this.

Hold on John
I think there's something good on
I used to read books but.....
It could be the news
Or some other amusement
Could be reusable shows.

Both sections exemplify the narrator's ignorance; rather than participating in meaningful exchange, he is inclined to "get pissed" or watch television. Too entranced by the action on the screen, he is unable to explain why he no longer reads books.

During the last verse the sense of haste is increased as the main riff is immediately repeated with every passing line. What were originally economic interests are now transformed into military ones, as the narrator demonstrates his intense patriotism and desire to assert his country's power:

Fuck all that we've got to get on with these
Got to compete with the wily Japanese
No need to worry about the Vietnamese
Got to bring the Russian bear to his knees
Well, maybe not the Russian bear

Maybe the Swedes[32]
We showed Argentina
Now let's go and show these
Make us feel tough
And wouldn't Maggie be pleased
Nah nah nah nah nah nah!

S'cusi dove il bar
Se para collo pou eine toe bar
S'il vous plait ou est le bar
Oi' where's the fucking bar John!

The song ends with the narrator exhibiting sophistication through his impressive multilingual display. The nature of this character carries solemn implications, however, in light of the statistics represented by polls conducted after the end of the Falklands conflict: with the Islands regained, satisfaction with the Government's handling of the crisis had reached 84 per cent *(Freedman 1988: 95)*.

Again Tam Dalyell's comments are enlightening:

...I came to the conclusion that Argentina's claims were far stronger than had been represented by Britain. However, when I tried to interest the press in my discoveries, only *The Times'* 'Diary' responded. From that brief mention arose a contact which was to confirm my doubts as to Britain's claim. It came from Dr. Peter Beck, an historian and international relations specialist, who had been researching into the Falklands dispute for several years....Dr. Beck had himself written a study indicating the uncertainty in the Foreign Office from 1910 onwards, which had been bought by *The Sunday Times*, but not published by them until after the British had retaken the Falklands—for patriotic reasons, the editor maintained.[33] *(Dalyell 1982: 25)*

The implication of Dalyell's criticism appeared again three years later in the Minority Report of the Foreign Affairs Committee:

> The overall conduct of the war, as we see it, has undermined confidence in the ability of this British Government to manage crises in the nuclear age when the calibre of leadership in the heat of a crisis should be demonstrated by a balance of diplomatic and military activity and not by over-readiness to press the red button. Nor do we believe that matters relating to the competing demands of secrecy and open government, of ministerial accountability to Parliament, can be solved by turning up the volume of the National Anthem. *(London: HMSO, 22 July 1985, cxvi Par 9.6)*

Besides pinpointing the troubling topic of nationalism, the Report raises concern about the issue of nuclear weapons—a concern which also provides the focus for the next piece.

As "Not Now John" fades away, the listener withdraws from the hammering chaos[34] into the peaceful calm of "Two Suns in the Sunset"—a contrast achieved primarily through the appearance of acoustic guitar, and by the reduction in dynamics and texture which accompanies it. The sounds of cars whizzing by, in combination with the song's first line, denote that the narrator of this song is driving.[35] The sense of serenity provided by the sunset's picturesque beauty is disturbed, nevertheless, by his disturbing premonitions:

> In my rear view mirror the sun is going down
> Sinking behind bridges in the road
> And I think of all the good things
> That we have left undone
> And I suffer premonitions
> Confirm suspicions
> Of the holocaust to come.

The disturbing idea of the possibility of mass destruction as a result of nuclear war is ushered in by Waters' thoughts about humanity's continued demonstration of its inability to utilise its potential for good. The advent of his premonitions coincides both with the first appearance of minor chords in the song, and with the departure of the comfortable riding rhythm of the drums. The sense of disturbance which is created is already anticipated, however, by the metric disruptions that occur. The straight four feel of the verse is constantly interrupted by the appearance of a fragment of the song's opening riff. These disruptions take place after the first and second lines are sung (a bar of seven-eight is inserted), and during the singing of the fourth (a bar of three eight is inserted).

This disturbing threat of the use of nuclear weapons was quite real at the time, as Paul Rogers remarks in reference to the Falklands conflict:

> Several different sources, in Government, in the Ministry of Defence and even from within the Polaris fleet, have informed Tam Dalyell and others that a Polaris missile submarine *was* ordered on patrol in the South Atlantic within missile range of Argentina during the Falklands War. *(Dalyell 1986: 19)*

If, in fact, this was the case then the implications discolour Britain's actions even further in light of Dalyell's observations:

> Britain (though not Argentina) had signed Protocol One of the Treaty of

Tlatelolco under which nuclear weapons were not to be used in the
South Atlantic. Moreover, the British Foreign Office had boasted that it
led the way in proclaiming that our country would never threaten to use,
let alone use nuclear weapons against a non-nuclear power. *(Dalyell
1987: 18)*

As Dalyell records, in any event, the Government has continually refused to
answer questions related to this issue, "taking sanctuary in the 'need for secrecy'" *(Dalyell 1987: 20)*.

The second verse of the song continues to imagine the scenario of a nuclear
holocaust, the lyrics portraying the image of someone "pushing the red button"
in a sudden fit of anger. Waters imagines driving toward what he thinks is the
setting sun, but suddenly remembering that he is driving east:

> The rusty wire that holds the cork
> That keeps the anger in
> Gives way
> And suddenly it's day again
> The sun is in the east
> Even though the day is done
> Two suns in the sunset
> Hmmmmmmmmmmmm
> Could be the human race is run.

The symbolic connotation of the day's end acquires special significance as
Waters contemplates the possibility of the human race being a thing of the past.

The middle section of the piece departs from Waters' calm narration. It features
sharp rhythmic shots and the alarming entry of a distorted guitar. Appropriately
the lyrics also feature a departure from the initial mode of the interior monologue to that of directly addressing the listener. Waters compares the remaining
brief moments to those one would have before experiencing a fatal traffic acci-
dent:

> Like the moment when the brakes lock
> And you slide toward the big truck
> You stretch the frozen moments with your fear
> And you'll never hear their voices
> And you'll never see their faces
> You have no recourse to the law anymore.

As demonstrated by the recorded sound effects, Waters invites listeners fully to
contemplate the situation by truly feeling what it might be like when they will
never again have the opportunity of contact with loved ones. Alluding to "The
Gunner's Dream" and the idea of being thankful that "everyone has recourse to
the law", Waters terrorises the listener with his observation that "the law" is
now superfluous because it no longer offers them protection.

The third verse reverts back to an interior monologue, and the composer again
adopts his calm narration of events:

> And as the windshield melts
> And my tears evaporate
> Leaving only charcoal to defend
> Finally I understand
> The feelings of the Few

Ashes and diamonds
Foe and friend
We were all equal in the end.

As portrayed through the passionate outburst in his voice, Waters conveys that he is finally *fully* able to understand the feelings of the returned RAF Hero (one of the "Few") and, in his own words, "all the other war casualties" *(Dallas 1987: 150)*. By imagining his own last remaining moments in the wake of a total nuclear holocaust, he is truly able to recognise the gift of human life and the devastating idea of its meaningless waste: to recall the words of the American, Captain Laurence Critchell, such senseless waste "shatters the integrity" of us all. And in the aftermath of the Final War—a war devoid of survivors—when all of our remains are eventually compacted into diamonds, the disputes that existed between "foe and friend" will be tragically redundant as we will all inevitably be truly equal.

The reason for Waters' placid tone throughout most of the song becomes clear. We can't continuously live in fear of such an occurrence, yet we should not forget its possibility. Nor should we forget those who died that we might live. As cars continue to whiz by him at the end of the song, it is clear that life goes on. The return of the main riff and its fading into perpetuity demonstrates that all we can do is strive to be happy—savouring the times of satisfaction represented by the riff's arrival at the tonic (D major), and braving those times of dissatisfaction where it returns to the sub-dominant (G major). Its awkward nine-eight metre seemingly reflects this inevitable discomfort which the human condition poses.

As the saxophone—the aural representation of the Gunner's post war dream—makes its reappearance, Waters encourages listeners to "hold on to the dream", even in the face of the bad news which is again heard on the radio as the piece fades out. This is, of course, a lesson that needs to be taught again and again both to present and future generations, a concept conveyed with the hearing of tomorrow's inclement weather: the news of scattered showers re-directs listeners back to the beginning of the album where the sound of car tires revealed that it either was, or had been, raining.

It is tempting to return to the symbolism that Waters employed on *The Dark Side of the Moon*: with the closing of the album the sun is still in the process of setting as he continues to make his way home. The unobstructed sun brilliantly shines its truth on his "moment of clarity" now, as he continues "holding on to the dream". As the world presented itself to Waters in the early 1980s, it did appear that this dream was, indeed, dead. *The Final Cut* remains his testament to its resurrection.

APPENDIX: Interview With Roger Waters

(Transcript of a conversation between
Phil Rose [PR] and Roger Waters [RW]).

[PR] I'm interested in your literary and poetic influences.

[RW] I suppose...I'm not a huge reader of prose, though I have read a number of novels in my life. I suppose the important ones, when I was an adolescent, would fall into two groups—one being a group of science fiction writers of whom, I suppose, the ones that were most important to me would have been Asimov, Arthur C. Clark, Ray Bradbury, Theodore Sturgeon and, most important of all, Kurt Vonnegut...I still love Kurt Vonnegut. I've read all of his novels several times. He's one of my great heroes. I think because of the lateral nature of his thinking. I think when you read Vonnegut he, by example, gives you permission to go laterally. Then, I suppose, Huxley was important...Herman Hesse...Thomas Mann to some extent....And of all contemporary novels, *Catch 22* was an important book for me when I was younger...Joseph Heller....More recently I've been very touched by Norman McLean's book, *A River Runs Through It*...and even more recently Cormack McCarthy's stuff, particularly *All The Pretty Horses*, but also *Blood Meridian* and some of his earlier things. So, there's a few books that have been important to me...not to mention—you mentioned later *One Flew Over The Cuckoo's Nest*. Of course, Kerouac and Kesey were very important when I was younger. I think the poetic influences were only really important in the late 50s with the beat generation in North America...Gregory Corsoe, and of course, Ginsberg...Ferlengetti and that team, because they made some kind of connection between the black music...between blues and intellect...which produced the melting pot out of which all the kind of middle- class English rock'n'roll developed I suspect.

[PR] I was interested in asking you whether you had ever read Thomas Hardy's poetry?

[RW] Thomas Hardy's poetry? No I haven't.

[PR] I was struck, when I began to read Thomas Hardy, how much he reminded me of you and vice versa...

[RW] Really?

[PR] Yeah...

[RW] Well I did, of course, read Hardy at school, because we had to...

[PR] ...I've never been a fan of his novels...

[RW] No I confess I found his novels...I think I had to do *Far From the Madding Crowd* and *The Mayor of Casterbridge* when I was a child, and I found it very dull fare.

[PR] Right. But I think his poetry I'm much more impressed with...

[RW] Well, maybe I'll look into that. I love Dorset...so maybe I'll look into his poetry.

[PR] It's interesting...because from his novels I don't find...I can't sense any of his actual personality, which I think you can derive from the poetry....In fact, that's basically what it all is for the most part, even when he is referring to other things. But I was quite curious whether you had ever...

[RW]   No. I don't know him.

[PR]   I shall be interested, perhaps sometime, in knowing what you think if you ever get a chance to check that out.

[RW]   Right. I was...As a younger person I was always really more interested in...I don't know...air rifles than I was in poetry.

[PR]   Have the following works acted as catalysts on your own pieces in any way? *One Flew Over the Cuckoo's Nest* (Ken Kesey), *Lord of the Flies* (William Golding), *Howl* (Allen Ginsberg), *The Trial* (Franz Kafka), *Animal Farm* (George Orwell).

[RW]   Oh, it's very hard to say. I mean, I loved *One Flew Over The Cuckoo's Nest*...I thought it was a fantastic novel. I've read it a number of times. Consequently I loathed the movie. I think it's a well made film, but when you love something and somebody changes it...when somebody reduces it to the popular taste in a way that...Douglas produced it, didn't he... Michael Douglas...?

[PR]   I can't remember...

[RW]   Yeah, he produced the movie, and I can't remember who...who directed it?...I can't remember now. Anyway, I felt, you know, the adding of the scenes for laughs really pissed me off...a whole bunch of stuff....All that business with the loonies playing basketball and things isn't in the book at all as I recall, but anyway....There was a whole history with the film because it was a big thing, I think, of Michael Douglas putting his father in his place, because Kirk Douglas had been trying to make it for years and years and years. It was always his great ambition to play Randall McMurphy. He too had fallen in love with the novel...

[PR]   I didn't know about that...

[RW]   ...Yeah, and I think, you know, a younger Kirk Douglas would have been a fantastic Randall McMurphy, I have to say...so yes, that piece is certainly a big love of mine.

[PR]   It was very interesting for me, because of the book's influence in bringing to the forefront all that questionable therapeutic sort of thing...shock therapy...lobotomy...

[RW]   I'd been aware of all the controversy about that, I think, long before I read *One Flew Over The Cuckoo's Nest*.

[PR]   So it was not necessarily something brought to your mind by that book...

[RW]   No, I just think that it's a beautiful piece of writing...it's a wonderful story and a fantastic piece of writing. *Lord of the Flies*, of course, I've read and I know quite well....I'm not sure that it had much...

[PR]   I was always interested in...it was in "Run Like Hell" when you say "the cockleshell shatters"...it almost seemed to me like the image of the conch that the boys have. I don't know...

[RW]   The cockleshell would have two references. One would be to the nursery rhyme..."Mary, Mary, quite contrary, tell me how does your garden grow? With silver bells and cockle shells, And pretty maids all in a row"..., though I wouldn't have been making any reference to the ideas in that. Of course, that lyric appears in "Walking the Dog"—the Rufus Thomas tune. It's the second verse of "Walking the Dog". [sings]"Baby's back. Dressed in black. Silver buttons all down her back. Hi ho, tipsy toe. She broke the needle, but she can sew. Walking the dog." The second verse quotes the nursery rhyme....The other thing that cockleshell means over here is...there was a movie made about a team of Marines—or maybe they were Special Boat Service—who went in kayaks up a Norwegian fiord to try and blow up either one of the German battleships or a German heavy water plant, and they...I think they actually failed, and they were all killed except one...one or two got out...or maybe they succeeded...I don't remember the history very well. But they were known as the cockleshell heroes. It was their kayak canoes...they were dropped by submarine and they went into this fiord, and their canoes were extremely frail craft, like cockleshells. So no it has nothing to do with conches, which are very solid things. They're brilliantly constructed and in fact incredibly powerful. Very hard to shatter.

[PR] In that book it kind of seemed to symbolise the order that they had during their meetings. And the lack of order...the degeneration of order corresponds to the breaking of the conch.

[RW] It was never a big deal for me...*Lord of the Flies. Howl*...again, you know, we all sat around in our darkened rooms and read that stuff when I was 15 or 16 years old. It was important culturally, but it was very much...I'm not sure how important the content and the work was, but the posing was very important. You know... the being "cool"...and pretending to like it [laughs].

[PR] I think it was Schaffner who notes that you use that device that Ginsberg uses in the poem of the repetition of "who" in the last lines of "Dogs". Was that a conscious... because it struck me immediately...the title "Howl" and a song called "Dogs"...

[RW] Right. No, no. I didn't make that connection. That's not to say it doesn't exist, of course.

[PR] No....In fact I've suggested that it might.

[RW] *The Trial* I've never read, though...clearly I know the story...because you get told the story in synopsis form every time anyone ever mentions the book. I've seen odd movies I think, or bits of them, but I've never actually read the novel.

[PR] So you didn't intend any allusion to that work in "The Trial" from *The Wall*?

[RW] No...absolutely no. "The Trial" from *The Wall* is just, you know, an internal self-examination. It's not based on any model...

[PR] I've not read "The Trial" myself either, but from some of Kafka's other stuff...I wouldn't have had any doubts if you had told me that you had meant some allusion to that work just because his work is very psychological...

[RW] *Animal Farm* I read when I was younger, and I was never very crazy about it.

[PR] No?

[RW] Well, it's O.K. It's a nice metaphor, I suppose. I'm not sure how well it's stood the test of time.

[PR] Yeah.... I was curious about that one because, to me, the hierarchy of animals in *Animals* seems to reflect the hierarchy that seems apparent in Orwell as well.

[RW] Yeah, well it's using characteristics as we perceive them of different animals in the same way... animals are very easy metaphors to use.

[PR] Did you name all the titles on *The Dark Side of the Moon*?

[RW] Well, I don't know...You tell me what the instrumental pieces are called, and I'll tell you what I know about them.

[PR] Well, there's "Speak To Me"...

[RW] "Speak To Me" definitely, yeah. That's a... it's one of my great regrets that I gave the publishing [rights] on that track to Nick Mason who had nothing to do with any of it.

[PR] Oh, really [laughter]?

[RW] Yeah [laughs]. He got... he was given that as a little gift for sitting in the corner and playing the drums while we were working on the piece. It's very galling to me when I read how he created this thing, because he was never anywhere near any of the machines when it was being done... when *I* was doing it. Anyway, that's neither here nor there...

[PR] It's funny how the books convey that, though, don't they...?

[RW] Yeah...well, don't forget I didn't speak to any of the people who wrote the books. I haven't spoken to anyone about any of this really, except in odd interviews and things.... I didn't speak to Schaffner and I didn't speak to Dallas. And I don't know who else has written books....But I didn't want to get into fights about things with people, so I just kept quiet and let them get on with it.... "Speak To Me" is something that a guy... one of the roadies... Chris Adamson, who is the guy whose voice you hear at the beginning, going "I've been mad for fucking years".... That's Chris Adamson's voice and it was a catchphrase of his. He used to say, "speak to me" when he wanted to be told what to do. So that's where that comes from. What's the next one?

[PR] "On The Run"... that one I'm not as concerned with... "The Great Gig In The Sky"?

[RW] I couldn't say... I can't recall. It sounds like me. But it sounds like anybody really. I think it's a phrase that had been used quite a lot. I mean...the Happy Hunting Ground...the great whatever-it-is in the sky... just to put "gig" it sounds like my kind of humour, but I wouldn't swear to where that came from really.

[PR] I guess the only other one is "Any Colour You'd Like". I'll tell you my theory, if you want to hear it first...

[RW] O.K.

[PR] I know that it was one of the questions you were asking people, was it not? "What is your favourite colour"?

[RW] Yeah, probably, one of the openers. Just to get people going... I wasn't interested in what their favourite colour was. I wanted to get people to just get on a roll of answering a question, simply so that when the questions that I *was* interested in came up, they answered them.

[PR] Well then, don't worry about my theory then, Roger [laughing]... How about we just hear yours then?

[RW] O.K. Well, it's.... I'll tell you where it comes from, so as I can.... I suspect I did think of the title, because it comes from... it's a Cockney thing, and maybe regional as well. At cattle markets and street markets—it's a street trader thing. In Cambridge where I lived, people would come from London in a van—a truck—open the back, and stand on the tailboard of the truck, and the truck's full of stuff that they're trying to sell. And they have a very quick and slick patter, and they're selling things like crockery, china, sets of knives and forks. All kinds of different things, and they sell it very cheap with a patter. They tell you what it is and they say,"It's ten plates, lady, and it's this, that and the other, and eight cups and saucers, and for the lot I'm asking NOT ten pounds, NOT five pounds, NOT three pounds...fifty bob to you!", and they get rid of this stuff like this. If they had sets of china and they were all the same colour, they would say, "You can 'ave 'em ten bob to you, love. Any colour you like, they're all blue." And that was just part of that patter. So, metaphorically, "Any Colour You Like" is interesting, in that sense, because it denotes offering a choice where there is none. And it's also interesting that in the phrase "any colour you like, they're all blue", I don't know why, but in my mind it's always they're all blue, which, if you think about it, relates very much to the light and dark, sun and moon, good and evil. You make your choice but it's always blue.

[PR] I see.... I was always thinking of it, perhaps, in relation to the album cover... just because it was interesting to me, you know, to break down the components of colour, and... I believe it was Schaffner who talks about it as the prism or the triangle being a symbol of ambition. Now I don't know how much involvement either yourself or anyone else had with the creation of the album cover?

[RW] The front sleeve just arrived as a fait accompli with about half a dozen other images, and we all went, "Oh, we like that one". That was it. I did the inside...the heart-beat, and the stuff for the gate-fold, but the outside was just... Aubrey Powell and Storm Thorgensen rolled up with it.

[PR] That's interesting because... yeah... the breaking down of the components of colour on the inside of the album is over the heart-beat, or the pulse.

[RW] Yes.

[PR] I kind of thought that it might also reflect "all these things in life"...you know these separate components of life, but they all...

[RW] Well it might, but now we're getting into your thesis...[laughs]. It's *your* thesis.

[PR] Right [laughter].... Alright then. In the last verse of "Dogs", are those lines questions or statements?

[RW] Right. I haven't listened to that for a while, but do you mean by...you know... (sings)"Who were da da by trained personnel"... that stuff?

[PR] Right. Right.

[RW] Those are statements... (sings)"Who was told not to spit in the fan. Who was told what to do by the man." Yeah... I'm sure they're statements.

[PR] I was curious because... you know how in Ginsberg's *Howl*, it starts off saying, "I saw the best minds of my generation..

[RW] "...best minds of my generation, destroyed... yeah"

[PR] I've never been quite sure... I mean... I know that they're referring to the first dog, right? It's the second dog giving his own back to the first dog, but I always imagined them as being questions rather than you know... like ironic questions, saying, "*Who* was dragged down by the stone"?

[RW] Well, if you want them to be, they can be. It's your thesis [laughs].

[PR] I'm not sure how it works when the companies put the lyrics down, and whether they take as much care as you would like with punctuation and stuff...

[RW] Well I always check that... so they should be right, yeah.

[PR] We shan't worry about that then. Did you write what Dallas refers to as "the official synopsis of *The Wall*"?

[RW] I've no idea... I haven't read the book...

[PR] I have a feeling he might have taken it off the cover of the video cassette or something...

[RW] It sounds like it was probably written by Alan Parker or somebody... I wouldn't dream of trying to write a synopsis of *The Wall*... I don't think.

[PR] Where did the musical influence for "The Trial" come from?

[RW] That's Kurt Weill... clearly. Pure Brecht... well Kurt Weill.

[PR] I don't know his stuff very well... but I remember having got a bunch of them out of the library... playing them as I was doing something...and there was one—I've not had the chance to go back and see which work it came from—but there was one which had a similar melody.

[RW] If you look at the credits from the album, you'll see that that track is credited as being co-written by Ezrin. That's the track where he's key. Most of the Kurt Weill influence came via him...so you'd need to ask him which particular thing he ripped it off from [laughing]... because I give him credit for that. It's very much in style anyway. I don't know Kurt Weill's work well enough to be able to identify specific pieces and name them... apart from *The Threepenny Opera*... which is the best known thing.

[PR] In "Your Possible Pasts" from *The Final Cut*, is the woman standing in the doorway a prostitute?

[RW] Yeah, that's the image. It's about lack of contact... not connecting.

[PR] In "The Gunner's Dream", is Max a fictional character or is he a real person?

[RW] That's a fictional character... hang on, let me think [sings the words]. Maybe Max... it must be the gunner's parents. The father must have had medals as well... or somebody... it's about medals. I don't know why I used the name Max, it's a strange name to use. It's very interesting because it's a Jewish name, isn't it? But it also sounds like Baron Richtofen in some strange way... or maybe that's because there was a movie called *The Blue Max* that was about First World War fighter pilots. I'm not saying that's where it came from but... I don't know. I don't know where that name came from, but anyway he's not a real person. Sometimes, you see, when I write songs—I write them in a consciously engendered state of complete passivity so that I try to put as little into the song as possible, and allow as much to come out as possible. And so words and names and things come out sometimes, and if they scan and sound alright, I'll leave them there even if I don't know what they are or where they come from really.

[PR] *The Pros and Cons of Hitchhiking* was based, in part, on actual dreams, wasn't it? I read somewhere that the "Yoko" portions were someone else's dream...

[RW] Yeah, I'll tell you who that was. Andy Newmark...drummer? He's drumming with Eric [Clapton] now. He did a lot of John Lennon's solo albums with him... wonderful drummer. That was his dream... terrible dream. He's actually from Bermuda so... eastern seaboard is actually closer to his geographical origins than it is to mine. My dream was just about driving about in eastern Europe... the sort of sense of foreboding. *The Pros and Cons of Hitchhiking* and the dreams that I can remember... the actual dreams that triggered the thing... and triggered the idea of writing a piece that was about forty-five minutes of sleep... the actual dreams have long been consigned to bits of memory that I don't care to get at—or can't get at—and am not interested in getting at anyway really... because they're not fundamental.

[PR] I guess you must have sort of kept a dream diary?

[RW] No, I don't write dreams down.

[PR] Was "The Pros and Cons of Hitchhiking" the only song on the album that was based on someone else's dreams?

[RW] Yeah.

[PR] Do you know if he felt any particular hostility towards Yoko Ono for any reason?

[RW] Well I don't know... I would assume so, having put her in his dream like that. I know I do. I have no right to really. I have that kind of "proprietorial thing" that fans have for their idols about Lennon. I kind of feel that she has betrayed a lot of what he stood for. We tend to idealize our dead heroes. All the stuff that she's done since he died is sort of alien, I would suggest, to the central beliefs and philosophies that are inherent in his work.

[PR] Did you harbour any of those type of feelings before his death?

[RW] They kept pretty much... I thought that all that making albums together, and her wailing and howling and things, was just kind of uninteresting musically but laudable emotionally. So I had nothing really against that, I just wasn't really very interested in it. I'm not interested in Yoko Ono's art... as is noone in the world... because it's worthless... as far as I can make out. That's not to say she hasn't got great worth... she has, as we all do. She just hasn't got anything interesting to say about anything, as far as I can tell. I find it very irritating that after he died, she kind of adopted his mantle and pretended that she had got interesting things to say. I was pretty upset by her parading the child around onstage round the world and things like that. I just thought it was unnecessary... and parading his power around, as if it was her own, I found upsetting at times but... that's a cross she has to bear... you know?

[PR] Is there an intentional musical quotation from "The Fletcher Memorial Home" in Clapton's slide guitar intro to the song "Go Fishing"?

[RW] No. I don't think there's any intention... it's just that people who write music tend to write the same thing over and over again [laughs]. I'm sure Eric wouldn't know "The Fletcher Memorial Home". Interestingly enough, at the moment I'm working on a kind of operetta... opera... I'm not sure how heavy it will turn out... about the French Revolution. It's where I'm only doing the music, the libretto's written by a friend of mine... a Frenchman...well actually he's Spanish, but he lives in Paris—a guy called Étienne Rodagil. I've been working on this thing, on and off, for four or five years. There's quite a lot of musical references in it to past pieces of work that I've just borrowed. I've just done a thing on a letter that Louis XVI sent to his cousin Bourbons D'Espagne...a fabulous letter, and the melody that I've used behind that is the melody from the end of *The Pros and Cons of Hitchhiking*.

[PR] You're also working on a stage production of *The Wall*?

[RW] Yeah. At the moment I'm looking for a collaborator, but I'm not looking all that hard because I have a sense that the story... is not quite finished. It's not quite over. I feel I need to arrive somewhere in my own life, and in my own mind, and in my own heart. I need to arrive.... It's been *so* long since I wrote *The Wall*... now... and I've come so far... and changed so much that... I feel I need to be standing four-square "outside the wall"... before I can complete a piece for Broadway. I'm not interested in it being as enigmatic as it is. It needs more light in it. If it's going to work as a play, I think it needs lots of humour and it needs more light, and it needs more explanation. It needs to be more accessible, easier to grasp, and it needs to have some kind of a conclusion...or else I don't think it's worth putting on.

[PR] So you don't intend to make that your focus at this point?

[RW] Well I do. I think it's almost there, you know... I think that things run in parallel.

[PR] This project that your working on... the operetta...

[RW] Let's call it an opera... sounds better doesn't it?

[PR]   ...is that going to be a rock-style operetta?

[RW]   Oh no, no, no... it's orchestra and chorus, and sound effects. It's a big orchestra, a big chorus and some soloists... no there's no electric instruments.

[PR]   What did you think of the McCartney oratorio?

[RW]   Oh I thought it was no better and no worse than *Give My Regards to Broadstreet*.

[PR]   Something I would like to talk to you about especially is your poetry. You're writing poetry and prose now is that right?

[RW]   Yeah, well I'm not writing a novel or anything. I've written a few short stories, and I've written... I don't know... maybe twenty or thirty poems... something like that.

[PR]   And are you planning to publish them eventually?

[RW]   I will publish at some point, yeah.

[PR]   Good, I look forward to that.

[RW]   You haven't heard it yet, you might not like it...[laughs].

[PR]   Yeah, I just assume that I will... [laughs]

[RW]   It's actually pretty good I have to say. I've rather surprised myself.

[PR]   Oh, really! Are you working more with short poems or longer poems or...?

[RW]   Some are quite long and some are... I mean I don't know what you call long, but some are sort of thirty or forty lines long, and some are only ten or fifteen lines long. There's nothing epic... there's no epic work. There all um... there all love poems. Well there's one or two hate poems, but... [laughs]. They're one or the other anyway....

* * *

NOTES

Introduction

1. For discussions of this issue by recent musicologists see (McClary and Walser 1990: 281), (Middleton 1990: 103-5), (Tagg 1982: 37-9) and (Moore 1993: 17-30).

2. This sentiment is supported in (Tagg 1982: 40).

3. Walser's sentiments are shared by Philip Tagg, who provides a comprehensive checklist of all of the various musical parameters (Tagg 1979: 69-70).

4. It is interesting to contrast Kramer's approach to hermeneutics to that of Philip Tagg who betrays a slight fear of what he calls the"unbridled application [of hermeneutics] ... degenerat[ing] into unscientific guesswork" (Tagg 1982:43).

5. This practice joins the tracks "Sergeant Pepper's Lonely Hearts Club Band" and "With a Little Help From My Friends" at the beginning of the album and "Good Morning Good Morning", "Sgt. Pepper's (Reprise)" and "A Day in the Life" at the album's close.

6. According to Karl Dallas, the first work that fits this description is the Pretty Things' *S.F. Sorrow* (1968) which, in turn supposedly inspired Pete Townshend to write Tommy (1969) (Dallas 1987: 21). I would suggest that the Pretty Things were predated by The Moody Blues with *Days of Future Passed* (1967).

7. Such projects included Barbet Schroeder's *More* (1969), Michelangelo Antonioni's *Zabriskie Point* (1970) and Schroeder's *La Vallee* (1972). Waters worked with Ron Geesin on music from *The Body* (1970) and more recently by himself on the soundtrack to *When the Wind Blows* (1986).

8. It can in fact be argued that, in Waters' hands, the concept album has become as much a literary genre as a musical one—a point I hope becomes apparent in this study. It is certainly significant that lyric sheets are included with *The Dark Side of the Moon* and all subsequent Pink Floyd/Roger Waters recordings.

9. Richard Wright, the group's keyboardist, told Crawdaddy Magazine (Volume IV, No. 5) in 1970, "I don't feel political. I play music. I see myself as a musician, turning people on to music, but I don't see myself as wanting them, or trying to make them change. I don't care about that".

10. On *The Dark Side of the Moon* (1973), all four Pink Floyd members (Roger Waters, David Giimour, Richard Wright and Nick Mason) are credited with compositions. By *Wish You Were Here* (1975) this has diminished to Waters, Gilmour, Wright and the latter two's contributions are limited to the suite "Shine on You Crazy Diamond". By *Animals* (1977) this has further diminished to Waters and Gilmour but the latter only contributes to the track "Dogs". Gilmour contributes to three of the twenty-six tracks on *The Wall* (1979) and *The Final Cut* (1983) is composed entirely by Waters.

Chapter 1 - The Dark Side of the Moon

1. (Durant 1984: 213).

2. Miles suggests, interestingly enough, that during the making of this album the songs were "put together quite quickly". According to Waters, "It had to be quick because we had a tour starting. It might have been only six weeks before we had to have something to perform" (Miles: 1980).

3. During the middle ages, the tritone was known as "the Devil's interval".

4. Remarkably enough the dollar coin in Canada is nicknamed "the Loony", a common slang version for lunatic (though originally the coin was so designated because of the loon which is featured on its face).

5. This viewpoint (especially because of the war imagery present in the song) provides, in part, the basis for *The Final Cut* (1983) which is a work expressing Waters' opposition to England's position and actions against Argentina in the Falkland Islands dispute of 1982.

6. Waters seems to have had these lines in mind once again during *The Wall* when expressing anger over the loss of his father in World War II: ("The generals gave thanks/ as the other ranks held back/the enemy tanks for a while./ And the Anzio bridgehead was held for/the price of a few hundred ordinary lives"—*When the Tigers Broke Free*).

7. In a game of chess which is well under way, both sides will often become interspersed on the board. If the distinction between black and white pieces were absent, players would experience difficulty in recognizing their own pieces.

8. According to David Gilmour, "'Us and Them' was a piece of Rick's—a piano piece that we initially had in 1969 funnily enough, and we were going to put on the film 'Zabriskie Point' by Antonioni over a riot at UCLA scene. It seemed to fit remarkably well, all this rioting and heads being banged by police in slow motion with that music..." (Redbeard: 1993). Waters appears to have retained the association of this music with violence and even drawn this section of lyric from the Antonioni scene.

9. As seems to be typical of successive American governments, these activities were not confined solely to the United States. The most serious incident with CIA involvement took place at McGill University in Montréal (see Marks: 1979).

10. From Led Zeppelin's *Misty Mountain Hop* which appeared on their untitled fourth album from 1971.

11. This "dark foreboding" of course became something of a reality in 1987 when Pink Floyd released their first album without Roger Waters who officially left, and unsuccessfully attempted to break up, the group in 1986 [see (White: 1988) and (Resnicoff: 1992)].

12. For readers who are too easily willing to accept the Freudian dogma, the author strongly recommends David Holbrook's *Human Hope and the Death Instinct* (1971).

Chapter 2 - Wish You Were Here

1. (Sedgewick 1975: 15).

2. Later, in the lyrics of "Welcome to the Machine", Waters also uses the guitar to represent the unauthentic "rock 'n roll dream". He seems to have in mind, partially, the expression "guitar hero", which appears to have come into use after Eric Clapton's rise to popularity in the mid-sixties. The common expression which coincided with Clapton's popularity was "Clapton is God".

3. Waters again suggests in *The Wall* that a withdrawal into the self does not provide a relief from one's sufferings.

4. See (Rockwell 1992: 492-499).

5. This is also reflected by one of the comments heard during the radio sound effects: "Derek, this star nonsense—what is it"?

Chapter 3 - Animals

1. (Eagleton 1976: 5).
2. As Karl Dallas suggests, this piece "is so alien to everything one associates with the Floyd that it comes like a douche of cold water to clear the mind for what follows" (Dallas 1987: 114).
3. It is interesting to note the frequency with which Waters uses drowning imagery. Besides here, and on *The Dark Side of the Moon* during "Breathe (in the air)" and "Brain Damage", it also appears on *The Wall* during the song "The Thin Ice". It always seems to coincide with a character's demise caused primarily by impending madness, suggested again by this character's "loss of control".
4. This awakening seems to relate to Waters' own realization about the falsity of the dreams of success which initially lured him into the music business, and which he subsequently documented in *Wish You Were Here*.
5. In "Pigs on the Wing (Part II)" the narrator refers to himself as a dog. Waters has said that this song is a love song addressed to his second wife Carolyne (Dallas 1987:117).
6. The "digging" image in the pig's creed is possibly derived from the song "Breathe (in the air)" (From *The Dark Side of the Moon*), where the addressee—portrayed as a rabbit—was indirectly told by the system through his brainwashed mother to "dig that hole forget the sun".
7. Pete Townshend, for example, can be heard playing one at the end of "The Rock", from *Quadrophenia* (1973), just before the beginning of the work's finale "Love Reign O'er Me".
8. See section CIII (41-44) of the poem.
9. The conditions observed by Waters have been, in large part, a result of the growing inequality which has been characteristic of the leading industrial nations since about 1973 to the present. With the continued globalization of liberalized trade, a major power shift has occurred in favour of monied interests. This has been exacerbated by the increasing depoliticization of the majority. See "Everything for Sale: The Virtues and Limits of Markets" (1997) by Robert Kuttner; "The Unconcious Civilization" (1995) by John Ralston Saul; and "Amusing Ourselves to Death" (1986) by Neil Postman.

Chapter 4 - The Wall

1. (Brody and Axelrad 1970: 42).
2. Brink defines ego as "the locus of intrapsychic activity, the governing centre of emotional life....Ego is a theoretical construct describing structure and topography to account for the individual's emotional development and activity....Fairbairn and Winnicott characterized the ego as a unitary governing system which incorporates all the features Freud mentioned while reflecting more exactly the developmental experience through which infants and children go" (Brink 1977: 34-5).
3. *The Wall* is an exceptional piece because it is not only a concept album, but also a film and an elaborate stage show. Reference will be made to the work in all of its forms wherever appropriate; but due to the discrepancies between media concerning the running order of songs, I shall follow that of the film for convenience. All musical discussions will consider the versions of the songs that appear on the original sound recording.
4. In World War II, allied forces landed at Anzio (a town of central Italy in the region of Lazio and the province of Rome) on January 22, 1944 and

formed a bridgehead, which, because of German resistance, did not link up with the main front until May 25, 1944.

5. I remember being staggered at a display of power I witnessed during a performance by The Rolling Stones in 1990 when, at one point, Mick Jagger raised his hands to clap above his head, the thousands upon thousands in the audience did likewise—a stunning sight at first, but then somehow troubling.

6. Most lullabies usually are in either three-four time or, like this one, six-eight.

7. (Reti 1978: 72).

8. The five stages of bereavement, according to Elisabeth Kuebler-Ross, are denial and isolation, anger, bargaining, depression and finally acceptance (Kuebler-Ross 1969: Ch. 3-7).

9. That the event has also profoundly effected Waters is apparent by the continual references to his father throughout his work, in particular the song "Free Four" from *Obscured by Clouds* (1972), *The Final Cut* (1983) and in the song "Three Wishes" on *Amused to Death* (1992).

10. As Karl Dallas notes, "the Tiger was the Wehrmacht Panzer Divisions' most potent tank in World War II" (Dallas 1987: 77).

11. On the recording, the teacher's approach is portrayed by the sound of an oncoming helicopter. His overwhelming presence is communicated by the helicopter's loudness which, as it gets closer, drowns out the sound of the kids playing in the schoolyard. The teacher's preying on Pink has a similar effect for him to that of being the victim of a helicopter assailant. During the '77 tour, interestingly enough, Waters purportedly arrived at the venue by himself via helicopter.

12. Waters' comments appear to give further support to Brink's thesis: "My father was a schoolteacher before the war....He taught physical education and religious instruction, strangely enough. He was a deeply committed Christian who was killed when I was three months old. A wrenching waste. I concede that awful loss has coloured much of my writing and my world-view" (White 1988: 162).

13. As Henry Biller observes, "[if] the father is absent, the probability of a pattern of maternal overprotection is often increased. The child's age at the onset of father absence is an important variable. The boy who becomes father absent during infancy or during his preschool years is more likely to be overprotected by his mother" (Biller 1974: 90).

14. On the recording this line is substituted for "Is it just a waste of time?", although it appears in the liner notes as it does here.

15. This disease, we find out later in "Comfortably Numb", is characterized by fever and a swelling of the hands. In a draft of the screenplay for the film, Waters writes: "We see YOUNG PINK, aged ten, ill in bed. His MOTHER tidies and fusses the bedclothes, and looks on anxiously as the DOCTOR stuffs a thermometer into his mouth, and tests his legs, as if for Polio" (G. R. Waters 1981). Polio is an infectious viral disease that affects the central nervous system and which can cause temporary or permanent paralysis—perhaps the physical equivalent to being "Comfortably Numb".

16. The sense of escape that is created by the entry of the guitar solo corresponds in the film with the image of Pink's marriage to a "dirty", rock and roll woman—definitely an act of rebellion against his mother's overpro-

tectiveness.

17. If one recognizes the common mythical association of the phallus with potency or power, Pink's apparent impotence can be seen analytically to coincide with the power struggle between he and his wife.

18. This message, which only appears on the recording, when played backwards says, "Congratulations. You have just discovered the secret message. Please send your answer to Old Pink, care of the Funny Farm, Chalfont".

19. See "Pigs on the Wing (Part II)".

20. "Axe" is a term commonly used by musicians to refer to their instrument, in this case guitar. In this context, however, its literal meaning makes its use somewhat frightening.

21. Walser seems to have excluded the locrian mode which shares this characteristic with phrygian.

22. The tritone, as has been said, is the most jarring and unstable interval in tonal music.

23. Here Waters alludes to *Animals*. In "Pigs on the Wing (Part II)", the narrating dog did not feel "the weight of the stone" which dragged down the first character in "Dogs"; he did not feel it because he was not isolated like the first dog. Because Pink is entirely isolated however, he feels the weight of the stone tremendously.

24. Waters again alludes to *Animals*. Pink realizes that he is merely a slave to the "Pigs" who reward his good work with "bones".

25. It is interesting that Waters seems to have partially modelled the character Pink on Syd Barrett. He says of this song that "there are some lines in here that harp back to the halcyon days of Syd Barrett...it's partly about all kinds of people I've known, but Syd was the only person I used to know who used elastic bands to keep his boots together, which is where that line comes from. In fact the 'obligatory Hendrix perm' you have to go back ten years before you understand what all that's about" (Vance 1979). Concerning the aetiology of Syd's condition, Gilmour made the comment to *Guitar World* that "[i]n my opinion, it's a family situation that's at the root of it all. His father's death affected him very heavily, and his mother always pampered him—made him out to be a genius of sorts" (Guitar World—Feb. 1993). Barrett lost his father at age twelve however.

26. "Gohill's" is a shoe store in Camden, North London.

27. "The function of the ego upon which Freud has laid most stress is its *adaptive* function—the function which it performs in relating primal instinctive activity to conditions prevailing in outer reality, and more particularly social conditions. It must be remembered, however, that the ego also performs *integrative* functions, among the most important of which are (1) the integration of perceptions of reality, and (2) the integration of behaviour. Another important function of the ego is discrimination between inner and outer reality. Splitting of the ego has the effect of compromising the progressive development of all these functions..." (Fairbairn 1962: 9).

28. *Harrison's Principles of Internal Medicine (13th ed.)* describes rat-bite fever: "High-grade fever, rigors, headache, vomiting, and myalgias followed by regional lymphadenopathy, arthralgias, and arthritis constitute the clinical syndrome. A maculopapular rash on the palms and soles may progress to petechial haemorrhages. If the patient is not treated, fever persists, and the patient may die" (Isselbacher et al. 1994: 570).

29. According to Karl Dallas, "when Sir Oswald Mosley's British Union of Fascists was having a last fling before World War II destroyed its mass support, this was precisely the technique that was used to isolate hecklers or outsiders at the mass rallies at places like Olympia and Earls Court—ironically, the latter the very hall where 'The Wall' was performed in London..." (Dallas 1987: 85).

30. Genocide, for the Nazis, was the "Final Solution of the Jewish question". It is effective that Waters alludes to what was perhaps the largest organized display of hatred in the history of mankind—a hatred which was exercised also in mass killings of other victims including Poles, Russians, gypsies, Jehovah's Witnesses, homosexuals, and political prisoners, among others. For a recent discussion of the activities of the Third Reich, see Richard Breitman's *The Architect of Genocide: Himmler and the Final Solution* (1991).

31. Although Fairbairn rejected Freud's concept of the id, he retained his basic conception of the super-ego—the part of the mind that acts as a conscience and responds to social rules.

32. This fear was expressed earlier by Pink when he was seen sitting in the toilet stall, before he sang "Stop": 'Do you remember the way it used to be,/Do you think we should have been closer?/I put out my hand just to touch your soft hair,/To make sure in the darkness that you were still there./I have to admit I was just a little afraid/Of the ones fiddling under their dirty old macs,/The ones that were pointing the guns at our backs...'. The revised excerpts of these lines eventually found their way into the songs "Your Possible Pasts" and "The Moment of Clarity"—from *The Final Cut* (1983), and Waters' first solo album *The Pros and Cons of Hitchhiking* (1984) respectively.

Chapter 5 - The Final Cut

1. From Led Zeppelin's "The Battle of Evermore" which appeared on their untitled fourth album from 1971.

2. The Argentineans refer to the islands as the Malvinas.

3. Waters seems to refer back to ideas presented in the reprise of "Breathe" from *The Dark Side of the Moon* where it appeared to be his suspicion that it was "the tolling of the iron bell", or fear of death, which predominantly "calls the faithful to their knees". Although it bears a dedication to its composer's father Eric Fletcher Waters (1913-44), the work's subtitle suggests that this is not a requiem for his absence, but for that of "the post war dream"—indicating that Waters' concerns are with conditions in the present life. For a similar criticism of Christianity's preoccupation with the afterlife, see the English Romantic poet William Blake's "Ah! Sunflower" (1794), from *Songs of Experience*, with its play on the word "sun" (Son).

4. The metaphor also effectively conjures the negative image of the first dog in "Dogs" from *Animals* (1977).

5. Nippon is the Japanese word for Japan. It means literally 'land of the rising sun'.

6. The Clyde is a river in Scotland. In the eighteenth century it was made navigable to the centre of Glasgow, which soon became the world's largest shipbuilding centre. As Waters recounts, the Clydeside shipyards, which bordered the river for 20 miles (32 km) below Glasgow, suffered severely from foreign competition after World War II.

7. The use of acoustic guitar would have given too warm an effect, countering that apparently desired by Waters in order to portray a lack of genuine human contact.

8. This notion foreshadows the focus of "The Fletcher Memorial Home".

9. The same effect was used at the end of "Hey You" from *The Wall*.

10. These lines are similar to the following from "Sexual Revolution": "Hey Girl/Don't point your finger at me/I am only a rat in a maze like you/And only the dead go free/So...please hold my hand/As we blunder through the maze/And remember/ Nothing can grow without rain".

11. The technique is the same as that used in the beginning of the solo which appears at the end of "Pigs (Three Different Ones)" from *Animals*.

12. Although the third and fourth lines are omitted from the recording, they are contained in the accompanying lyric sheet.

13. For a reproduction of this poster see (Barker 1981: 46).

14. The guitar's melody quickly slides from the minor third through both the major and minor second scale degrees, but the ear is more apt to record the last tone (the flattened second) before the tonic is reached.

15. As has been previously noted, the tritone is the most jarring and unstable interval in tonal music.

16. Note the piano's use of word painting which occurs after the word "rise"— the piano responds with an ascending scale figure.

17. The top medal is the *Distinguished Flying Medal*, and from left to right the other three are the *1939-45 Star*, the *Africa Star* and the *Defence Medal*.

18. The insights provided by Robert Walser concerning rock guitar solos are widely applicable to other instruments. See (Walser 1993: 53-54).

19. This aural effect seems similar to a common cinematographic effect; one imagines the camera zooming out from its focus on the agonized Bomber on to the speaking narrator.

20. In Britain "brown and mild" is an alcoholic beverage which mixes brown ale and mild beer, also referred to as "half and half".

21. Soviet troops were deployed in the North of Afghanistan where Islamic rebels were engaged in fierce fighting against government forces. Moscow feared that the Moslem rebellion would spread to its own Moslem population in Central Asia, and consequently did not withdraw their occupation of the country until the beginning of 1989. The Israeli attack was aimed at the Palestine Liberation Organization (PLO), and the country was severely criticized for its refusal to withdraw from the Lebanon until September 1983.

22. Before the sinking of the *Belgrano*, no British blood had been spilt in the conflict; two days later, however, an Argentine fighter bomber destroyed the British destroyer *Sheffield* in retaliation.

23. The Government sought purposely to mislead the Committee, but this was revealed to Dalyell from within the Ministry of Defence, an event leading to the arrest of Clive Ponting in mid-July 1984 (Dalyell 1986: 13). Mysteriously and conveniently, the Control Room log-book of *HMS Conqueror* vanished the very day the Defence Secretary of the time was due to give evidence related to the *Belgrano* to the Select Committee on Foreign Affairs (Dalyell 1987: 16).

24. The files are to be released to the Public Record Office in the year 2013 (Freedman 1988: 122).

25. Waters produced a "Video EP" for *The Final Cut* which featured visuals for "The Gunner's Dream", "The Fletcher Memorial Home", "The Final Cut" and "Not Now John". The video for "The Fletcher Memorial Home" depicted a father, who had lost his son in the Falklands conflict, wreaking his vengeance on Margaret Thatcher.

26. Alexander Haig, Jr. was the American secretary of state from the beginning of the Reagan administration in 1980 until he resigned in 1982. Ian Paisley is a militant Irish Protestant leader who co-founded the Democratic Unionist Party in 1971, and who was elected to a seat in the British House of Commons in 1970. Joseph McCarthy (d. 1957) was a U.S. senator, who in 1950 led a severe anti-communist campaign in the U.S. for 4 years, blacklisting hundreds of people until he was censured by the senate in 1954. Richard Nixon was the 37th President of the United States, who was forced to resign after being linked to Watergate—the greatest political scandal in American history.

27. Waters, by leaving Galtieri out of the Home, seems to share the viewpoint of the former Soviet Union with regard to the Falklands conflict. The U.S.S.R. dropped its original position of neutrality, suggesting that the American mediation mission (conducted by Haig) was merely a "smoke-screen" for Britain's efforts to preserve its "colonial" position in the islands (Facts on File 1982: 261).

28. The first use of this expression may have been by Abraham Lincoln in his *Reply to the Missouri Committee of Seventy* (1864): "I desire so to conduct the affairs of this administration that if at the end, when I come to lay down the reins of power, I have lost every other friend on earth, I shall at least have one friend left, and that friend shall be down inside me".

29. The discomfort which this figure creates is even more pronounced over minor chords, where the interval between the second and third of the chord is a semi-tone rather than a tone. The first line of text is sung over an A minor chord where the second is altered from B flat to B natural—a note outside the song's key which therefore creates an even more dissonant effect.

30. In England the name "John" corresponds to the North American use of the name "Mac" or "Jack"—a name that is often used to address someone who the speaker does not know. Therefore "John" could represent *anybody*. As we shall see, it is likely that Waters perceived "John" as a representation of *everybody* (see below).

31. Bingo, of course, is a game whose sole objective is to win money.

32. This line brings a further sense of poignancy with the knowledge that Sweden has pursued a neutral foreign policy since the early 19th century, which, incidentally, kept it out of both world wars.

33. Dalyell also tells how the University of Stirling invited all 71 Scottish MPs on 24 April 1982 to a one-day seminar ("over which they had taken considerable trouble, with a number of distinguished speakers"), which would provide them with background to the current crisis. Dalyell reports that he was the only MP to show up (Dalyell 1982: 22).

34. Appropriately the main riff of "Not Now John" is a reccurrence of the claustrophobic Figure B from *The Wall*.

35. According to Waters, the ideas presented in the song actually occurred to him while driving home one night (Dallas 1987: 150).

Works Cited and Consulted

Barker, Ralph (1981) *The RAF at War*, Alexandria, Virginia: Time-Life Books.

Biller, Henry (1974) *Paternal Deprivation*, Lexington, Massachusetts: D.C. Heath and Company.

Bilton, Michael and Peter Kosminsky (1989) *Speaking Out: Untold Stories from the Falklands War*, London: André Deutsch Limited.

Boyle, Kevin (1989) *The Crime Of Blasphemy—Why It Should Be Abolished*, London: no publisher.

Brazier, Chris (1979) 'Floyd: The New Realism', *Melody Maker*, December 1: 29.

Brink, Andrew (1977) *Loss and Symbolic Repair*, Hamilton, Ontario: The Cromlech Press.

Brink, Andrew (1982) *Creativity as Repair*, Hamilton, Ontario: The Cromlech Press.

Brody, Sylvia and Sidney Axelrad (1970) *Anxiety and Ego Formation in Infancy*, New York: Innternational Universities Press, Inc.

Brown, Bertram, Wienckowski, Louis and Bivens, Lyle (1974) *Psychosurgery: Perspective On A Current Issue*, U.S. Department of Health, Education, and Welfare—National Institute of Mental Health.

Brown, Mick and Kurt Loder (1982) 'Behind Pink Floyd's Wall', *Rolling Stone*, September 16: 14-16.

Chavkin, Samuel (1978) *The Mind Stealers: Psychosurgery and Mind Control*, Boston: Houghton Mifflin Company.

Chidester, David (1988) *Patterns of Power: Religion and Politics in American Culture*, New Jersey: Prentice-Hall.

Clarke, Paul (1983) "'A magic science': rock music as a recording art", *Popular Music* 3, 195-213.

Considine, J.D. (1987) Rev. of *Radio K.A.O.S.* by Roger Waters, *Rolling Stone* July 16-30: 134.

Cook, Nicholas (1994) 'Music and meaning in the commercials', *Popular Music* 13(1), 27-40.

Coppage, Noel (1980) Rev. of *The Wall* by Pink Floyd, *Stereo Review*, March: 110.

Dallas, Karl (1982a) "Just Another Flick of 'The Wall'", *Melody Maker*, July 17: 14.

Dallas, Karl (1982b) 'Floyd's Soundtrack Becomes New Album', *Melody Maker*, August 7: 4.

Dallas, Karl (1983) 'A Hitchhiker's Guide to Roger Waters', *Melody Maker*, March 26: 3.

Dallas, Karl (1987) *Bricks in the Wall*, New York: Shapolsky Publishers.

Dalyell, Tam (1982) *One Man's Falklands...*, London: Cecil Woolf Publishers.

Dalyell, Tam (1983) *Thatcher's Torpedo: The Sinking of the 'Belgrano'*,

London: Celil Woolf Publishers.

Dalyell, Tam (1986) *Thatcher: Patterns of Deceit*, London: Cecil Woolf Publishers.

Dalyell, Tam (1987) *Misrule*, London: Hamish Hamilton Ltd.

Dillard, Dudley (1963) 'Capitalism', *Encyclopaedia Britannica* (1963 ed.), Chicago: Encyclopaedia Britannica Inc.

Dillon, G.M. (1989) *The Falklands, Politics and War*, New York: St. Martin's Press.

Douglas, Adam (1992) *The Beast Within*, London: Orion Books.

Durant, Alan (1984) *Conditions of Music*, London: MacMillan.

Eagleton, Terry (1976) *Marxism and Literary Criticism*, London: Methuen & Co.

Eagleton, Terry (1983) *Literary Theory: An Introduction*, Oxford: Basil Blackwell.

Edmunds, Ben (1975) 'The Trippers Trapped: Pink Floyd in a Hum Bag', *Rolling Stone*, November 6: 63- 64.

Everett, Tod (1977) Rev. of *Animals* by Pink Floyd, *Hi Fi/Mus Am*, May: 118.

Fairbairn, W. Ronald D. (1962) *Psychoanalytic Studies of the Personality*, London: Tavistock Publications Limited.

Freedman, Lawrence (1988) *Britain and the Falklands War*, Oxford: Basil Blackwell Ltd.

Fricke, David (1984) 'Roger Waters Can't Top the Wall', *Rolling Stone*, August 30: 38.

Fricke, David (1987a) Rev. of Roger Waters in Concert, *Rolling Stone*, October 22: 21.

Fricke, David (1987b) 'Pink Floyd: The Inside Story', *Rolling Stone*, November 19: 44-46.

Fricke, David (1992) 'The Dark Side of Amused', *Rolling Stone*, September 17: 28.

Frith, Simon (1983) *Sound Effects*, London: Constable.

Fuller Torrey, E. (1974) *The Death of Psychiatry*, New York: Penguin Books.

Gilmore, Milal (1977) 'Pink Floyd's Optic Nerve', *Rolling Stone*, June 30: 124.

Goldman, Brian (1983) 'The fight to refuse treatment', *Maclean's*, December 19: 36.

Guntrip, Harry (1969) *Schizoid Phenomena, Object Relations and the Self*, New York: International Universities Press, Inc.

Guntrip, Harry (1971) *Psychoanalytic Theory, Therapy, and the Self*, New York: Basic Books, Inc.

Hamilton, Edith (1942) *Mythology*, Boston: Little, Brown and Company.

Hillburn, Robert (1980) Rev. of Pink Floyd in Concert, *Melody Maker*, February 16: 31.

Hoberman, J. (1982) 'Off the Wall', *Village Voice*, August 31: 44.

Hogan, Richard (1980) 'Up against the wall of secrecy with Pink Floyd', *Circus*, April 15: 24.

Holbrook, David (1971) *Human Hope and the Death Instinct*, Oxford: Pergamon Press.

Humphries, Patrick (1981) 'Pink Freud Slip', *Melody Maker*, June 20: 29.

Isselbacher, Kurt and Eugene Braunwald, eds (1994) *Harrison's Principles of Internal Medicine* (13th edition), New York: McGraw-Hill, Inc.

Jenkins, Mark (1984) Rev. of *The Pros and Cons of Hitch Hiking* by Roger Waters, *Melody Maker*, May 5: 23.

Jones, Allan (1980) 'Troubled Waters', *Melody Maker*, August 9: 15.

Kaplan, Michael (1987) Rev. of *Radio K.A.O.S.* by Roger Waters, *Rolling Stone*, June 4: 29.

Kramer, Lawrence (1990) *Music as Cultural Practice, 1800-1900*, Berkeley: University of California Press.

Kuebler-Ross, Elisabeth (1969) *On Death and Dying*, New York: MacMillan.

Laing, Dave (1969) *The Sound of our Time*, London and Sydney: Sheed and Ward.

Laing, R.D. (1965) *The Divided Self: An Existential Study in Sanity and Madness*, Harmondsworth, Middlesex: Penguin.

Lee, Robert (1986) 'The Uses of Form: A Reading of *Animal Farm*', *Critical Essays on George Orwell*, Ed. Bernard Oldsley and Joseph Browne. Boston: G.K. Hall & Co.

Levin, Sidney (1966) 'Depression and Object Loss', *Journal of the American Psychoanalytic Association* (XIV): 142.

Loder, Kurt (1980) "Pink Floyd: Up Against 'The Wall'", *Rolling Stone*, February 7: 75-76.

Loder, Kurt (1983) 'Pink Floyd's Artistic Epiphany' *Rolling Stone*, April 14: 65-66.

Loder, Kurt (1984) 'Roger Waters Walls Himself In', *Rolling Stone*, June 7: 49.

London: HMSO, (22 July 1985) *Third Report from the Foreign Affairs Committee. Session 1984-85. Events Surrounding the Weekend of 1-2 May 1982*, HC II.

Marks, John (1979) *The Search for the Manchurian Candidate—The CIA and Mind Control*, New York: Dell Publishing.

McClary, Susan and Walser, Robert (1990) 'Start making sense! Musicology wrestles with rock', in S. Frith and A. Goodwin (eds) *On Record*, London: Routledge.

McDonough, Jack (1970) 'Pink Floyd-The Inter Stellar Band', *Rolling Stone*, November 26: 20.

McKee, Alexander (1982) *Dresden 1945: The Devil's Tinderbox*, New York:

E. P. Dutton, Inc.

Meyer, Leonard (1956) *Emotion and Meaning in Music*, Chicago: The University of Chicago Press.

Middleton, Richard (1990) *Studying Popular Music*, Philadelphia: Open University Press.

Middleton, Richard (1993) 'Popular music analysis and musicology: bridging the gap', *Popular Music* 12(2), 177-189.

Mieses, Stanley (1977) Rev. of *Animals* by Pink Floyd, *Melody Maker*, July 16: 18.

Miles, Barry (1980) *Pink Floyd*, New York: Quick Fox.

Miles, Barry ed. (1986) *Allen Ginsberg: Howl*, New York: Harper & Row.

Milward, John (1983) Rev. of *The Final Cut* by Pink Floyd, *Hi Fi/Mus Am*, July: 91-92.

Moore, Allan (1993) *Rock: The Primary Text*, Philadelphia: Open University Press.

Morrison, Wilbur H., *Fortress Without a Roof: The Allied Bombing of the Third Reich*, New York: St. Martin's Press.

Mullins, Stephanie (1978) 'Biography', *Britannica Book of the Year*, Chicago: Encyclopaedia Britannica Inc.

Neaman, Judith (1978) *Suggestion of the Devil: Insanity in the Middle Ages and the Twentieth Century*, New York: Octagon Books.

Newman, Peter C. (1982) 'The Challenge of Japan', *Maclean's*, March 8: 3.

Oldfield, Michael (1983) Rev. of 'Pink Floyd - The Wall' (Film), *Melody Maker*, April 30: 26.

Orwell, George (1983) *Animal Farm*, New York: Penguin.

Pareles, John (1980) 'Pink Floyd Can't Stand Themselves', *Village Voice*, January 28: 61.

Parker, Alan (1982) 'Pink Floyd The Wall: The Making of the Film Brick by Brick From My View', *American Cinematographer*, October: 1025.

Picarella, John (1983) 'The Last Labor of Pink Floyd' *Village Voice*, June 7: 59.

Pinguet, Maurice (1993) *Voluntary Death in Japan*, Cambridge: Polity Press.

Pink Floyd at Pompeii (1972), Dir. Adrian Maben: RM Productions.

Pink Floyd—The Wall (1982), Dir. Alan Parker. Screenplay by Roger Waters: Tin Blue Ltd.

Pond, Steve (1980) "Pink Floyd: Up Against 'The Wall'", *Rolling Stone*, April 3: 76.

Pond, Steve (1981) "Pink Floyd To Film 'The Wall'", *Rolling Stone*, October 1: 81.

Pond, Steve (1990) "Roger Waters on 'The Wall'", *Rolling Stone*, August 9: 29.

Redbeard (1993) "The Twentieth Anniversary of *The Dark Side of the Moon*", *In the Studio*, broadcast March 30 in Toronto on CILQ FM (Q107).

Resnicoff, Matt (1992) 'Roger and Me', *Musician*, December: 38.

Rochlin, Gregory (1973) *Man's Aggression: The Defense of the Self*, Boston: Gambit.

Rochlin, Gregory (1980) *The Masculine Dilemma: A Psychology of Masculinity*, Boston: Little, Brown and Company.
Rockwell, John (1992) 'The Emergence of Art Rock', *The Rolling Stone Illustrated History of Rock and Roll* (ed. Anthony Decurtis, et al.), New York: Random House.

Rose, Frank (1977) 'Floyd's Feckless Fauna', *Rolling Stone*, March 24: 56.

Roud, Brian James (1966) 'Biography', *Britannica Book of the Year*, Chicago: Encyclopaedia Britannica Inc.

Ruhlmann, William (1993) *Pink Floyd*, London: Bison Books.

Schaffner, Nicholas (1991) *A Saucerful of Secrets: The Pink Floyd Odyssey*, New York: Harmony Books.

Sedgewick, Nick (1975) 'A rambling conversation with Roger Waters concerning all this and that', *Wish You Were Here—Songbook*, Pink Floyd Music Publishers.

Shepherd, John (1994) 'Music, culture and interdisciplinary: reflections on relationships', *Popular Music* 13(2), 127-141.

Sherrill, Helen Cecil (1991) *The Quality of Childhood Conciousness and Its Significance*, PhD thesis, Emory University.

Silverstein, Red (1982) 'Pink Floyd - The Wall', *Variety*, June 2: 18.

Solt, Andrew and Egan, Sam (1988) *Imagine—John Lennon*, New York: Macmillan.

Sutherland, John (1980) 'The British Object Relations Theorists', *The Journal of the American Psychoanalytic Association*, Vol. 28, No. 4: 829.

Tagg, Philip (1979) *Kojak—50 Seconds of Television Music: Towards the Analysis of Affect in Popular Music*, PhD thesis, University of Gothenberg.

Tagg, Philip (1982) 'Analysing popular music: theory, method and practice', *Popular Music*, 2, 37-67.

Tarasti, Eero (1979) *Myth and Music*, The Hague: Mouton Publishers.

Thorgerson, Storm (1992) *Pink Floyd: Shine On*, London: Pink Floyd Music.

Tracey, Michael and David Morrison (1979) *Whitehouse*, London: The MacMillan Press Ltd.

Valenstein, Elliot S. (1973) *Brain Control: A Critical Examination of Brain Stimulation and Psychosurgery*, New York: John Wiley & Sons.

Vance, Tommy (1979) 'Interview with Roger Waters', broadcast November 30 1979, BBC Radio One.

Walser, Robert (1993) *Running With the Devil: Power, Gender, and Madness in Heavy Metal Music*, Hanover/London: Wesleyan University Press.

Waters, G. Roger (1981) *Draft of Screenplay for 'The Wall'*.

Watts, Michael (1971) 'Michael Watts talks to ex-Pink Floyd man Syd Barrett', *Melody Maker*, March 27: 34.

Watts, Michael (1980) 'Up Against The Wall', *Melody Maker*, August 2: 4-5.

White, Timothy (1988) 'Pink Floyd', *Penthouse*, September: 158-163, 166, 215.

White, Timothy (1992) "Roger Waters''Death' And Rebirth", *Billboard*, August 1: 5.

Whiteley, Sheila (1992) *The Space between the Notes*, London: Routledge.

Wicke, Peter (1990) *Rock Music: Culture, Aesthetics and Sociology*, Cambridge: Cambridge University Press.

Willis, Garry (1990) *Under God: Religion and American Politics*, New York: Simon and Schuster.

Discography

Pink Floyd

Meddle..Harvest SMAS 832, 1971.

The Dark Side of the Moon ....Harvest SMAS 11163, 1973.

Wish You Were Here ....Columbia PC 33453, 1975.

Animals ....Columbia JC 34474, 1977.

The Wall ....Columbia PC2 36183, 1979.

The Final Cut ....Columbia QC 38243, 1983.

Waters, Roger

The Pros and Cons of Hitch Hiking ....Columbia FC 39290, 1984.

Radio K.A.O.S. ....Columbia CK 40795, 1987.

Amused to Death......................................Columbia CK 47127, 1992.

The author and publishers acknowledge with thanks the permission to quote the following:

FOR USE OF LYRICS

DARK SIDE OF THE MOON

Breathe (In the Air); Time; Money; Us And Them; Brain Damage; Eclipse.

All lyrics by Roger Waters;

©1973 Pink Floyd Music Publishers Ltd., for the world, excluding USA & Canada.

TRO ©1973 Hampshire House Publishing Corp., New York, NY (used by permission), for Canada & USA.

WISH YOU WERE HERE

Shine On You Crazy Diamond Part 5; Shine On You Crazy Diamond Part 7; Welcome To The Machine; Have A Cigar; Wish You Were Here.

All lyrics by Roger Waters,

©1975 Pink Floyd Music Publishers Ltd., for the world.

ANIMALS

Pigs on the Wing (Part I); Dogs; Pigs (Three Different Ones); Sheep; Pigs on the Wing (Part II).

All lyrics by Roger Waters,

©1977 Pink Floyd Music Publishers Ltd., for the world.

THE WALL

In the Flesh?; The Thin Ice; Another Brick in the Wall (Part I); The Happiest Days of Our Lives; Another Brick in the Wall (Part II); Mother; Goodbye Blue Sky; Empty Spaces; Young Lust; One of My Turns; Don't Leave Me Now; Another Brick in the Wall (Part III); Goodbye Cruel World; Hey You; Is There Anybody Out There?; Nobody Home; Vera; Bring the Boys Back Home; Comfortably Numb; The Show Must Go On; In the Flesh; Run Like Hell; Waiting for the Worms; Stop; The Trial; Outside the Wall.

All lyrics by Roger Waters,

©1979 Pink Floyd Music Publishers Ltd., for the world.

THE FINAL CUT

The Post War Dream; Your Possible Pasts; One of the Few; The Hero's Return; The Gunner's Dream; Paranoid Eyes; Get Your Filthy Hands Off My Desert; The Fletcher Memorial Home; Southampton Dock; The Final Cut; Not Now John; Two Suns in the Sunset.

All lyrics by Roger Waters,

©1982 Pink Floyd Music Publishers Ltd., for the world.

FOR USE OF MUSICAL EXCERPTS

DARK SIDE OF THE MOON

The Great Gig in the Sky. Written by Richard Wright.

©1973 Pink Floyd Music Publishers Ltd., for the world excluding USA & Canada.

TRO ©1973 Hampshire House Publishing Corp., New York, NY (used by permission), for Canada & USA.

WISH YOU WERE HERE

Shine On You Crazy Diamond Part 3. Written by Roger Waters / David Gilmour/Richard Wright.

Shine On You Crazy Diamond Part 5. Written by Roger Waters.

THE WALL

In the Flesh; The Thin Ice; The Happiest Days of Our Lives; What Shall We Do Now?; Don't Leave Me Now; Another Brick in the Wall (Part III); Hey You; Is There Anybody Out There?; Vera; Waiting for the Worms. Written by Roger Waters.

THE FINAL CUT

The Final Cut. Written by Roger Waters.